AFRICAN ETHNOGRAPHIC STUDIES
OF THE 20TH CENTURY

Volume 12

THE POSITION OF THE CHIEF IN THE MODERN POLITICAL SYSTEM OF ASHANTI

THE POSITION OF THE CHIEF IN THE MODERN POLITICAL SYSTEM OF ASHANTI

A Study of the Influence of Contemporary Social Changes on Ashanti Political Institutions

K. A. BUSIA

Routledge
Taylor & Francis Group

LONDON AND NEW YORK

First published in 1951 by Oxford University Press for the International African Institute.

This edition first published in 2018
by Routledge
2 Park Square, Milton Park, Abingdon, Oxon OX14 4RN

and by Routledge
711 Third Avenue, New York, NY 10017

Routledge is an imprint of the Taylor & Francis Group, an informa business

British Library Cataloguing in Publication Data
A catalogue record for this book is available from the British Library

ISBN: 978-0-8153-8713-8 (Set)
ISBN: 978-0-429-48813-9 (Set) (ebk)
ISBN: 978-1-138-49224-0 (Volume 12) (hbk)
ISBN: 978-1-138-49227-1 (Volume 12) (pbk)
ISBN: 978-1-351-03082-3 (Volume 12) (ebk)

Publisher's Note
The publisher has gone to great lengths to ensure the quality of this reprint but points out that some imperfections in the original copies may be apparent.

Disclaimer
The publisher has made every effort to trace copyright holders and would welcome correspondence from those they have been unable to trace.

THE POSITION OF THE CHIEF IN THE MODERN POLITICAL SYSTEM OF ASHANTI

A STUDY OF THE INFLUENCE OF
CONTEMPORARY SOCIAL CHANGES ON
ASHANTI POLITICAL INSTITUTIONS

BY

K. A. BUSIA

Published for the
INTERNATIONAL AFRICAN INSTITUTE
by the OXFORD UNIVERSITY PRESS
LONDON   NEW YORK   TORONTO
1951

Oxford University Press, Amen House, London E.C. 4

GLASGOW NEW YORK TORONTO MELBOURNE WELLINGTON
BOMBAY CALCUTTA MADRAS CAPE TOWN

Geoffrey Cumberlege, Publisher to the University

PRINTED IN GREAT BRITAIN

DEDICATED TO MY LATE WIFE

AMMA

WITHOUT WHOSE HELP
AND ENCOURAGEMENT
THIS WORK WOULD NEVER
HAVE BEEN COMPLETED

CONTENTS

FOREWORD

THE present work, with minor alterations, is a thesis accepted by the University of Oxford for the Degree of Doctor of Philosophy.

The original subject of my research was 'Family, Clan, and Kinship. A study of the influence of contemporary social changes on Ashanti society'.

I obtained permission to spend a year in Ashanti to do my field-work. Work on the field convinced me that the political problem centring round the position of the chief was a crucial one for Ashanti. In order to be able to deal more comprehensively with this problem than I could otherwise have done, I applied to the Board of the Faculty of Anthropology and Geography, when I returned to Oxford, to grant me leave to write on 'The position of the chief in the modern political system of Ashanti. A study of the influence of contemporary social changes on Ashanti political institutions'.

In writing the thesis, therefore, I have confined myself to this subject, although I covered a wider field in my research. The political organization is necessarily connected with other aspects of the whole society—religion, land-tenure, and economic activities—and I have treated these subjects only in their relation to the political institutions.

My field-work was done in 1941–2. I divided the time between Mampong, Wenchi, and Kumasi, but paid short visits to other towns. In Kumasi I was able to meet chiefs and elders from all parts of Ashanti, and so I obtained information about areas which I was unable to visit.

I entered the Administrative Service in September, 1942, and although I was posted away from Ashanti I was able to keep in touch with events there by correspondence, and by reading official reports and the Minutes of the Confederacy Council.

Before I returned to Oxford in April 1946 I spent a month in Ashanti. At that time the Asantehene was writing a history of Ashanti with the help of a small committee of acknowledged authorities on Ashanti tradition and political life. The Asantehene gave me permission to meet this committee on many occasions, and the help and information I received in that short time was equivalent to many months of field-work.

I have tried to do two things. First, to give a picture of Ashanti political institutions as they were before the British administration, and secondly, to indicate the changes that have taken place since British administration was established.

It seemed to me convenient to take 1900 as the dividing line. The British fought their last battle against Ashanti in 1895, and expatriated the king to the Seychelles Islands in 1896. In 1900 there was a rising in Ashanti because the Governor demanded the surrender of the Ashanti Golden Stool. It was after this rising had been quelled that the British administration of Ashanti really began.

I have tried to reconstruct the political system of Ashanti as it was at the close of the nineteenth century on the basis of what remains of the old culture, from tapping the memories of old informants, and from studying historical records.

Much of the old culture remains, for the British administration of Ashanti is barely fifty years old, and, moreover, the policy of indirect rule has sought to adapt rather than destroy Ashanti institutions.

As to historical records, my main source has been the works of Rattray. He stands mid-way between my 1900 landmark and 1942, the time of my field-work. When Rattray did his researches twenty years ago many of his informants had known the period immediately before the British administration, and remembered it well enough to give him accurate information about it. It was still largely a part of their lives. I deliberately chose to spend most of my time in Mampong, where Rattray had worked, as I have regarded his work as the foundation for my own. Two of my informants, now old men, were among Rattray's friends and informants. I have quoted Rattray frequently because I was able to check up his information in the same area in which he worked, and I found him to be generally correct and accurate.

In the few instances where I found him wrong, mainly in recording traditional history, he had been deliberately misinformed, as one of his informants admitted to me. That difficulty besets all field-workers in Ashanti as regards any attempt to collect traditional history. There are different branches of every royal lineage, and the chiefs are jealous of the parts their own ancestors have played in the wars of the tribe. Tradition is the basis of the respective claims of the different branches of a royal lineage to the office of chief. What one is told depends on which branch of the royal lineage is in power at the particular time.

There is one point of interpretation on which I find myself unable to accept Rattray's views. Rattray interpreted Ashanti society through the concepts of English Law of Real Property and English medieval feudalism. I think this approach erroneous, and have discussed it in the chapter on 'Chiefship and Land-tenure'.

I have also quoted from Bowdich's *Mission to Ashantee*. The mission was undertaken in 1817. Bowdich strikes me as a careful observer, and where he wrote from his own observation his descriptions tally remarkably with existing survivals.

On one or two historical incidents I have referred to Claridge's *A History of the Gold Coast* and Ward's *A Short History of the Gold Coast*.

With regard to the changes that are now taking place, I have relied on my own field-work, on Government Reports, and on the Minutes of the Ashanti Confederacy Council.

The then Chief Commissioner of Ashanti, E. G. Hawkesworth, Esq., C.M.G., kindly gave me access to Government files, but in writing my thesis I have only quoted from published reports.

The Minutes of the Ashanti Confederacy Council are records of each session taken down by the Secretary to the Council. I attended meetings of the Council, and I am able to say that the minutes are accurate accounts of the council's discussions. I have quoted frequently from the minutes, because I have thought it best to give as much documentary evidence as possible of what the chiefs themselves have said on the issues which face them in Ashanti to-day.

I have mentioned a large number of place-names, some of them quite small villages, in the text. Of the two accompanying maps, one shows the administrative districts of Ashanti as they were in 1942, and the other the communications, the capital towns of all the Divisions, and some of the larger towns and villages. To have included every village mentioned in the text would have considerably reduced the usefulness of the maps.

The spelling of place-names in Ashanti presents some difficulty. The name of the same town has been spelt differently at different times in official reports and maps, and in some cases different spellings still exist for the same town, as Asumegya and Essumeja,

Tekiman, Techiman. I have used the more common spelling even when I think it unsatisfactory from the point of view of the way in which the Ashanti themselves pronounce the names. The place-names require official revision and standardization.

I have kept Ashanti expressions down to a minimum, and have given them only where they throw light on or give evidence of the way the people themselves regard certain things.

Rattray's works and the numerous books written on the British campaigns in Ashanti have put that country on the map as well for the anthropologist as for the general reader, and I have thought it unnecessary to give the usual introductory remarks about the geography of the country. Such knowledge of the history as is necessary for understanding the position of the chief has been woven into the text.

Important constitutional developments, some of them fore-shadowed in my analysis, have taken place since this work was originally written; but I have thought it best to get it published as it stands, as an analysis of the position before the post-war changes began. Constitutional changes are continuous, and already there are some very far-reaching changes on the way. When in a decade or so the then existing structure comes to be re-analysed, this work may be of some value as a point of departure.

My thanks are due to the Carnegie Research Fund Committee of the University of Oxford for the generous award of Carnegie Research grants; to Nuffield College, Oxford, for the award of a Studentship; to the Gold Coast Government for a grant towards publication; to the Asantehene, Nana Sir Osei Agyeman Prempeh II, K.B.E.; the Mamponghene, Nana Owusu Sekyere Abunyewa II, for providing me with authoritative information; to the many informants who gave me of their time and knowledge; to my tutor and friend Dr. M. Fortes for invaluable assistance and advice; to Professor Daryll Forde, Director, International African Institute, for making many helpful suggestions and for arranging publication; and finally to my late wife, Amma Abrefa Busia, to whose memory this work is gratefully dedicated, for the help, encouragement, and inspiration she gave me in my study.

UNIVERSITY COLLEGE OF   K. A. BUSIA
THE GOLD COAST
1951

CHAPTER I

THE CONSTITUTIONAL ASPECT OF CHIEFSHIP

The matrilineal bond

ASHANTI chiefship is based on the lineage system. The theory of procreation held in Ashanti is that a human being is compounded of two principles: the 'blood' (*mogya*) which he inherits from the mother, and the other 'spirit' (*ntɔrɔ*) which is derived from the father. Corresponding to this dogma of descent, an individual derives certain rights and duties through his mother, and others through his father. In Ashanti a child is bound by religious and educational ties to his father, but the greater part of his rights and duties are derived through his mother. For political purposes the matrilineal bond is the more significant.

Descent is traced through the mother, for the traditional conception is that physical continuity between one generation and another is maintained by the blood which is transmitted through her. A man is therefore legally identified with his maternal kinsmen: his maternal grandmother and her brothers and sisters, his mother and her brothers and sisters, and his own brothers and sisters. It is his membership within this group that determines his succession to different offices or property, and his jural rights and obligations.

In this group the closest bond is that which exists between siblings: children of the same parents or of the same mother.[1] A man's potential successors are his brothers in order of age, his mother's sister's son, his sister's son, his mother's sister's daughter's son, his sister's daughter's son, his mother's sister's daughter's daughter's son, his sister's daughter's daughter's son, or his mother's sister's daughter's daughter's daughter's son, in that order of preference. This may be represented diagrammatically (see p. 2).

The diagram represents four generations, the number usually contemporaneous. Ego's potential successors in his own generation are B, D, and E. In the first generation of descendants, F and

[1] See p. 127.

G, in the second generation H and J, and in the third generation K and L. B, D, F, H, and K in the direct line have within their own generations preference over E, G, J, and L who are descended from Ego's mother's sister. Seniority in age is given consideration, but it is not the sole criterion. The members of the lineage appoint anyone they consider most suitable from the potential heirs.

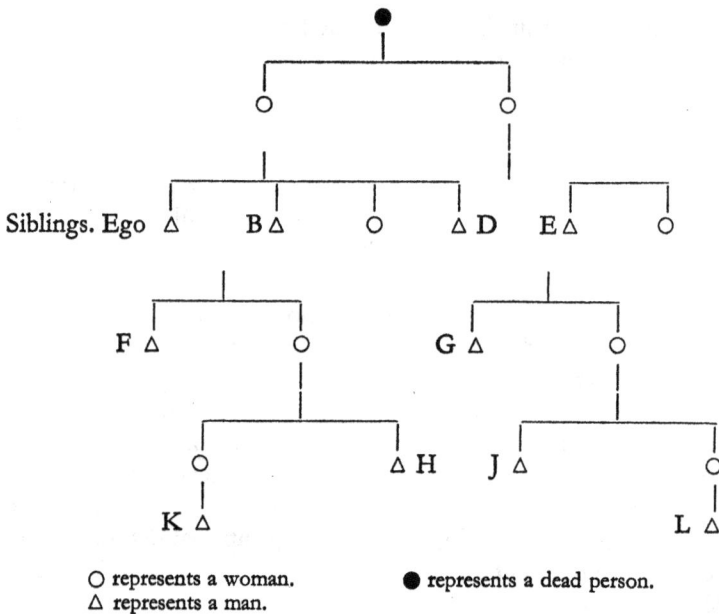

O represents a woman.   ● represents a dead person.
△ represents a man.

As the diagram shows, a man has several potential heirs, descendants of his own mother or his mother's sisters. There is a tendency for a lineage to split up into a number of branches, descended from sisters of the same mother. The lineage is a group of men and women who trace their descent in the matrilineal line to a common ancestress. Some lineages, especially those of chiefs, can sometimes trace their ancestry as far back as ten or twelve generations, and have several branches.

In Ashanti succession to property as well as to political offices is handed down in the matrilineal line. Succession to these offices is made by selection by the lineage from its members. There is thus a combination of kin-right and selection.

Wenchi as an example of Ashanti constitutional practice

In *Ashanti Law and Constitution*[1] Rattray recorded the Constitutions and histories of seven of the important Divisions of Ashanti and stated the general principles of the Ashanti Constitution.

As a further illustration of the Ashanti Constitution an account of the Constitution of Wenchi in North Ashanti is given below, as an addition to the seven which Rattray has recorded.

According to the tradition, the site of the town of Wenchi has changed several times in the course of its history; but whenever it was rebuilt on a new site the old aggregations were preserved. The town was always built in three main sections: north, centre, and south, or, as they were called, *Kɔntɔn* (in the valley), *Bokorɔ* (by the single stone), and *Asere* (the name of a clan).

Each section consisted of several lineages. In Wenchi each lineage inhabited a particular area of the section. The members of the lineage had their houses close together, grouped around the house of the lineage head. First the area and later the lineage itself came to be distinguished by the name of a tree said to have been found near the first settlement of the ancestors of the lineage. Thus there were the following lineages:

Bokorɔ

Kyeasefo	people under the *akyea*-tree (a tree like the cashew nut) in the Bokorɔ section.

Kɔntɔn

Ababaafo	people under the roofing-cane.
Sisiriasefo	people under the *sisri*-tree (a tree which bears red flowers: Christaller suggests that it might be a tulip-tree[2]) in the Kɔntɔn section.

Asere

Nyaasefo	people under the silk-cotton tree (*onyina* or *onyan*: silk cotton).
Abɛasefo	people under the palm-tree.
Nkwaduasefo	people under the banana-tree.
Sɔfoasefo	people under the *Sɔfo*-tree.

All the last four lineages lived in the Asere section. This gives seven quarters, and is characteristic of the Asere (Asenie) Clan of Ashanti to which Wenchi belongs.

The Nkwaduasefo and the Sɔfoasefo were also called Yefrefo

---

[1] Chaps. ix–xiii.
[2] Christaller, *Dictionary of the Asante and Fante Language*, 1933.

(i.e. indigenous or original settlers). The tradition is that their ancestors founded Wenchi. They 'came out of a hole and settled at Ahwene', the people say, hence, *Yefre*, the etymology of which is *Ye-firi* (we come from, or out of). The lineage from which Wenchi chiefs are selected is of the Yefrefo, or group of indigenous settlers as they regard themselves.

Migrations

As the distinction *Yefrefo* indicates, the tradition is that some of the lineages are descendants of later immigrants.

According to the tradition, the first group of immigrants were fugitives from Adanse, fleeing from the victorious forces of Ntim Gyakari of Denkyira. This confirms Ward's account: 'In the first place, the Denkyira's had first had a war against the Adansis in which the Adansis were beaten: many Adansis fled to Ashanti, and Osei Tutu received them kindly and protected them from Denkyira.'[1] This was about the beginning of the eighteenth century. Osei Tutu ruled Ashanti from 1697 to 1731.[2]

Other immigrants came from Techiman when that country was defeated by Opoku Ware, King of Ashanti, 1731–4. They were joined later by fugitives from Nkoranza. More immigrants migrated to Wenchi from Forikrom and other parts of Ashanti as a result of inter-tribal wars.

A large group of immigrants are believed to have come from the region of Bontuku in the Jaman Kingdom, now part of French Ivory Coast. The tradition is that the group consisted of about 300 men armed with bows and arrows. They came to Wenchi during the reign of Wenchihene Gyane who ruled between 1780 and 1818. Osei Bonsu, King of Ashanti fought against Jaman at this time, and these men were believed to be fugitives from the defeated armies of the King of Jaman.[3]

When the immigrants were numerous enough to form separate villages, they were given land near Wenchi where they lived under their own leaders; but in every case one of the elders of Wenchi was placed in charge over the village. When they were not numerous enough to form separate villages they were settled in one of the three sections of the town, in Bokoro, Konton, or Asere. Thus

[1] Ward, *A Short History of the Gold Coast*, 1935, p. 42.
[2] Claridge, *A History of the Gold Coast and Ashanti*, 1915, vol. i, chap. xi.
[3] Ibid., chap. xvi. Ward, op. cit., chap. xi.

the village of Gyansoso consisted entirely of immigrants who
were placed under the Akwamuhene; but as the immigrants from
Forikrom were not numerous enough to form a separate village,
they were settled in the Bokoɔ section.

This tradition shows that the people think that their Division
was built up by successive migrations. This probably happened

ASHANTI

SCALE 1:3,000,000

MILES 10 5 0   10   20   30   40   50 MILES

_____ ...Roads

● TECHIMAN...Capitals of Divisions
○ Sunyani ....Other towns

all over Ashanti in the eighteenth and nineteenth centuries. King-
doms broke up, lineages dispersed, some tribes expanded, others
diminished owing to wars and migrations. This would explain
why the ties of kinship and clanship form a criss-cross pattern con-
necting widely separated lineages and groups all over Ashanti.

The village

Where the immigrants formed a separate village, as in the case
of Gyansoso or Awisa, their original leader became the *Odekuro*
(owner of the village), responsible to the elder under whom the
Wenchihene placed him. If the Wenchihene wanted to communicate with the immigrants at Gyansoso, he did not send to them

direct, but he communicated with them through his elder, the *Akwamuhene* who was placed over that village.

Other villages were founded in the Wenchi Division, probably through people moving out in search of farm land, and being followed later by other members of their lineage. The Wenchi Division came to comprise the villages of Akrobi, Gyansoso, Drɔboso, Yoyoano, Adantase, Koase, Awisa, &c.

Each village consisted of a number of lineages which formed a political community under the *Odekuro*, who belonged to one of the first lineages to settle there. The affairs of the village were managed by the *Odekuro* and the heads of the lineages of the village. But the *Odekuro* was also responsible to an elder who lived at the capital in Wenchi. Thus Gyansoso came under the *Akwamuhene*, Yoyoano under the *Gyasehene*, Akrobi under the *Adɔntenhene*, Awisa under the *Kurotiahene*, and Koase came directly under the Wenchihene. The headmen of the villages were linked with the Wenchihene through the elders to whom they were responsible.

The elders

The elders (*Mpanyimfo* or *Asafohene*) were themselves heads of the different lineages residing in Wenchi; that is, heads of the Nyaase, Abɛase, Sisiriase, and the other lineages.

These elders used to be distinguished by the names of their lineages as Nyaasehene, Abɛasehene, Bokorɔhene, and the like; but later their lineage names were superseded by the titles which indicated the positions of the lineage heads in the military organization. So names like *Benkumhene* (leader of the left wing), *Nifahene* (leader of the right wing), *Kyidɔmhene* (leader of the rearguard) came into more general use.[1]

Lineage ties

Both in the town of Wenchi, and in the villages, lineage ties were the basis of communal life. The members of a lineage lived close together.[2] It was the practice for all the men of a lineage to eat together daily in the house of the lineage head. When the men

---

[1] Cf. Rattray, *Ashanti Law and Constitution*, 1929, p. 77, 'After Feyiase, we have the inauguration of a whole series of new and high-sounding titles to designate these "Elders". . . . All these were titles having reference to a military organization.'

[2] Cf. account of Wenchi settlement on p. 3.

were married, their wives carried the evening meal to the house of the lineage head where all the men, married and single, met and ate together. Kinship ties were strengthened by this regular practice of eating together.

Moreover, members of a lineage assisted one another in building their houses and making their farms, and performed many corporate acts in communal affairs such as clearing paths, or in funeral rites centring round their ancestors.

Lineage ties were so strong that, even when a man had to spend most of his life in another town or Division, he looked upon the village of his lineage as his home. That was where he looked forward to being buried when he died, so that he might join his ancestors. It is still the desire of many Ashantis to be buried in the village of their ancestors, and the relatives of a dead man regard it as a solemn duty to bury their kinsman in the ancestral village. Dead bodies are conveyed many miles at great expense in order that this obligation may be fulfilled.

The men and women of a lineage were expected to help one another in every possible way. Their unity was most conspicuously expressed when a member of the lineage died. Then they all came together to perform the funeral rites and share the expenses.

The duty of the elder or head of the lineage was to maintain peace and amity within this corporate group, and to represent it in its relations with other groups of the village community. The head of the lineage had political duties also, for the lineage was a unit for political action.

Election of an elder

The heads of the important lineages were the chief's councillors. Each of them held a hereditary office, the symbol of which was a stool. The man who was chosen to be the head of a lineage was not necessarily the most senior member. When an elder died, the chief sent a message to the senior woman and the senior man of the lineage, requesting them to elect a man to be the head of their lineage. This man would on his election also become the chief's elder. All the grown-up men and the senior woman of the lineage then held a meeting to select a candidate. They considered the sons of all the women of the lineage whose children had a kin-right to the office. When they had decided on one they sent to the father and mother of their chosen candidate to 'beg them for their son'. If the parents agreed they said, 'We give him to you.' The members of the lineage, including all the men and women, met again in the house of the senior woman. The candidate was informed that he had been selected to become the head of the lineage. 'We put you in the place of our ancestors.' The male members one by one swore to 'serve you whom we have chosen to occupy the stool of our ancestors, so that you in turn may serve the chief'. The senior man then sent to tell the chief that they had chosen a man to be head of their lineage. If the chief accepted the nomination, a day was fixed when the lineage could present their head to the chief and his elders. If the chief did not like the nominated candidate, he gave his reasons and asked the lineage to elect one with whom 'I could look after the state'. On the appointed day the candidate, accompanied by the senior members of his lineage, was brought to the chief's house where the chief and his elders would have met already. The senior man of the lineage, on behalf of himself and the other members, presented the candidate to the chief and his elders as their chosen head, and took the oath of allegiance as follows: 'I beg to swear by Thursday (the forbidden oath),[1] this man we have brought to you, if he does anything wrong, and I do not advise him, if I do not serve him well so that he too may serve you well, then have I broken my oath.' The candidate swore a similar oath to serve the chief faithfully. The chief then directed that a stool should be given to the candidate so that he might sit down. After he had sat down, the *Ɔkyeame Panyin* (head spokesman) claimed the *aseda*[2] (thanksgiving fee) from him. This was usually £4. 10s. and a bottle of rum. After the rum had been drunk by the assembled elders, the chief's spokesman, on behalf of the chief, gave the lineage stool to the candidate whom he admonished never to rebel against the chief. The candidate was then carried away from the chief's house on the shoulders of his friends to the music of the *fontomfrom* drums, and the singing of the *ose* (jubilant song) of the members of the lineage, thanking the Supreme Being, whose day is Saturday.[3] The candidate was thenceforth the head of his lineage and an elder or councillor of the chief.

---

[1] For the meaning of the oath see Chap. IV, pp. 75 ff.

[2] On *aseda* see n. 2, p. 12.

[3] 'Ose e, Yee! Ose e, Yee! Tweaduampon Nyame e, Yɛda ase O, Yɛda ase amene O, Yɛn na Yɛn ni O.' Cf. Rattray, *Ashanti Law and Constitution*, p. 104.

Election of the chief

The head of the Wenchi Division, the chief or Wenchihene, was himself similarly elected from the Suffoase lineage of the Yefrefo. This lineage traces its descent from Affia Atoa, the founding ancestress.

When a chief died and a new one had to be appointed, the elders held a meeting at which the Kontihene[1] presided. At the meeting the elders selected two from among themselves to approach the queen-mother and ask her to nominate a candidate for the stool.

The queen-mother then held a meeting with all the adult men and the senior women of the branches of the royal lineage. They considered the eligible candidates in turn and chose the one they thought most suitable. The necessary qualities were intelligence (*adwempa*), humility (*ahobrε-ase*), generosity (*ne yam ye*), manliness (*abooduru*), and physical fitness (*dεm biara nni ne ho*). When they had decided on a candidate, the queen-mother sent to inform the Kontihene. The latter summoned a meeting of the elders and told them of the queen-mother's nominated candidate. The elders sent a message back thanking the queen-mother, and adding that they could not say whether or not the candidate was acceptable, but that a meeting of the whole Division (*Ɔman*) would be summoned to consider the candidate. A day was appointed for this meeting, and the queen-mother was informed.

The Kontihene then sent a message to all the heads of villages through the respective elders, asking them to be present for the election of the chief. This was an important affair in which everyone took a keen interest, and all the headmen, elders, and commoners came to the meeting on the appointed day.

The role of the commoners[2]

The commoners or young men (*mmerante*), as they are called in Ashanti, played an important part in the election.

They would come as members of their respective lineages, but they also formed an unofficial body having a recognized and effective way in which they expressed their will not only about the election of the chief but on all matters affecting the tribe.

---

[1] See under 'The Personnel of a Division', p. 18 below.

[2] I use 'commoners' to denote the citizens (free men) who were not councillors or elders.

In every village the commoners had an association of their own. They did not hold regular meetings, but whenever any matter of importance was discussed by the elders, it became known and was talked about. The commoners would meet to discuss such matters.

They had a recognized leader or spokesman, the Nkwankwaahene.[1] He was not a member of the chief's official council, and his office was not a hereditary one. The commoners chose any one of themselves whom they considered brave and eloquent. When so chosen he became a recognized leader, and the commoners would submit their disputes to be settled by him in arbitration, and on any question of importance he presented the views of the young men to the elders.

Rattray uses the term Nkwankwaahene for an unconfirmed Divisional chief,[2] that is, a chief who has not yet taken the oath of allegiance to the Asantehene. This was used of a chief, because, until he had taken the oath of allegiance to the Asantehene, his position in the national council was not officially recognized. His position was then similar to that of the Nkwankwaahene[3] *vis-à-vis* a Divisional council.

Although he had no official place in the council of elders, the Nkwankwaahene was recognized as the representative of the commoners, and the elders considered any representations he made to them. His position was of political importance as it enabled the commoners to criticize the Government. The elders and the chief formed the Government and were jointly responsible for any decisions they made affecting the tribe. An elder could not oppose unpopular measures without exposing himself to the charge of disloyalty. The chief had an effective weapon against that. He could call on any elder to 'drink the gods', that is, to swear an oath to testify that he was not plotting against him, if he had cause to suspect him of any subversive intentions. Public opinion or criticism of the Government was therefore expressed through the Nkwankwaahene.

When the elders and headmen met on the appointed day for the election the commoners were also present. They sat as a body

[1] *Nkwankwaa* is synonymous with *mmerante* and means youth, or young men; hence *Nkwankwaahene*: chief or leader of young men.

[2] *Ashanti Law and Constitution*, p. 87.

[3] In 1936 the Ashanti Confederacy abolished the position of *Nkwankwaahene* in Ashanti.

behind their Nkwankwaahene. The elders and headmen took their places round the Kontihene who presided over the meeting.

The queen-mother and the members of the royal lineage met separately in the queen-mother's house, or sat a short distance away from the general meeting.

The spokesman (*Ɔkyeame*) told the general meeting of the Division (*Asetena Kɛse*) the name of the candidate the queen-mother had nominated. On the announcement of the name, demonstrations of approval or disapproval were unmistakably given by applause, grunts, hisses, laughter, or silence.

The elders would appear to deliberate over the matter, and then ask the commoners what they thought about it. The Ɔkyeame would say: 'Thus has the queen-mother said. What do the people say?' The commoners would reply, 'We would like to hear what the elders have to say first.' The commoners would then approve or disapprove of the decision of the elders. If the candidate was not accepted, the queen-mother was informed and the royals[1] proceeded to make another nomination. If after three nominations the queen-mother's candidate was still unacceptable, the Divisional Council nominated a candidate from the royal family. It was for the queen-mother to say whether or not the popular candidate had a kin-right to the stool. Both parties usually agreed on one of the eligible candidates. In case of disagreement, the popular candidate, that is, the one who had the backing of the Divisional Council, won. '*Ɔdehye nsi hene*' is the Ashanti maxim on such a situation: 'a royal does not install the chief!' That is the privilege of the commoners who have to serve him.

After a candidate had been elected and accepted, all the adult men and women of the royal lineages held a meeting with the chief-elect in the queen-mother's house. They settled any disputes or differences there might be between the chief-elect and any member of the royal family. After this the adult male members each swore an oath of allegiance to the chief-elect, promising to serve him as the chosen occupant of the stool of their ancestors, and to support him in his administration as chief of the Division. This precaution, besides expressing the solidarity of the royal lineage, imposed the moral and religious sanction of the oath on any member of the royal lineage who might feel injured on being passed over, to prevent him from working against the chief.

[1] Members of the lineage from which the chief is selected.

A day was then appointed for the installation of the chief. All the elders and headmen and their followers assembled in Wenchi. The Kontihene, through the Ɔkyeame, formally sent for the chief-elect, who came to the assembly dressed in an *adinkra* cloth, signifying that he was in mourning, accompanied by the members of the royal lineages. The Ɔkyeame addressed the chief-elect as follows:

Konti, Akwamu, Bokorɔ, Kɔntɔn, Asere, Kyidɔm, Benkum, Twafo, Adɔnten, Nifa—all the elders say that I should give you the Stool. Do not go after women. Do not become a drunkard. When we give you advice, listen to it. Do not gamble. We do not want you to disclose the origin of your subjects. We do not want you to abuse us. We do not want you to be miserly; we do not want one who disregards advice; we do not want you to regard us as fools; we do not want autocratic ways; we do not want bullying; we do not like beating. Take the Stool. We bless the Stool and give it to you. The Elders say they give the Stool to you.[1]

The chief-elect thanked the elders and gave them their *aseda*[2] (token of thanks) of £20 or £25. He also gave £4. 7s. for the *afona* (ceremonial sword) with which he took the oath to his elders. Standing before the Kontihene and Akwamuhene he said: 'I ask your permission to speak the forbidden oath of Thursday. I am the grandson (i.e. descendant) of Anye Amoampon Tabraku. To-day you have elected me: if I do not govern you as well as my ancestors did; if I do not listen to the advice of my elders; if I make war upon them; if I run away from battle; then have I violated the oath.'

The elders then each in turn took the oath of allegiance to the chief. After the elders had taken the oath of allegiance, the chief sent them rum and palm-wine (*nsua-nsa*). The chief was then carried shoulder-high from one end of the town to the other, the people following behind singing the *ose*.

The following day, the solemn acts of enstoolment took place in the stool-house.[3] The elders, Kontihene, Akwamuhene, Gyase-

---

[1] Cf. Rattray, *Ashanti Law and Constitution*, p. 82. The same formula is still in use.

[2] In Ashanti it is customary to acknowledge the gift of a valuable present, e.g. a house or a farm, by making the donor a small present. It is evidence that the gift has been made and accepted, and that the object has changed hands.

[3] There is a room in the chief's house in which the ancestral stools are kept. It is a sacred place.

hene, the Ɔkyeame Panyin, and the queen-mother attended. The Nifahene, Adɔntenhene, Benkumhene, and the Adekurofo of Akrobi and Koase might also attend. They took with them a sheep and a bottle of rum. The Ɔkyeame informed the ancestors whose stools were in the stool-house that a new chief, their own descendant in the matrilineal line, had been elected to take their place and govern the Division. The Kontihene held the right hand of the chief, the Ɔkyeame Panyin his left, and the queen-mother his waist. Three times they lowered him gently on to Anye Amoampon's stool and raised him again. Anye Amoampon came from the Suffoase Yefre line and was the first Chief of Wenchi. The Ɔkyeame then poured libations, and prayed for the new chief, and for prosperity and increase for the Division during his reign. The sheep was killed, and its blood was sprinkled on the blackened stools. It was then cut up and distributed: one hind-leg to the chief, the waist to the queen-mother, the head and legs to the stool-carriers; the rest was shared among the elders.

On the same day, after the ceremony in the stool-house, another sheep (*nyame-dwane*: sheep for the Supreme Being) was killed in the open yard in front of the stool-house. The chief first prayed that the Division might prosper and increase during his reign, and that the Supreme Being might help him, so that his reign might be successful. The Ɔkyeame Panyin, his son, or the head stool-carrier then poured libations on the ground. The oldest of the sons of chiefs (*Ahenemma Panyin*) killed the sheep. It was cut up and shared amongst the sons of chiefs and the younger royals. It was taboo for any other person to eat of the meat.

After this the chief was the acknowledged successor of his ancestors and head of the Division. He visited each town in his Division in turn to thank his people, and to show himself to the gods at Gyansoso, Akrobi, and Drɔboso.

The functions of the chief

Before 1900, when there were tribal wars, the military duty of the chief and the elders was important. They led different sections of the army. The military formation of Wenchi conformed to the type common to all Ashanti.[1] It consisted of scouts (*akwansrafo*), and an advance guard (*twafo*) in front, followed by the main body

[1] See Rattray, *Ashanti Law and Constitution*, chaps. xvi–xxiii.

(*adɔnten* and *konti*), the chief's body-guard (*gyase*), a rearguard (*kyidɔm*) with the right- (*nifa*) and left- (*benkum*) wing flanks.

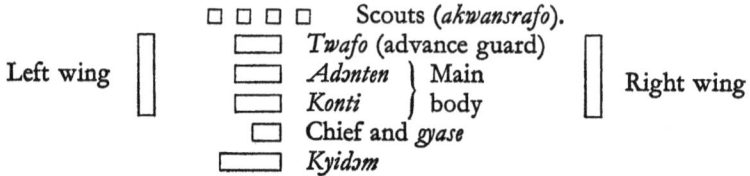

Left wing   □ □ □ □   Scouts (*akwansrafo*).
                               ☐   *Twafo* (advance guard)
                               ☐   *Adɔnten* ⎫ Main
                               ☐   *Konti*   ⎭ body   Right wing
                               ☐   Chief and *gyase*
                               ☐   *Kyidɔm*

Each section was under the leadership of an elder. The chief commanded the whole army.

The chief and the elders were responsible for the administration of the Division. They performed the necessary sacrifices for the welfare of the people. They were responsible for seeing that law and order were maintained and that the customs were followed. These two aspects, the religious and the judicial, will be examined in separate chapters.

The chief was bound by his oath to consult the elders on all matters, and to obey their advice. The government thus consisted of the chief and the elders. They met regularly, for it was the duty of every elder to visit the chief every morning. In this way the elders met informally to discuss the business of the day and other affairs of State. Each elder was interested in matters affecting the lineage he represented and the villages under him. The chief, on the other hand, was responsible for the whole Division. He therefore had to reconcile the sectional interests of the elders.

To show how the Division was administered I select different topics discussed on different mornings at the chief's house during 1933. One morning it was reported that the neighbouring people of Kyeraa were encroaching on Wenchi lands. The report was made by the Kontihene, who had received the information from one of his subjects who had a farmstead near the boundary. The chief and the elders discussed what action was to be taken. The chief was responsible for the protection of the land of the Division, and he had to guard it from encroachment by others. It was decided to send reliable messengers to the spot to ascertain what had actually taken place. The Gyasehene was asked to provide two men. These were called at once to the chief's house, and were given their instructions by the Okyeame.

On another morning the Gyasehene reminded them that the

Odwera ceremony[1] was only two weeks ahead, and that the necessary arrangements had not been made for its celebration. The chief and the elders discussed this, and the necessary orders were given.

On yet another morning the Akwamuhene reported that he was worried about the number of deaths that had taken place within a short time at Koase. Some of the elders shared his alarm, and regarded the deaths as a grave misfortune. They asked the Akwamuhene to go to Koase and meet the Odekuro and his elders and find out more about the cause of these deaths. A sacrifice was subsequently made by the chief and his elders at the shrine of Drɔbo in the village of Drɔboso to avert the misfortune (*yi mmusuo*).

One morning was spent in settling a dispute between the Adɔntenhene and the Ɔkyeame Panyin, each of whom claimed some palm-trees to be within the land of their respective lineages. The elders discussed the matter, and decided that the palm-trees were on the Ɔkyeame's land.

Often they discussed matters of a general nature: the prospects of the yam harvest, the meat supply, the state of the paths and roads, whether the court should sit that day or not. So important were these informal meetings for the administration of the Division that it was obligatory for every elder to call at the chief's house every morning 'to greet the chief'. Failure to do so without explanation was regarded as disaffection towards the chief. The first sign of disaffection on the part of an elder was his failure to go to the chief's house in the morning. A chief whose elders relaxed in this duty, or abstained from going to his house in the morning, surmised that there was something brewing against him, or that the elders were displeased with him. If at a morning meeting it was decided that no court or other business would be done during the day, the elders went and worked on their farms, or visited one of the villages directly under them.

If other meetings were necessary in addition to the morning meetings to discuss matters of importance, the chief sent a messenger to call the elders, usually in the evenings, after the day's work had been done. The chief had to keep strictly the injunction that he was to act only on the advice of his elders. There were rare occasions, however, when in an emergency he could act on

[1] See Chap. II, pp. 29 ff.

his own initiative. One such instance was the following: at about 7.30 o'clock one night the Zongo quarter of the town of Wenchi caught fire. This was reported direct to the chief by one of the men who had seen the fire from a distance. The report should normally have been made to an Ɔkyeame, who would have told the chief. The chief caused a drum to be beaten at once, and soon his house was crowded with people who had obeyed the summons conveyed by the drum. The chief instructed the young men to follow him to the scene of the conflagration and help to beat down the fires. The women were told to fetch their water-pots and follow later. This was a matter calling for immediate action, and no one questioned the chief for acting without first consulting his elders.

A chief could also appoint anyone to be an elder or an Ɔkyeame. He would inform the elders of his choice, but he was not bound to take their advice in such a case.

After meetings of the chief and his elders, decisions about which the people had to be informed were made public by the beating of *gongong* in the evenings, when all the people would have returned from their work on the farms. The town crier began these proclamations, 'All you people, *Nana*[1] bids you good evening; he says . . .': then followed the information or order. The people were called out in this way to do communal labour on the roads or to work on the chief's farm.

The elders were responsible for seeing that orders or decisions affecting the villages under their direct rule were made known to their people. They sent messengers to inform the village headmen (*Adekurofo*), who summoned meetings of their elders and told them; and then in the evening the villagers were informed by the village crier. But when important executive proposals or laws had to be passed, the chief was obliged to summon the Divisional Council to discuss and pass them.

The Wenchihene's obligations to the Asantehene

The Wenchihene and his elders had charge of all the internal affairs of Wenchi; but as the Wenchi Division was within the Ashanti Union, the Chief of Wenchi incurred certain obligations to the Asantehene.[2]

---

[1] *Nana*, i.e. the chief.
[2] The king or head of the Ashanti Federation; see Chap. V.

Like other chiefs in Ashanti he owed military service to the Asantehene. Wenchi contingents fought in the wars against Adinkra (1818), in the Awuna wars under Kwaku Dua I (1838–67), and in the wars against the British (1873–4, 1896, and 1900).

Another obligation of the Chief of Wenchi was to provide the elephant skin on which the Golden Stool was placed. When the Asantehene wanted an elephant skin he sent gunpowder and lead to the Wenchihene, who sent his hunters out to kill an elephant for the Asantehene. One informant said that during the reign of Kwame Bene (died about 1900) the Asantehene sent three kegs of gunpowder and forty bars of lead. The elephant was killed near Drɔboso, and its skin was taken to the Asantehene.

The Wenchihene was also forbidden to make war on another Division without the permission of the Asantehene. Proof of this was given by an incident which occurred during the reign of Nkatia Kwasi, about 1800. The Wenchihene sent messengers to buy small gourds (used for storing the gunpowder, and carried by the men in their belts (*ntoa*)) from a place called Mansera in Bontuku. The Chief of Mo also sent messengers on a similar errand to the same market. A quarrel broke out between the messengers of the two chiefs, during which the messengers of the Chief of Mo insulted the Wenchihene. This was reported to the latter, who declared war against the Chief of Mo. When the Asantehene heard this he sent for the two chiefs. He found the Wenchihene guilty for declaring war without first informing him. This, it was said, made the Wenchihene so ashamed that he died at Amowi on his return from Kumasi. His body was conveyed to Wenchi for burial.

The Chief of Wenchi also had to attend the periodic *Odwera* festivals held in Kumasi. Wenchi was so far away and the communications so poor that attendance at the *Odwera* took the people away from Wenchi for three to four months. Those who attended took plenty of food with them, including peas, dried cassava, and game. At the *Odwera* ceremony any destoolment which had taken place was reported to the Asantehene and a new chief took the oath of allegiance.

In judicial matters the Wenchihene could not execute the death sentence. This required the permission of the Asantehene. He could hear cases in which the Great Oath was sworn, but a report of the case was made to the Asantehene, and half of the *aseda* (fee

paid by the innocent party) was sent to him. A person dissatisfied
with the judgement at Wenchi could appeal to the Asantehene by
swearing the Great Oath on the Wenchihene's Kyeame (spokesman) who delivered the judgement.[1]

The personnel of a Division

In the above account mention has been made of the elders who
formed the personnel of an Ashanti Division. The principal office-
holders and their functions have been recorded by Rattray.[2]

The officers of a Division are the following: the chief, the
queen-mother, the Kontihene, Akwamuhene, Adɔntenhene (com-
mander of the main body), Nifahene (leader of the right wing),
Benkumhene (leader of the left wing), Gyasehene (in charge of
the chief's household), Kyidɔmhene (leader of the rearguard),
Ankɔbeahene (one who does not go anywhere; created to guard
the town when the chief goes to war; when the Ankɔbeahene
does go to war, he is the leader of the chief's personal body-guard),
the Abusuahene (head of the chief's lineage), and several Akyeame
(spokesmen).

These were all heads of lineages. It is, however, handed down
by tradition that Osei Tutu created two captains whom he called
Kontihene (created because of war), and Akwamuhene (in memory
of Akwamu, the place of his sojourn),[3] and that they ranked as
the two most senior elders in Kumasi. The other Divisions are
believed to have copied Kumasi in the appointment of an Akwamuhene and a Kontihene. These two elders are generally the most
senior in a Division.

Precedence amongst the other elders depends on the history of
each Division. Their titles indicate their respective places in the
military organization, and not seniority among themselves.

The Ɔkyeame (spokesman) is a busy official in every Division.
A Divisional chief has several spokesmen. The office of the head
spokesman (*Kyeamehene* or *Kyeame Panyin*) is usually hereditary
and the holder, like other elders, is the head of his lineage.
The Ɔkyeame's stool is then a lineage stool. But there are other
spokesmen whom a chief may appoint because of their personal
merit and fitness for the post. They hold office at the chief's

[1] See Chap. IV.   [2] *Ashanti Law and Constitution*, chap. xi.
[3] See Chap. V.

pleasure. Anyone desiring to lay a complaint before the chief must do so through an Ɔkyeame. At public meetings it is the Ɔkyeame who speaks, and not the chief. At ceremonies an Ɔkyeame must always be present to offer the prayers when a libation is poured or sheep are sacrificed to the ancestors. In judicial matters it is the Ɔkyeame who delivers the judgement of the court. When a chief wants to communicate with a neighbouring chief he sends his Ɔkyeame. The Ɔkyeame may also be sent to represent his chief at official meetings of the Ashanti Union or Confederacy. He has to be skilful at diplomacy and negotiations, to be eloquent and well spoken. He is also expected to be well versed in the lore and history of the tribe, and many Akyeame are the acknowledged authorities on their tribal history and lore.

The Gyasehene, as Rattray has described, supervises the numerous officials of the chief's household. The list of these officials[1]—spokesmen, stool-carriers, drummers, horn-blowers, umbrella-carriers, caretakers of the royal mausoleum, bathroom-attendants, chief's soul-washers, elephant-tail switchers, fan-bearers, cooks, hammock-carriers, floor-polishers, treasurers, eunuchs, heralds, sword-bearers, gun-bearers, shield-bearers, minstrels, and executioners—gives some idea of the chief's household, and of the organization built up around him.

The Queen-mother

Rattray was the first to point out how important the queen-mother's position was in Ashanti.[2] The brief information he gave may be supplemented.

The queen-mother is described as the 'mother' of the chief. She is more often his sister, but constitutionally she is regarded as the chief's mother, hence her title, Ɔhemmaa (female monarch), is usually translated queen-mother.

She is expected to advise the chief about his conduct. She may scold and reprove him in a way none of his councillors can. Two queen-mothers of Juaben, Ataa Birafo and Afua Kobi, were destooled for not advising their sons (i.e. the chiefs) well.

When a chief's stool becomes vacant, it is from the queen-mother that the elders ask for a man to fill the vacant stool. As the 'mother' of the members of the royal lineage she is regarded as

---

[1] Rattray, *Ashanti Law and Constitution*, p. 91.
[2] Rattray, *Ashanti*, 1923, pp. 84–5.

the authority on the kinship relations of the lineage, and, therefore, questions as to whether or not any candidate possesses a legitimate kin-right to the stool are referred to her. But, as has been shown in the account of the election of the Chief of Wenchi, it is not her wishes but those of the elders that prevail in the selection of a candidate.

The queen-mother is consulted on the matrimonial affairs of the royal lineage. If any man of the lineage wishes to marry any particular girl he informs the queen-mother, who then asks the girl's family. Anyone wishing to marry a girl of the royal lineages also asks the queen-mother.

In Wenchi the queen-mother examines any girl who reaches the age of puberty, during the celebration of the girl's puberty rites, to make sure that she is not enceinte.

Queen-mothers have their own stools, on which they pour libations and offer food and sheep on an *Adae*.[1] They have their own elders and spokesmen, and hear household cases (*efisɛm*), usually matrimonial cases or disputes between members of the royal lineage. The queen-mother was a member of the chief's court, and was given her share of court fines and fees.

It is a common belief that in the olden days it was women who were chiefs. The traditional histories of Wenchi, Mampong, Juaben, and other Divisions in Ashanti tell of women who were chiefs. But, according to a well-known tradition, when war broke out and they were sent for, or sometimes when they were required for important meetings, they would say 'My menstrual period is on (*m'akyima*)'[2] and they could not perform their duties. 'So', said one informant, 'we asked them to give us men who would be chiefs in their place. That is why the elders ask the queen-mother to nominate a candidate.'

Every lineage has its own senior woman (*ɔbaapanyin*) responsible for the women of that lineage, and concerned with matters dealing with the marriage and divorce of the members of that lineage. The queen-mother does not control all the women in a Division. '*Mmaa nyinaa nsom no*' (It is not all the women who serve her) declared the Asantehene's spokesman.

But in the days when there were wars, when all the men had gone to fight, the queen-mother as head of the royal lineage

---

[1] See Chap. II.
[2] Ashantis regard women in their menstrual period as ceremonially unclean.

superintended the rites and dirges of the women praying for victory and the safe return of their men (*mmomome*).

Ashanti constitutional practice

The account of Wenchi confirms the main features of Ashanti constitutional practice presented in Rattray's accounts of seven of the Ashanti Divisions.[1]

Chiefship in Ashanti was based on the lineage system. Each lineage was a political unit, and the lineage head represented it on the council. The chief was chosen from one of the lineages by the heads of the other lineages. Kin-right and popular selection were combined.

The chief was bound by custom to act with the consent and on the advice of his elders, who were themselves representatives of lineages, and were subject to similar restraints from the members of their own lineages.

The chief was subject to checks from the elders, but they were jointly responsible for the administration of the Division. They formed the Government. Public opinion and criticism was expressed by a loose association of the commoners (*mmerante*) through their leader, the Nkwankwaahene, or through the elders.

Destoolment of a Chief

The Ashanti had a constitutional practice which ensured that the will of the people was given consideration. They had ultimately the constitutional right to destool a chief. As the fundamental principle was that only those who elected a chief could destool him, a destoolment required the consent of the elders. Sometimes they initiated a destoolment themselves when, for example, a chief repeatedly rejected their advice, or when he broke a taboo, or committed a sacrilegious act. The kind of offences for which chiefs were destooled may be gathered from the following instances of destoolments recounted in the traditional histories of the Divisions.

Chiefs Kwabena Aboagye of Asumegya, Kwabena Bruku, and Kwasi Ten of Nsuta were destooled for drunkenness; Kwame Asonane of Bekwai for being a glutton (*adidifurum*); Kwame Asona, also of Bekwai, for dealing in charms and noxious medicines; and Akuamoa Panyin of Juaben for his abusive tongue, and

---

[1] *Ashanti Law and Constitution*, chaps. ix–xi.

for not following the advice of his elders. In Kokofu, Osei Yaw was destooled for being fond of disclosing the origin of his subjects (i.e. reproaching them with their slave ancestry), and Mensa Bonsu for excessive cruelty.

A chief was also destooled if he became blind, or impotent, or suffered from leprosy, madness, or fits, or if his body was maimed in a way that disfigured him.

Two important characteristics of Ashanti constitutional practice brought out by Rattray[1] need to be emphasized here.

The chief was the axis of the political relations of the different elders and their subjects. There was no link between one elder and another except their common allegiance to the chief. Without a chief the elders, and the lineages and villages under their respective control, were isolated units. Communication from one to the other lay through the chief, and it was under him as the head that they formed a political unit.

The tribe or Division was administered on a policy that Rattray summed up in the one word 'decentralization'.[2] The chief communicated directly with the elders, they in turn with the headmen of the villages under them and they with their subjects. When the system functioned well it was democratic. There was an aristocracy of rulers, but they were constitutionally elected, and they were under popular control through the right of destoolment vested in the electors. Everyone was represented on the council through the lineage system. Legislation and major executive or administrative proposals were submitted for the approval of the representatives of the whole people meeting in the Divisional Council (*Asetena Kɛse*). We saw an example of this in the description of the election and installation of the Chief of Wenchi.

The efficiency of the system depended on the chief acting with the concurrence and advice of his elders, on an effective popular control of both the chief and his elders, so that they discovered and realized the will of the people in their legislative and executive functions, and finally on the adequacy of the lineage system to give representation to all the members of a tribe or residents of a territorial Division. To a large extent these conditions were satisfied in Ashanti until after 1896.

[1] *Ashanti Law and Constitution*, chaps. xii and xxxviii.
[2] See Chap. IV.

CHAPTER II

THE RELIGIOUS ASPECT OF CHIEFSHIP

The world of spirits

In *Ashanti* and *Religion and Art in Ashanti*[1] Rattray described the religious ceremonies of the Ashanti in detail.

The religion of the Ashanti is mainly ancestor-worship, and the position of the chief gains significance within the organized ceremonies by which the people express their sense of dependence on their ancestors.

The Ashantis believe in a world of spirits (*asaman*) where all their ancestors live in very much the same way as they lived on earth. This conception of a life after death similar to life on earth is implicit in their funeral ceremonies.

When a man is dying, water is poured down his throat. This is to help him climb the steep hill into the world of spirits. When he has died, food (*kraduane*) is set before the dead body. Relatives and friends give presents of gold-dust, cloths, blankets, mats, and pillows for the deceased to take into the world of spirits, where it is believed he will need these things as on earth.[2] Not so long ago, when a chief died, attendants were killed to accompany him into the world of spirits to continue their services to him.

The deceased goes to join his kinsmen who have preceded him. He is buried in the portion of the village cemetery reserved for members of his lineage. It is the wish of every Ashanti that he should thus be buried beside his ancestors.

But death does not sever the ties of kinship. Between the dead and their living relatives the bond of kinship is believed to persist.

At the graveyard, before the coffin is finally covered, the deceased is addressed by a member of his lineage:

'You are leaving us to-day; we have fired guns; we have given you a sheep; we have performed your funeral. Do not let any of us fall ill. Let us get money to pay the expenses of your

---

[1] *Ashanti*, chaps. iv–xx; *Religion and Art in Ashanti*, 1927, chaps. i–xx.

[2] This is based on my own observation, which confirms Rattray's account in *Religion and Art in Ashanti*, chap. xiv.

funeral. Let the women bear children. Life to all of us. Life to the chief.'

The ancestors are believed to be always watching the behaviour of those they have left behind on earth, sending them help and protection, or punishing them with misfortune if they do not act well.

To the Ashanti the world of spirits is very close. He has his ancestors constantly in mind. At meals the old Ashanti offers the first morsel to the ancestors. He also gives them the first drops of his drink. Even very young children are encouraged to leave a small morsel of food in the dish for the ancestors.

Intervention of the ancestors

In every Ashanti village stories are always circulating about the ancestors. Very often it is in connexion with the death of some-one who is believed to have been punished by his ancestors.

Two recent examples may be quoted.

In 1946 the Akwamuhene of Ankaasi, a village near Kumasi, died. Forty days before, he had given evidence at court in a case in which another man had been accused of murdering the Akwamuhene's own father. The accused person was acquitted chiefly on the evidence of the Akwamuhene, who a few days later fell ill. On the twenty-eighth day of his illness he confessed to a friend that he believed his father's ghost was punishing him because he had given false evidence at the trial. He did not recover from his illness, and died. No other explanation was required, for it was the general belief that his father had punished him for his conduct.

Another death also occurred recently (1946) at Wenchi. In 1940 an elderly man died there. His funeral rites were curtailed because some of the members of the lineage were away. It was decided that the full rites should be performed later. This was not done for six years. Then another member of the lineage, a nephew of the elderly man, fell ill and died. A native physician declared that the death had been caused by the spirit of the elderly man because the lineage had not performed his funeral rites. This was generally held to be a sufficient explanation for the death.

The ancestors are believed to be the custodians of the laws and customs of the tribe. They punish with sickness or misfortune those who infringe them.

An incident which occurred in 1942 may be told to illustrate this. A slave woman bought by a former chief had two daughters. The original purchaser's successor, a chief, married the older daughter; the other was married to a commoner. The chief's wife had four children, and her sister two. When the chief died, both women refused to live with his sisters, with whom they had lived all their lives. They went and lived in a village three miles away. Within a short time the chief's former wife lost two of her children, and her sister lost both of hers. When they consulted the local god (*ɔbosom*) to find out the cause of this misfortune, the priest told them that since they had left the chief's house the ancestral spirits were angry and no longer protected them. If they wished to avoid further deaths they should give a sheep to the chief's sister to be sacrificed to the ancestral spirits, and they should return to the house. I was present at the piacular sacrifice subsequently made.

Constantly before the Ashanti, and serving to regulate his conduct, is the thought that his ancestors are watching him, and that one day, when he rejoins them in the world of spirits, they will ask him to give an account of his conduct, especially of his conduct towards his kinsmen. This thought is a very potent sanction of morality.

The ancestors are believed to send help to their descendants. I translate a story told me by the sister of a paramount chief who had died four years before the incident narrated here occurred.

I was dangerously ill. I became dumb and could not speak. For two weeks I had not spoken. I could not eat or drink. I could only drink a little soup, which had to be pushed down my throat. One night I became very stiff. It took six strong men to hold me down. Then I went off to sleep. I dreamt, and in my dream I saw my brother, the late chief. He looked very angry. He told me he had always warned me about my bad temper, and that I should show proper respect to my elder sister, who was now the head of the house and served food to the ancestors. I had been afflicted with sickness because the ancestors were displeased with me. He threw me a medicine-ball (*dufa*), and asked me to give it to my sister in the morning, and direct her to dissolve a little in water for me to drink. Next morning, when my sister came, I could not speak to her. But I lifted my pillow. The medicine-ball was there. I gave it to her, and showed her by signs what she was to do. When I drank it, I became well. I have still got the rest of the medicine-ball.

The wishes of the ancestors are believed to be made known

more often through the priests of the gods (*abosom*) than through dreams. But these stories show how close the Ashantis conceive the bond to be that exists between the living and their dead kinsmen.

At one *Adae*[1] ceremony I attended at Mampong I stood among the crowd of spectators watching the dances. An elderly man, one of the sub-chiefs, suddenly got up and asked leave to go home. As he passed he explained to me: 'The *samanfo* (spirits) have come; they are all about here; it is too much for me. I am going home.'

Although few would claim this power of seeing the dead, the old man was expressing a common belief among the Ashantis that at these ceremonies, held in memory of the dead, the ancestors come to join their living descendants in the celebrations.

The Chief as intermediary

The Ashanti believe that the well-being of a society depends upon the maintenance of good relations with the ancestors on whom the living depend for help and protection. Each lineage keeps in touch with its own ancestors through ritual sacrifices. Every lineage has its blackened stool which is the shrine of its ancestors. During ritual ceremonies the elder places sacrifices on the stool, and pours libations on it, and prays for the welfare of his lineage, which is represented at these ceremonies.

It is believed that the tribe as a whole is protected by the spirits of the dead rulers. The chief is therefore appointed to act as the intermediary between his royal ancestors and the tribe.

As has been described, the esoteric rite of the chief's installation is when the chief-elect is led into the stool-house where the blackened stools of his ancestors are kept. There, more than in any other place, the spirits of the ancestors are believed to be present. Upon the blackened stool of the most renowned of his ancestors the chief is lowered and raised three times. He is then enstooled. He has been brought into a peculiarly close relationship with the dead. Thenceforward he becomes the intermediary between the tribe and his royal ancestors without whose aid misfortunes would befall the community.

From the moment that the chief is enstooled his person becomes sacred. This is emphasized by taboos. He may not strike, or be

[1] See pp. 27 ff. below.

struck by, anyone, lest the ancestors bring misfortune upon the tribe. He may never walk bare-footed, lest when the sole of his foot touches the ground some misfortune befall the community. He should walk with care lest he stumble. If he does stumble, the expected calamity has to be averted with a sacrifice. His buttocks may not touch the ground: that again would bring misfortune. All these taboos remind the chief and everybody else that he occupies a sacred position. He is the occupant of the stool of the ancestors (*Ɔte nananom akonwa so*). For this reason he is treated with the greatest veneration.

In conversation, chiefs frequently refer to themselves as 'I who sit upon the stool of so-and-so', mentioning the name of a great ancestor. To chiefs and subjects alike it is a significant fact that the chief is one who 'sits on the stool of the ancestors'. It is in that capacity that he offers the sacrifices deemed necessary for the welfare of the tribe.

The Adae *ceremony*

It is in his role as the intermediary between the tribe and the ancestors that the chief becomes the central figure at the organized religious ceremonies which have been described by Rattray.[1] Of these ceremonies the most frequent is the *Adae*, which is still performed in the same way as when Rattray described it twenty years ago. As he correctly defined it, the *Adae* refers to 'those ceremonies at which the spirits of departed rulers of the clan are propitiated, their names and deeds recalled, and favours and mercy solicited'.[2]

There are two *Adaes*, one held on Sundays (*Kwesidae, Adae Kese*), and one held on Wednesdays (*Wukudae*). To-day, just as Bowdich observed in 1817, 'the customs are alternately called the great and little Adai, the former taking place always on a Sunday, the latter on a Wednesday; and it appeared to me, from calculation, that there were six weeks between each great Adai, and six weeks between each little one, so that the custom was generally held every twenty-one days.'[3]

The period is calculated in North Ashanti as follows: A prefix is attached to each day of the week; but as there are only six prefixes, and seven days in the week, one prefix occurs twice in

[1] *Ashanti*, chaps. v–ix.   [2] Ibid., p. 92.
[3] Bowdich, *Mission from Cape Coast Castle to Ashantee*, 1819, p. 281.

each week; by continuing the prefixes in cycle the starting-point is reached again on the forty-third day, thus:

	Prefix	Day of week	
1.	*Fɔ*	*Dwo*	Monday
2.	*Nwona*	*Bena*	Tuesday
3.	*Nkyi*	*Wukuo*	Wednesday
4.	*Kuru*	*Yao*	Thursday
5.	*Kwa*	*Fie*	Friday
6.	*Mono*	*Mene*	Saturday
7.	*Fɔ*	*Kwasi*	Sunday (1st prefix repeated)

The cycle then begins in the succeeding week at *Nwona-Dwo*, and continues *Nkyi-Bena*, &c., each prefix moving up one step. From one *Nkyi-Wukuo* to the next *Nkyi-Wukuo* takes six weeks. It actually occurs on the forty-third day.

So every twenty-one days an Ashanti chief offers libations to his royal ancestors on behalf of his subjects, praying that the soil may be fruitful and the tribe increase. As these *Adae* ceremonies have been fully described by Rattray,[1] only the main features need be recalled here.

Preparations are made on the previous day. The stools are cleaned, and the necessary money, drink, sheep, and other things collected together. In the evening the drums announce the approach of the *Adae* celebration. The esoteric rite takes place in the stool-house with only a few people present. These usually include the chief, an Ɔkyeame, a stool-carrier, and one or two of the elders. Here the chief is the servant. With the sandals off his feet, his shoulders bared, he reverently offers drink and meat to his ancestors with the prayer: 'To-day is *Adae*, come and receive this and eat; let this town prosper, let the bearers of children bear children; may all the people get riches; life to me; long life to the nation (*Ɔman*).'

At such a ceremony the office of the chief as an *Ɔhene Kɔmfo* (priest chief), priest to the ancestors, is most in evidence. As servant of the ancestors he shows them the same reverence and pays them the same courtesies as he is accustomed to receive from his subjects, because he is the one who 'sits upon the stool of the ancestors'.

After the rites in the stool-house the public ceremony is held.

[1] Rattray, *Ashanti*, chaps. v–ix.

The drums recite the brave deeds of the chief's ancestors, while the minstrels (*kwadwomfo*) drone into his ear 'the names and deeds of dead kings and queens, as far back as their traditional history has any record'.[1]

When the chief takes his seat in the public assembly all the elders, each accompanied by his subjects and the members of his lineage, pay their respects to him. He then sends drink to each elder and his followers.

The rest of the afternoon is spent in dancing and drumming, in which everyone joins. The old men think of past *Adae* ceremonies at which the performers were different. They recall actors whose places are now filled by their sons, brothers, or nephews. They think of the future when they, too, will be looking on such scenes from the world of the spirits, where they hope to join their ancestors.

The *Adae* ceremonies do not complete the chief's religious functions. There are the *Odwera* ceremonies, the periodic sacrifices to the national gods, especially during the harvest season, and special sacrifices during emergencies or misfortunes.

The Odwera *ceremony*

Both Rattray and Bowdich have described the big national ceremonies which centred round the Asantehene and his royal ancestors.[2] No *Odwera* has been held in Kumasi for a long time owing to the expatriation of the Asantehene, the late Nana Prempeh I, to the Seychelle Islands in 1896. But the *Odwera* ceremony is still held in Wenchi, North Ashanti, and in other Divisions in Ashanti. A description is given below of the ceremony as observed in Wenchi.

Bowdich and Rattray both pointed out certain features of the ceremony. In the old days it was a feast of the dead, it was closely connected with first-fruits, it was a cleansing of the nation from defilement and a purification of the shrines of the ancestral spirits and the national gods. All these features are present in the ceremony I describe below. The account is from my own observations and from details supplied later by the chief's mother, who offered the food and libations at the ceremony.

[1] Rattray, *Ashanti*, p. 103.
[2] Rattray, *Religion and Art in Ashanti*, chap. xii; Bowdich, op. cit., Part II, chap. v.

Explaining the beginnings of the custom, the old woman said:
'The chief's *Odwera* is held when the last of the Wenchi gods has
eaten yam. In the old days all the gods (*abosom*) lived in the chief's
house (i.e., their shrines were kept there). Then they said Nana
G— had wronged them, so the gods were angry, and Nana G—
died. Fiema, a woman, then became chief as well as queen-mother.
She distributed the gods to the various towns where they are now
found. To the principal gods, Guakuro, Drɔbo, and Gyanso she
gave presents, a miniature golden stool to one, a golden gun to
another, and a sword of gold to a third. At first there used to be
famine in the land. So when we planted yams, and we got a good
crop, we first gave some to the gods. The yam is mashed with
palm-oil and eggs. The eggs are presented by the people who live
in the town in which the god dwells.

'When Drɔbo eats yam, the Odekuro of Drɔboso gives him a
sheep; the Chief of Wenchi also gives a sheep and some yams.
These and the shrine of the god are carried to the river near the
village. The shrine, the sheep, and the yams are all washed. Some
medicinal leaves (*sommɛ*) are mixed in water in a brass pan; a
switch made of cow's tail is dipped into the water, and the shrine
is sprinkled with it. The sheep are brought home and killed. One
foreleg is given to the people of Akrobi (the seat of the shrine of
Guakuro); the people of Drɔboso are given the waist; the blood
is poured on the shrine. The men struggle for the rest of the meat.
Many people from other towns in Wenchi attend the ceremony.
Plenty of food is cooked by the women of Drɔboso and given to
the guests, some of whom stay a whole week for the celebrations.

'About six or seven women fetch clay from the river, and on
the Friday, which is Drɔbo's day, they daub the house of the shrine
with the clay. The chief takes a bottle of rum to the god. This is
offered to him by the priest who, as he pours the libation, says:

' "Drɔbo, to-day the edges of the year have met (*afe ano ahyia*).
The Chief of Wenchi has given you yams, he has given you sheep,
he has given you eggs, and now he has brought this drink. Let
Wenchi prosper. May the women bear children; do not let our
children die; those who have gone to trade, may they get money.
May there be peace and prosperity during the present chief's
reign."

'The gods celebrate their yam-eating festivals in succession, and
the people go from one town to the other to attend them.

Guakuro's is the last, and forty days after his celebration the chief's *Odwera* celebrations begin.'

After all the gods have been offered their sacrifices of the first-fruits of yam, the ancestors are offered theirs. This is what is done at the *Odwera* ceremony. It is a feast of the dead. The approach of the *Odwera*, which is an annual festival, is described as *akonwa bedi bayerε* (the stool is going to eat yam) or *ohene betwa dwera* (the chief is going to celebrate the *Odwera*). Until the ceremony has been held, and some of the year's harvest of yams have been offered to the ancestors, the chief may not eat any yams because his royal ancestors have not yet eaten.

The rites last over a week, during which the chief does not sit in court or deal with any political or administrative affairs of the Division. The Kontihene takes over the administration.

The chief, the elders, and the Adekurofo prepare for the celebrations by collecting together meat and yams. To get the meat they distribute gunpowder, which they save up for the purpose, to their subjects, for hunting. Farmers and hunters throughout the Division, as well as the elders and Adekurofo (village headmen) bring presents of yam and meat to the chief.

The *Odwera* festival observed began on a Tuesday (*Adapaa*) preceding a Wednesday *Adae* (*Wukudae*). That night there was continuous drumming in the chief's house from 9 p.m. till about 4 a.m. The women met there and sang till far into the night. Their songs were songs of thanksgiving to the gods, to the Supreme Being, and to the ancestors for the gift of a good harvest, for life and children, or prayers for these same things.

On the following day, the *Wukudae*, the elders met in the chief's house at about seven in the morning. Led by the head stool-carrier, the Ɔkyeame Panyin (chief spokesman), the chief, the queen-mother, the Gyasehene, and one attendant entered the stool-house. They slipped their sandals off their feet as they entered the room, bared their shoulders, and bowed, saying, 'Good morning to you, grandsires'.

The Ɔkyeame poured libations of rum and offered as sacrifice a sheep provided by the chief. The Ɔkyeame mentioned by name each chief who had a blackened stool in the room and said, 'Here is drink' as he poured the libations, or 'here is meat' as he offered the meat. 'All of you, grandsires, by your help the year has come round again; your grandson (the chief) has come this morning to bring you a sheep and drink; grant him health; prosperity to the Wenchi people; let the celebrations about to begin pass peacefully. Blessing, blessing.'

The entrails of the sheep were placed on the stools. The rest was cut up and distributed. Each elder got a portion. The three quarters of the town (Asere, Bokorɔ, Kɔntɔn) each received a portion; the Gyase people, the chief, stool-carriers, horn-blowers, umbrella-carriers, and drummers all received their portions.

I recorded the following allocations at the time: one leg went to the people in the Kɔntɔn quarter, one shoulder went to the Gyase people, a leg and the heart to the chief; the feet and skin were given to the stool-carriers, the jaws to the horn-blowers and drummers, the rest of the entrails to the umbrella-carriers, the waist to the queen-mother, the lungs to the court-crier (Ɛsɛn).

All through the Wednesday the Adekurofo (village headmen) in the outlying villages and their subjects, men, women, and children, thronged into the town. The day was spent in drumming and dancing.

The central rite of the celebration was held on the Monday of the second week. At about 3 p.m. there was a long procession to a place a mile from the town, called Kaamu. This was the burial-place of the chiefs. The procession was led by a row of women carrying cooked food in brass pans. The food consisted of different dishes of mashed yam, rice, maize, meat, and fish—'every kind of food grown on the land', as the chief told me. A row of boys carrying palm-wine and beer brewed locally from maize corn followed. No spirits were used at this ceremony. Any drink except palm-wine and maize-corn beer was tabooed. Next followed the chief's own mother who, as occupant of the founding ancestress's stool, officiated at the ceremony. She was joined by the queen-mother, the senior women of the royal families, and the senior women of the three principal lineages in the town—Brafo Kwame's lineage, Gyane's lineage, and the Gyansoase lineage. The chief and the elders and their retinues followed next, with the drummers and horn-blowers immediately behind. When the procession reached Kaamu it stopped near a tree called sofoase, underneath which were three broken pots of earthenware stuck fast in the ground. This was the sacred place where the offering of food and drink was made annually to the ancestors. The chief's mother sat beneath the sofoase-tree and the food that had been brought was lined up in front of her. Two bearers fetched water from the Adaagye stream near by. The chief and his elders took their seats near the tree. The chief's mother said, 'We are now going to offer food to the ancestors'. The drums stopped beating. All the people stood up. The chief and the elders rose from their seats, bared their shoulders, and squatted. The chief's mother took some mashed yam with a wooden ladle, and dropping some near each of the three earthenware pots she said, mentioning each departed chief and then each queen-mother by name: 'Here is food: all of you receive this and eat; the year has come round again; to-day we celebrate it; bring us blessing; blessing to the chief who sits on your stool; health to the people; let women bear children; let the men prosper in their undertakings; life to all; we thank you for the good harvest, for standing behind us. Blessing, blessing, blessing.' The whole company repeated in chorus: *Kosɛ, kosɛ, kosɛ* (blessing, blessing, blessing). Next the chief's mother took a pot of palm-wine, and went through the same ceremony as before, substituting 'here is drink' for 'here is food'. When she had finished, the chief and the elders resumed their seats. The drums sounded again in praise of the chief and his ancestors. The corn-beer and palm-wine were distributed to the company under the direction of the Ɔkyeame (spokesman). After drinking this the procession returned to the town, leaving the food under the *sofoase*-tree. The chief's mother was the last to leave.

The following day the stools 'ate yam'. About 10 a.m. a dish of mashed yam and some corn-beer were offered to the stools in the stool-house by the spokesman in the same manner as has been described, the chief, the Ɔkyeame, the stool-carrier, the queen-mother, and the chief's mother being present. After this ceremony the chief's mother performed a similar ceremony in the queen-mother's stool-house. The chief killed a cow and four sheep. A large amount of food was cooked by the chief's wives, and distributed to the elders and people attending the ceremony from the outlying villages, each lineage receiving a present. In the evening, the principal black[1] stool was brought out of the stool-house, wrapped in a blanket (*ɲsa*) and carried on the nape of the neck of the head stool-carrier. Two rows of men armed with Dane-guns marched on either side of the stool. The chief and his elders

---

[1] 'Black' from the blood of sheep with which it has been besmeared at many ceremonies.

followed immediately behind. Outside the chief's house the drummers, horn-blowers, and all the men and women took their places in the procession. The stool was carried round the town, the whole crowd following. This action was a symbolic expression of the watch that the ancestors kept over the town all the year round.

The following day the *mfodwofa* was held. This was a ceremony in which only the 'royals', i.e. members of the chief's lineage, took part. They and the chief went again to Kaamu, the burial-place, where a black hen was offered to the ancestors. A black hen was an unusual sacrifice, a spotless white hen being what the priests usually demand for sacrifice to the gods. The black hen was really a 'scapegoat'— a piacular offering to the ancestors on behalf of the people for the sins of the past year. It is best understood in relation to the rite of purification which followed it on the Saturday of the second week of the celebrations.

At about 4 p.m. that day the chief and his wives and the royals came out all dressed in white cloth (calico). Behind them came the stool-carriers carrying the brass pans, the white stools,[1] and the other paraphernalia of the stool-house. Next came the elders, the queen-mother, the chief's mother, and their followers. A sheep and three chickens were carried by attendants who brought up the rear. The procession marched again to Kaamu. When it got there, the chief's 'soul-washer' (*kradwarehene*) sent for water from the Adaagye river. This was the river from which the Wenchi people obtained their drinking-water. It was a ritual obligation to use its water for the ceremony. When the water was brought, some leaves (*kra-ha* or 'soul-leaves') were mixed in it, and the chief's soul-washer bathed him in this water, using a new sponge and fresh soap. The soul-washer tied the chief's wrists and ankles with *kra-ha* leaves and daubed white clay on his toes and chest. The procession then returned to the chief's house. The three chickens and the sheep, which had been washed in the river, were killed. Fresh wood was used for making a fire, on which three new pots were placed. One large yam was cut into seven pieces and cooked in one of the pots. The three chickens were cooked in the second pot. The sheep was cut up and the heart, liver, intestines, jaw, kidneys, shoulder, neck, and a leg were cooked in the third pot. No salt or pepper was used, as the spirits are believed not to like them. The yam was mashed. The chicken soup was poured into

---

[1] Stools in regular use, which had never been besmeared with blood.

a big brass bowl, the mutton into another. The Ɔkyeame offered some of each to the ancestors and to the gods, repeating the same prayers that had been used at Kaamu. After this, everyone present was invited to share the feast. There was a rush, everyone trying to take as much as he could. He who partook of this had shared a meal with the ancestors and would receive strength and health.

Not till these rites were held could the chief or his wives eat of the new crop of yam.

The above account may be compared with the ceremony described by Bowdich more than a hundred years ago, when he visited Kumasi. It will show how these rites have persisted down to the present day.[1]

About ten days after the custom, the whole of the royal household eat new yam for the first time, in the market place, the King attending. The next day he and the captains set off for Sarrasoo before sun rise, to perform their annual ablutions in the river Dah. Almost all the inhabitants follow him, and the capital appears deserted; the succeeding day the King washes in the marsh at the south-east end of the town, the captains lining the streets leading to it on both sides. He is attended by his suite, but he laves the water with his own hands over himself, his chairs, stools, gold and silver plate, and the various articles of furniture used especially by him. Several brass pans are covered with white cloth, with various fetish [i.e. shrines] under them. About twenty sheep are dipped, (one sheep and one goat only are sacrificed at the time) to be killed in the palace in the afternoon, that their blood may be poured on the stools and doorposts. All the doors, windows, and arcades of the palace are plentifully besmeared with a mixture of eggs, and palm-oil; as also the stools of the different tribes and families. After the ceremony of washing is over, the principal captains precede the King to the palace, where, contrary to usual custom, none but those of the first rank are allowed to enter, to see the procession pass. The King's fetish men walk first, with attendants holding basins of sacred water which they sprinkle plentifully over the chiefs with branches, the more superstitious running to have a little poured on their heads, and even on their tongues. The King and his attendants all wear white cloths on this occasion. Three white lambs are led before him, intended for sacrifice at his bed chamber. All his wives follow, with a guard of archers.

I have described the *Odwera* ceremony at length because the cycle of rites observed during the celebrations contains all the essential elements of Ashanti religion.

[1] Bowdich, op. cit., p. 279.

The meaning of the rites

The dominant desire of the people is for increase and fertility. They want the earth to be fruitful, the women to bear children, the men to prosper in their undertakings. These are desired so that the race may continue. Those who give these things are the gods, the Supreme Being, and the ancestors.

When the people come together for these ceremonies they express their solidarity in relation to the chief and his ancestors, on whom their common loyalty is focused. Their joint participation in these ceremonies strengthens their unity and cohesion.

The symbols which are used in the sacrifices are the objects of common interest on which the life of the tribe depends. As the chief's mother explained, these rites were held because 'in the old days, there used to be famine'. Food was and is a matter of common interest, so is the desire for the continuance of the race. So the tribe comes together to ask for food and for increase—for fertility of the soil and for the procreation of children.

Chiefship is a sacred office

Only the chief could bring all the lineages together and sacrifice to his royal ancestors on behalf of the community as a whole. To the people this was his most important function. Before they came together to settle in a town as a community the chief first sacrificed on their behalf. An example of this was given me by the elders who narrated to me the history of Mampong. The people of Mampong at one time lived at Behenease between Nsuta and Juaben. They decided to look for another place in which to live because they found Behenease too small. The Chief of Mampong then was Nana Akuamoa. He sent his hunters to look for a suitable site. They found the site of the present Mampong. An area was marked out near the River Tadie. The chief then sent a sheep and some palm-wine. The sheep was sacrificed to the river, and the wine was used for pouring libations. The chief and his people were coming to live beside the river, so he prayed that the spirit of the river might guard his people. After this, the people moved to settle there.

Chiefship in Ashanti is a sacred office. This has been shown by the rites of the chief's enstoolment and by his part in ceremonies such as have been described. As long as he sits upon the stool of the ancestors his person is sacred. As the successor of the ancestors he performed various rites for the welfare of his people. With that office were joined other functions which may be described as administrative, executive, judicial, and military. If he abused his power, he was divested of it by having his special connexion with his ancestors, established on his enstoolment, severed. This happened when he committed or was made to commit one of the tabooed acts. His sanctity was violated and he was no longer able to sit on the stool of the ancestors. Thus, the Ashanti destool a chief by bumping his buttocks on the ground, or taking his sandals off his feet, or by mutilating his body. After such an act the chief was no longer in special contact with the ancestors, and having lost his sanctity he became automatically divested of all the other functions pertaining to the office of chiefship.

Chiefship in the Gold Coast

The sacred nature of the chief's office is a characteristic feature of chiefship throughout the Gold Coast.

Recently (1946) the paramount chief of Aowin[1] was destooled. There was no precedent, as no paramount chief had ever been destooled. The Aowin Constitution is very similar to that of Ashanti. All the elders except those who were closely related to the chief agreed that the administration of the paramount chief was unsatisfactory and that he should give up the stool. This the chief agreed to do. A public meeting was held at which the Gyasehene, on behalf of the elders, gave the reasons why they had all agreed to destool the chief. The chief in reply said that he was the direct matrilineal descendant of the founding ancestress of Enchi, and that his ancestors had always ruled the State. He had never heard of such an incident. But he did not wish to be the cause of any disturbance in the State and he was willing to hand over the stool since all the elders were united against him. The Gyasehene walked up to the chief, took off his sandals so that his feet touched the ground, and declared him thereby destooled.

That chiefship is a sacred office in the Gold Coast generally is also illustrated by the following example. Manya Krobo is a State in the Eastern Province of the Gold Coast. The social organization there is different from that of Ashanti in that the lineage system is

---

[1] In the Western Province of the Gold Coast.

based on patrilineal and not on matrilineal descent. But the chief occupies the same sacred role as in Ashanti. I asked the paramount chief, who is literate, what procedure they had for destooling a chief. He wrote:

We do not recognize destoolment in Krobo as there are no cases in our history. No *Konor* (paramount chief) has ever had the misfortune of being destooled. There was, however, a case about twenty years ago when a sub-chief was brought by his clan heads, who complained to the *Konor* in council that the sub-chief was persistent in his refusal to maintain the dignity and sanctity of his position, and had violated several rules. He was tried, but before the end of the trial, when he found that it was a losing battle, he abdicated by taking off his sandals and sitting on the ground in open council. This was not our accepted form, but it did mean that by doing before the open council what he knew was taboo was to declare his inability to hold his sacred post and trust. He did not lose any civil rights as a citizen except his right ever to consider himself for the stool again.

No one could be an adequate chief who did not perform the ritual functions of his office. There have recently been elected as chiefs in different parts of Ashanti men who are both literate and Christian. But they have all felt an obligation to perform the ritual acts of their office. They were enstooled in the stool-house, where they poured libations to the ancestors whom they had succeeded. They owned that they felt the reality of their contact with the ancestors during these rites of installation. I have attended ritual ceremonies at Wenchi, Bekwai, Mampong, and Kumasi, where the chiefs who were the principal actors were literates. It is as successors of the ancestors that they are venerated and their authority respected, and they could not keep the office without maintaining contact with the ancestors through the traditional rituals.

Literates and illiterates, Christians and pagans have participated in ritual *Adae* ceremonies, and shared the sentiments they expressed or symbolized. I have questioned literate and Christian young men who have been privileged to attend the pouring of libations to ancestors, or have witnessed the sacrifices at *Adae* and similar ceremonies. Their answers were in many instances, 'I felt its reality' or 'I was deeply moved'. The Ashanti expression often used '*Ɛtɔɔ me so*' describes a very exalted feeling of awe.

The ritual position of the chief in Ashanti and the ceremonial rites connected with chiefship have remained unchanged. Ceremonies that Bowdich (1819) and Rattray (1923) described are still observed in the same way.

Although there are constitutional checks for the proper exercise of the chief's powers, the office is essentially sacred. Ancestor-worship is based on the lineage system, the members of a lineage forming a cult-group in relation to their own ancestors. The tribe as a whole is a cult-group in relation to the chief's ancestors.

In the ritual, as in the constitutional aspect of his life, the chief is the focus of the unity of the tribe. His ritual functions are connected with ceremonies through which the people express their reverence for the ancestors and gods and their sense of dependence on them, and also their sentiments of solidarity and continuity. This accounts for the persistence of the ritual ceremonies in the face of revolutionary changes in the political system. The chief's position is bound up with strong religious sentiments.

CHAPTER III

CHIEFSHIP AND LAND-TENURE

Beliefs about the Earth

K INSHIP, reverence for the ancestors, and belief in the spiritual power of the Earth have combined to give land tenure in Ashanti its peculiar character.

The Ashanti believed that the Earth had a power or spirit of its own which could be helpful if propitiated or harmful if neglected. This power in the Earth was conceived as a female principle, *Asase Yaa* (Earth) whose natal day is Thursday.[1]

Rattray translated *Asase Yaa* as 'Thursday, Earth Goddess', and spoke of the 'Cult of the Earth Deity'[2]. This was not a very accurate rendering of the Ashanti conception. The Earth has no priests or priestesses, nor do the Ashanti consult her for divination in case of illness or need as they do other gods (*abosom*). The Ashanti say '*Asase nyɛ bosom; ɔnkyerɛ mmusuo*' (The Earth is not a goddess, she does not divine).[3] The conception is rather that of a power or principle possessed by the Earth.

Thursday was regarded as the natal day of the Earth. She was not to be disturbed on that day.[4] To avert misfortune work on the land on Thursdays was prohibited. It was desirable to be on good terms with the spirit of the Earth.

Every *Adae* ceremony the drummer addressed the Earth:

> *Asase damirifa*
> *Asase damirifa*
> *Asase ne mfuturu*
> *Twereduampon,*

---

[1] The Ashantis establish a connexion between many things, e.g. rivers and gods, and days of the week.

[2] Rattray, *Ashanti*, chap. xxi.

[3] *Asasenkyerɛ mmusuo*: literally, 'the Earth does not advise sacrifices'.

[4] In this connexion this extract is rather interesting: 'On April 15th (1870) we were awoke by the rocking of our bedroom from a sharp shock of earthquake. Some years before, on a like occurrence, human sacrifices had been immediately offered to appease the Spirit, but Prince Ansa had explained to the King that this was happily discontinued; but field work was forbidden on a Thursday because of an earthquake which had once happened on that day.' Ramseyer and Kühne, *Four Years in Ashantee*, 1875, pp. 166-7.

Asase merebewu a
  Medan wo
Asase mete ase a
  Medan wo
Asase a odi afunu,
Odomankoma kyerɛma se
  Ɔkɔɔ baabi a
Wama ne ho mene so oo,
Wama ne ho mene so.

Earth, condolences,
Earth, condolences,
Earth and dust,
The Supreme Being
I lean upon you.
Earth, when I am about to die
I lean upon you.
Earth, while I am alive
I depend upon you.
Earth that receives dead bodies,
The Creator's Drummer says
From wherever he went,
He has roused himself,
He has roused himself.

The sense of dependence expressed in this drum language is also given expression in certain rites.

Rattray has recorded the old Ashanti custom when at the commencement of cultivation the farmer offered the Earth a sacrifice of yam and fowl.

The farmer stands upon the land and wrings off the neck of his offering, allowing the blood to drip upon *etɔ* (mashed yam) and upon the earth, and speaks as follows: 'Grandfather So-and-so, you once came and hoed here and then you left it to me. You also, Earth, Ya, on whose soil I am going to hoe, the yearly cycle has come round and I am going to cultivate; when I work, let a fruitful year come upon me, do not let the knife cut me, do not let a tree break and fall upon me, do not let a snake bite me.'[1]

When the Earth granted a good harvest, the farmer was expected to return thanks by pouring libations or making a sacrifice. In 1942 a farmer, who had cultivated a very large farm and had an

[1] Rattray, *Ashanti*, p. 215.

unusually good crop of yams, died at Wenchi before it had all been harvested. His death was attributed to his failure to propitiate the Earth which had given him such a good yield.

The drummer referred to the 'Earth that receives dead bodies'. Libations were poured to her when a grave was dug for the burial of a dead person. At one such ceremony, at Daho near Mampong, the deceased was an old woman who had been baptized a Christian in the Anglican Church six weeks before her death. She was to be buried by the roadside. The Ashanti believe it to be a bad thing to bury a solitary person by the roadside. Her spirit would feel lonely, and she would cause the death of some of her relatives so that they might keep her company in the spirit world. This, the family desired to avert. A libation of palm-wine was poured at the spot where the grave was dug and the following prayer was offered:

> *Asase Yaa, gye nsa nom,*
> *Wo nana . . . na wawu*
> *Yɛbɛsrɛ wo ha abɔ amena*
> *Mma bone bi nka yɛn,*
> *Abusuafo nkye*
> *Eha yi a yɛde . . . abɛto yi,*
> *Mma obi mmɛka ne ho.*

> Earth, whose day is Thursday, receive
>   this wine and drink,
> It is your grandchild . . . that has died,
> We have come to beg you for this spot
>   so that we may dig a hole;
> Do not let any evil befall us.
> Let the relatives live long.
> Here where we are laying . . .
> Do not let another join her.

Among the participants at this ceremony was the literate chief.

The land belongs to the ancestors

The Earth was regarded as possessing a spirit or power of its own which was helpful if propitiated, and harmful if neglected, but the land was also regarded as belonging to the ancestors. It is from them that the living have inherited the right to use it. The farmer's prayer (p. 41, above), when he offered his sacrifice of mashed yam and fowl, began: 'Grandfather . . . you once came

and hoed here and then you left it to me.' It was because his ancestor had hoed there that he had inherited the right to farm there.

It was believed not only that the ancestors owned the land, but
also that they constantly kept watch and saw to it that it was used
properly and fairly.

A farmer cut himself while felling trees on his farm at the village
of Gyansoso, near Wenchi, and died shortly after he had been
conveyed home. The *obosom* (god) of the village, when consulted,
declared that the farmer had died because his ancestors who had
farmed there before him were dissatisfied with him. He was a
greedy person who did not share his food with his relatives, and
had even neglected his sacrifices to the ancestors.

Another man when on his death-bed (this occurred in 1942)
made a dying declaration giving one of his cocoa-farms to his son,
and swore an oath enjoining his brother, who was his successor,
to see that the gift was honoured. 'If you do not give it to him',
said the dying man, 'I shall call you before the ancestors for our
case to be judged.' A man's property should normally go to his
maternal kinsmen, and his brother had the right to succeed to it
all. A man was permitted by custom to make a gift of part of his
farm to his son. This was valid if it was made in the presence of
witnesses, and if the gift was acknowledged by the offer and
acceptance of *aseda* (token of thanks) in money or drink. But the
gift was subject to the approval of the maternal kinsmen, who
were thereby deprived of part of their inheritance.

The man died and his brother succeeded to his property, but
refused, with the concurrence of the other members of the family,
to give the cocoa-farm to his deceased brother's son. Three months
later a fire broke out in the village. The surviving brother fell
from a roof while helping to put out one of the fires, and sustained
an injury to his leg from which he subsequently died. Before he
died, he told his family that he believed his deceased brother was
summoning him to the spirit world to answer for his conduct in not
honouring his brother's death-bed declaration. The general belief
was that his death was due to his failure to carry out his deceased
brother's instructions. The next successor to the property duly
gave the cocoa-farm to the son to whom it had been left.

This idea that the land belonged to the ancestors made the
Ashanti unwilling to sell his land. There was always the dread that
the ancestors would summon him to account for such conduct.

The belief that the land belonged to the ancestors and that they had passed it on to the living for their use was of political significance. As the land belonged to the ancestors it was a link between them and their living descendants. In Ashanti the object which symbolized the unity of the ancestors and their descendants was the stool which the chief occupied. In any Ashanti village the inquirer was informed, 'The land belongs to the stool', or 'The land belongs to the chief'. Further investigation revealed that both expressions meant the same thing: 'The land belongs to the ancestors.'

The Chief is custodian

The chiefs were the custodians of the land. The following illustration makes this clearer. There was a boundary dispute between two neighbouring Divisions in Ashanti. The best-informed person in one of the Divisions was an ex-chief who had been ruler in the Division from 1900 to 1904, when he was destooled. He and the ruling chief had been on bad terms for years. The ruling chief sent a bottle of gin to the ex-chief, desiring reconciliation, and asking if he would give evidence if the land dispute came before the court. The ex-chief's reply was as follows: 'Tell him I do not want his drink. As to the land, it is not his; it belongs to the ancestors whom I hope soon to rejoin. If I do not give evidence and so save the land for the use of their grand-children, it is the ancestors that I wrong, and they will ask me about it when I join them. So tell him I shall give evidence, because the land belongs to the ancestors and not to him.'

The custodianship of the chief entailed certain rights and responsibilities. The chief was responsible for the defence of the land at law or by arms. He had also certain defined rights which were coexistent with the rights of lineages and individuals in his Division.[1] In case of extreme need he could sell the land, but not without the consent of his council and a sacrifice to the ancestors. The chief had a right to portions or skins of certain wild animals killed on the land of the Division. He was entitled to tributes of fish from those who fished in its rivers; to a certain amount of work on his farm from his people, and to an annual tribute of food, meat, or fish at the *Odwera* ceremony. He had a share in any

[1] I have found Dr. Max Gluckman's concept of 'cluster of rights' in African Law most helpful. See his *Essays on Lozi Land and Royal Property*, 1943.

treasure-trove found on the land. This was evidence of his rights in any minerals mined or discovered in his Division. But over the same land his people had rights of usufruct. Any piece of land to which no lineage had the claim of usufruct came directly under the chief in his official capacity. Strangers wanting land on which to settle or farm would ask the chief, who would give them portions of these lands.

The chief also had political rights such as the right of jurisdiction over the land of his Division. He had also the right to impose specific levies, with the consent of his council, on the subjects who lived on his land.

When an Ashanti said that the land belonged to the chief or the stool, he meant that the chief had these rights, but he was also aware that the subjects of the chief, grouped according to lineages, had recognized rights in the land too. These were the principles of Ashanti land-tenure. The practice is described below.

Early settlements

There is not enough reliable evidence from which to reconstruct accurately the formation of towns and villages in Ashanti. Such historical evidence as there is supports the view that the communities lived in large groups at first; but there were also small scattered settlements. There was probably a cyclical process of 'fission and fusion', to use Professor Evans-Pritchard's phrase,[1] people breaking away from a large settlement to live in small villages, or smaller villages uniting or growing into large settlements.

According to tradition the first settlements of Kumasi, Bekwai, Juaben, and Kokofu were all at Santemanso, whence the community spread out to form separate settlements. Rattray, who visited Santemanso, testified to this tradition as follows:

Myths and traditions are strangely substantiated in some respects by visible proofs. In the vicinity of this spot is an area of dense primaeval forest. The keen observer will note there are no clearings, and no cocoa-trees, and if the mounds through which every now and then the motor road cuts, are minutely examined, they will be found not to be ant-hills, but 'kitchen middens' from which project fragments of ancient pottery in which I found many neolithic instruments. The forest around

[1] E. E. Evans-Pritchard, *The Nuer*, 1940.

for miles is dotted with these mounds, and the whole of this area along the banks of the Asuben River must, at some remote period, have been the site of a great settlement, larger by far than any Ashanti town or villages of the present day. No one is permitted to cultivate the soil or clear the forest at this place.[1]

An old man who told me the history of Mampong began: 'The people of Mampong first appeared at Adanse. Nana Asiama Guahya, the founding ancestress, was the mother of Kwakye Panin, Baafo Antiedu, Twentɔ, and Nana Afua Kaafena. Kwakye Panin was the first to rule at Adanse. When we (i.e. our ancestors) left Adanse, the first town we came to was Amoafo Ankaase, then we came to Aboɔntam, and thence to Behenease. At Behenease we did not feel happy, because we were hemmed in between Nsuta and Juaben, so the chief of Mampong decided to move again. It was Nana Boaten Akuamoa who first came to found Mampong; but after his hunters had surveyed the land for the new settlement, and he had sacrificed a sheep and some palm-wine to the River Tadie, which was near the selected site, he died. Atakora Panin, his successor, continued his work. The settlement was so large that people who saw it exclaimed 'Ɔman pon bɛn na apue ha yi' ('What big nation is this that has appeared here'). Hence the name Mampong (ɔman—nation, pon—big).

The traditional history of Wenchi conforms to this pattern. The narrators told me: 'When our ancestors came out of the hole in the ground, they first settled at Ahwene. It was a large town with seventy-seven quarters.' The mounds at Ahwene give evidence of a settlement much larger than any town in the Wenchi Division to-day.

The general picture then is that the communities first lived in large settlements. There is in Ashanti to-day within each political unit a central village which gives the impression of being the place from which the people wandered into the smaller villages surrounding it. This village is usually the capital where the chief lives. From this central village the chief sent out his hunters to view the surrounding country. A large area usually distinguished by natural boundaries such as rivers, rocks or trees was demarcated. The chief made a sacrifice to the Earth and the rivers of this locality on behalf of the community. The area thus demarcated

---

[1] Rattray, *Ashanti*, pp. 121–2.

became stool land, under the care of the chief. It was tribal land. This is how, according to the tradition, Mampong was founded.

From the central village, a lineage group, or a man and a few of his kinsfolk, went out to found a new village within the tribal land in order that they might farm there. This process has been repeated in modern times by people seeking land for growing cocoa.

Kinship confers rights over land

If any farmer were asked how he came to possess the right to farm where he did, he sought to establish his right by tracing his descent in the matrilineal line to an ancestor known to have farmed there before him. His right to farm where he does is conferred by his kinship with this ancestor.

The ancestor may have been one of the original settlers of the land, or one who was rewarded by the chief with land after a successful war so that he might farm on it, or 'eat on it', as the Ashanti put it. The right to use the land was inherited from the original settler or donee, like other property and jural rights, by his maternal kinsmen. It was a whole lineage that acquired the right of usufruct over the land. The lineage might occupy it, build houses on it, and generally exercise the right of usufruct over the land in perpetuity, but they could not sell it.

The elder or head of the lineage was the custodian of this lineage land. He saw to it that every member of the lineage had a portion for his farm. Sometimes a farm was made jointly by the members of the lineage, for it was difficult work. The farms had to be cultivated in virgin forest with huge trees and thick undergrowth. There is a tradition that very long ago the people used stone axes for farming. Later they used cutlasses, as they still do to-day. The making of a farm therefore required the help of every able-bodied member of the domestic unit, brothers, sons, nephews, sisters, as well as wives. The crops and fruits which were raised with the joint labour of the group were owned by the head of the family, but the members could collect food from it. Crops, like kola, were passed on as inheritance within the lineage. Individual members could cultivate farms on the lineage portion of the land, and own individually the crops they grew. They could do what they liked with these. But they could not sell the farmland, or any economic trees like kola or palm-trees standing on it, without the consent of the lineage.

The obligation of military service based on kinship

The head of the lineage who inherited the land was one of the chief's elders. Every elder was under an obligation to assist the chief to defend the land. On becoming an elder a man took an oath of allegiance to his chief.[1] 'As you have put me on this stool, if I do not render you good service, if I do not give you good help to rule this people, if I tell you any falsehood whatsoever, I swear the oath, then may the Sky and the Earth "get" me (i.e. harm me).'

The elder was expected to give the chief military service. In the event of war he took his place in the army at the head of his subjects. These were his kinsmen who had settled on his land. The ties of kinship, which gave a man the right to farm where he did, imposed on him the obligation to fight under his lineage head or elder in defence of the land.

Kinship was what determined military service. An Ashanti who had lived for many years away from his home, the place where his kinsmen lived and his ancestors lay buried, and did not therefore use the lineage land for farming, still considered himself a subject of his lineage head, and under an obligation to fight under him. In the same way, service to a chief was personal. Wherever a man might wander he owed allegiance to the chief of his native Division.[2] Within the same Division a man might settle on the land of an elder other than his own lineage head. But in time of war he fought with his kinsmen under his own lineage head.

If people went from one Division to settle permanently in another, then they became liable for military service in the Division in which they settled. An informant explained this by saying: 'When he came to settle on your land, he became your kinsman' (*Ɔbɛbɔɔ wo abusua*). The obligation to military service was phrased in terms of kinship.

Service due to a Chief

In addition to military service, the subjects of a stool were liable for various levies for certain specific purposes. A special levy was raised when necessary to defray the expenses of a chief's

[1] Cf. Rattray, *Ashanti*, p. 225.

[2] Cf. Casely Hayford, 'The essential feature of allegiance is that it is a personal relationship which has nothing to do with property rights' (*Gold Coast Native Constitutions*, pp. 55–6).

funeral (*ayitoɔ* or *asekantoɔ*), or for paying the expenses of a war (*apeatoɔ*) or for purchasing a cow or sheep for a sacrifice on behalf of the tribe (*mmusu-toɔ*) or for paying a stool debt, or buying stool paraphernalia (*akonwa-toɔ*). All these levies were raised only with the concurrence of the chief's council, and after they had been approved by the people.[1]

Any treasure-trove found on the land belonged to the stool, for the soil, the minerals, the rocks, and trees were stool property. So anyone who found a treasure-trove had to take it to the chief. The finder was usually given a small share. One of my informants told me: 'At Mampong, near the site of the present Trade School, a woman found a pot of gold-dust while she was harvesting her groundnuts. She took it to the chief Nana Sɛkyerɛ. Her hand was held (my informant demonstrated by gripping the back of his right hand with his left hand) and she dipped it three times into the pot of gold. She kept what she was able to hold. The rest belonged to the stool.'

The subjects of a chief were also liable for service of an agricultural nature. They worked on the chief's farm several days each year. At Wenchi this service was performed on every *Wukudae* (Wednesday *Adae*), that is, about six times a year. At Enchi, in Aowin, where the service is still performed (1946), the surrounding villages take it in turn to work on the chief's farm. The number of days on which this service was given varied from place to place from two to eight days in the year with twenty to a hundred or more men working on any one day. There do not appear to have been any stipulated times in most areas. The chief asked his men when he needed their help, and provided them with food and drink while they worked for him.

During the *Odwera* ceremony, the chief received yearly tributes of 'first-fruits' from his subjects: yams, rice, palm-oil, meat, and snails.

A hunter who killed an elephant or an antelope on the chief's land sent the chief his portion as fixed by tradition. In the case of an elephant, the foreleg, ear, tail, and one tusk were the chief's portion. If a hunter who was the chief's subject killed an antelope he gave the foreleg to the chief; if the hunter was a stranger, he gave the chief the hindleg. A hunter who killed a leopard gave the chief

---

[1] See Rattray, *Ashanti Law and Constitution*, pp. 42–3, where the method of collection is described. Also Chap. IV below.

its skin. The chief's share of all the wild animals found on his land was known and fixed by custom.

A palm-wine cutter sent the chief a pot of palm-wine daily (*ahen nsa*) for entertaining his guests.

In short, pithy sentences, characteristic of the old Ashanti, one of my informants summarized the basic traditional rules of land-tenure in Mampong as follows:

'The people of Mpenem, for example, came from Ekuansa and begged for land from us. We[1] gave them land where the Girls' School now stands. Then they removed from there, and went to the Chief of Nintin who gave them land at Mpenem. We used to collect first-fruits: rice, yam, and oil from them annually. The plantains and cocoyams you plant are yours. The land is the chief's. You cannot sell the land. You may mortgage your kola. Only the stool can sell land. In the old days everyone who lived on your land was your subject, and so he accompanied you and fought in your wars. Because, when he came to settle on your land, he became your kinsman. When a stranger buys land, he buys the surface; that is, the right to use it. Every year the chief claims money from him, if he has cocoa. If he has no cocoa, he provides a sheep for the stool.'

The chief also received other services necessary for the upkeep of his household. The Gyase people provided him with his attendants—horn-blowers, drummers, gunners, hammock-carriers, elephant-tail switchers, sandal-bearers, pipe-bearers, wine-cup bearers. All these attendants gave their services without wages, but obtained their food from the chief.

The subjects of a chief were responsible for providing him with a house, and for maintaining it in good repair. In Bekwai, for example, the Kyidom built one of the four 'pato' rooms surrounding the kitchen. The remainder were built by Akwamu, Kontire, and Twafo. The *Asokwafo* (horn-blowers) were responsible for roofing the harem. Each of these groups (*fekuo*) provided the labour and materials necessary for the section of the building for which it was responsible.

Chief rich in services, not in transferable wealth

The chief was wealthy in terms of the services which he received, but he could not accumulate capital for his personal use. The

---

[1] The narrator was a member of the royal lineage. 'We' means 'my ancestors'.

tribute of first-fruits which he received at the *Odwera* ceremony was redistributed as presents to the elders and their subjects. The palm-wine sent him was used to entertain all and sundry. The food and meat went to feed the large number of attendants in the royal household, and anyone who cared to go to the chief's house for a meal. One of the strict injuctions given to a chief on his enstoolment was that he should be generous. Over a century ago when Bowdich visited Kumasi he noted:

About twenty pots of white soup, and twenty pots of black (made with palm nuts) are cooked daily at the palace, (besides those for the consumption of the household) for visitors of consequence, and a periguin of gold (about £8 in English currency) is given daily to Yokokroko [Yaw Kokroko], the Chamberlain for palm wine. This would have appeared too large a sum, had I not witnessed the vast consumption and waste of it.... A large quantity of palm wine is dashed to the retinues of all the captains attending in the course of the day; much is expended in the almost daily ceremony of drinking it in state in the market place; and our party was always well provided for in the course of the evening.[1]

On a more modest scale, each chief according to his status and means, but with the same obligation to generosity, had to entertain his subjects and elders.

The chief was not allowed to have personal property of his own. He could not own land in a private capacity. Everything he possessed—gold-dust, wives, slaves, farms—became stool property on his becoming a chief. 'No one places leaves inside the elephant's mouth and takes them out again' is the Ashanti maxim governing this custom.

The specific levies collected and paid into the chief's treasury circulated again to the people. The weavers, carvers, goldsmiths, metal-workers, and the like, who worked for the chief were never paid wages, but they fed at the chief's expense while working for him, and received *aseda* (token of thanks) after they had finished. The thanks were usually expressed by a gift equivalent to the value of their products.

The services and tributes which the chief received were to enable him to fulfil the obligations of his office, but not to enrich him personally.

[1] Bowdich, op. cit., p. 292.

The Ashanti Union and services to the Asantehene

When the Ashanti Union[1] was formed, the Asantehene also secured certain rights. The land in every Ashanti Division continued to belong to the stool of that Division, and no change was made in the existing cluster of rights of chief, lineage, and individual in the use of land. But the chiefs incurred certain obligations to the Asantehene. The historical development of the Union throws some light on the position.

The traditional histories of Kumasi, Mampong, Asumegya, Juaben, and Aduaben indicate a segmentary society with autonomous groups bound by ties of clanship. An impetus to a closer social solidarity was provided by the existence of the enemy State of Denkyira. According to their own tradition it was the desire to break away from Denkyira that brought the separate groups together in a Union, which was soon strengthened by the addition of Bekwai, Kokofu, and Nsuta, all of which had ties of kinship with Kumasi.[2]

The present Asantehene, Nana Sir Agyeman Prempeh II, gives the etymology of the word 'Asante' as follows: when the King of Denkyira heard of the Union of the five nations under Osei Tutu, he said he was certain that it had been formed for the purpose of making war on him (*Osa-nti: Osa*—war; *nti*—because of). So he called the members of the Union Sa-nti-fo. This etymology is interesting as indicating that the Ashantis have always thought of themselves as warlike, and of Ashanti national unity as connected with war. Traditional history supports the view that the aim of Osei Tutu and his successors was not the acquisition of land, but the formation of a strong army. Membership in the Union did not affect the land rights of the chiefs of the various Divisions.

There were Divisions like Techiman, Nkoranza, Dormaa, and Jaman which became part of the Union through conquest. But even in these Divisions the rights of the chiefs over their lands remained the same after, as before the conquest.[3] The chiefs were

---

[1] I use the term Ashanti Union of the Union of Ashanti States prior to 1900, and Ashanti Confederacy of the Union as restored by Government in 1935.

[2] See Chap. V.

[3] Cf. Casely Hayford, *Gold Coast Native Institutions* (1903), p. 39: 'In all my several years of practice at the Bar, I have not come across a case where title to land has been based upon a right of conquest. The usage of war amongst the aborigines would seem to be that after the conclusion of peace the vanquished still retained their land.'

required to pay a war indemnity, and they also incurred the obligation to military service.

When the Asantehene defeated Juaben after its rebellion under Asafu-Adjaye in 1879,[1] he did not confiscate the lands of the Juaben Stool and bestow them upon a henchman of his own choice. Yaw Sapon, the heir to the Juaben Stool, was captured during the war and taken to Kumasi. After the war, the Asantehene returned all the prisoners of war to Yaw Sapon and sent him back to rule in Juaben, thus keeping the stool in the same lineage.

There was, however, a distinction between the lands of the Divisional chiefs (*abirempon*) and the lands of the elders and captains (*asafohene*) of the Kumasi Division. The rights of the Asantehene over lands in the Kumasi Division were the same as the rights exercised by the Divisional chiefs in their own Division. But over the lands of the Divisional chiefs the Asantehene exercised no rights. The present Asantehene at a meeting of the Confederacy Council in 1941 said *à propos* of a measure to appoint a committee to hear appeals in land cases then under discussion: 'I would repeat that in introducing this measure I do not intend to interfere with the right of any chief to his land. You all know that custom does not permit me to litigate with any chief for any land.'[2]

Although they retained possession of their lands, the Divisional chiefs incurred obligations to the Asantehene. They were obliged to attend the periodic *Odwera* ceremonies held in Kumasi, and they brought gifts of food and meat to the Asantehene on these occasions. They accepted limitations on their judicial powers, and death sentences were authorized by the Asantehene only.

In pursuance of the main objective of the Union every Divisional chief vowed military service. On his installation a Divisional chief went to Kumasi to take the oath of allegiance to the Asantehene. A newly enstooled chief usually waited until he went to Kumasi for the *Odwera* ceremony before he took the oath of allegiance. This information was given me in Wenchi, and I afterwards discovered that it confirmed information that had been given to Rattray who wrote: 'At this gathering [i.e. *Odwera*] of all the heads of the great territorial divisions, the oath of allegiance was taken

[1] Claridge, op. cit., vol. ii.
[2] Minutes of the Confederacy Council (1941).

by any one who had not already done so, and problems of State were discussed.'[1]

The ceremony of taking the oath is still the same as described by Rattray.[2] The oath taken by the Divisional chief is as follows:

I speak (the day of the chief's own oath), I speak the Great Oath, that if I do not help you to administer this nation, if ever I am false to you, if you call me by night, if you call me by day, and I do not come, then have I broken the Great Oath and . . . (the chief's own oath).[3]

The Asantehene's reply to this oath is noteworthy: *Sε woyε me dɔm da a, abosom nku wo* (If ever you rebel against me, may the gods kill you).

Rattray asserts,[4] 'Besides the taking of the oath of fealty, the acknowledgement of the Kumasi *Hene* as King of Ashanti implied that his vassals held office, Stools, and land from the King, and could be removed by him.'

This statement is erroneous as regards the Divisional chiefs. They held their office and stools by kin-right and their selection by the elders and people of their own Divisions. By virtue of that office they were custodians of the lands of their Divisions. They could only be removed by the people who elected them.

What the oath did imply was that the Divisional chiefs were bound to answer the call to military service when so bidden by the Asantehene, by day or night. The Asantehene could compel obedience by the superior forces he could put into the field. An historical illustration of this is the case of Juaben, already alluded to.[5] After the battle between the Ashanti and the British in 1874, Asafo Agyei, the Chief of Juaben asserted his independence and tried to break away from Kumasi. This ultimately led to a war between Juaben and Kumasi during the reign of Mensa Bonsu. Bekwai and Kokofu decided to help Kumasi. Mampong and Nsuta did not actually take part in the fight, although their sympathies were with Kumasi. In any war between Kumasi and another Division, Kumasi could count on the support of some at least of the other Divisions. At first the Juabens were so successful that

---

[1] Rattray, *Religion and Art in Ashanti*, p. 132.

[2] Rattray, *Ashanti Law and Constitution*, p. 102.

[3] *Meka . . . , meka ntam kεsε sε mammoa wo me ne wo ammu Ɔman yi, na sε metwa wo nkontompo, sε meyε wo dɔm da, sε wofrε me anadwo, sε wofrε me awia, na sε mamma yaa meto ntam kεse meto. . . .'*

[4] *Ashanti Law and Constitution*, p. 104.

[5] Claridge, op. cit., vol. ii; Ward, op. cit., pp. 189–91.

many of the Kumasi captains, among whom were the Adumhene, the Anantahene, and the Nseniahene of Kumasi, blew themselves up.[1] The Juabens were eventually defeated, as Kumasi was able to put larger armies in the field, and many of them fled to Kibi.

If a Divisional chief broke the oath of allegiance, physical force could be used to compel obedience. But a new sanction was provided by the concept of national unity focused on the Golden Stool. The Golden Stool belonged to the Divisional chiefs as much as to the Asantehene. The sanction for fulfilling the oath of allegiance became a religious sanction which superseded the secular sanction of physical force. The breach of the oath became an offence against the gods. It became an *akyiwade*, a taboo. 'If ever you rebel against me, may the gods kill you.' The penalty for breaking the oath was death. If war became necessary, before the death penalty could be exacted, it was fought; but the aim was to punish the rebel by death, not to confiscate his lands. Death was the penalty meted out in Ashanti for offences against the gods— sacrilege, murder, incest, or 'cursing the king'. The misfortune which these crimes were believed to cause was palpable enough in the case of the breach of the oath of allegiance—national annihilation. Hence, its breach incurred the moral reprobation of the whole people, and the Asantehene was sure to find supporters among the other Divisional chiefs.

A recent incident showed how powerful this sanction was. The Chief of Bekwai in a letter dated 12 March 1945, signed by himself and his elders declared: 'We the undersigned (representatives of Bekwaiman) have the honour to inform you that Bekwai has withdrawn her membership from the Confederacy Council as from to-day's date.' This letter was read to the Confederacy Council at its meeting the following day. The Mamponghene presided over the meeting, as the Asantehene was absent. The Council decided to refer the letter to the Asantehene. But before delegates were sent to take the letter to the Asantehene, the Kokofuhene swore the Great Oath and testified that he was innocent of the Bekwai people's decision to secede, and affirmed his allegiance to the Golden Stool. All the other members of the council 'also solemnly swore the Great Oath to declare their innocence of the Bekwai perfidy and pledge their unrelenting support to any move pro-

---

[1] A defeated Ashanti captain was always expected to commit suicide. Death, to the Ashanti, was preferable to disgrace.

posed to meet the situation'. The Mamponghene as chairman replied, 'I thank all of you for reaffirming your loyalty to the Golden Stool by swearing the Great Oath.'[1]

The general reaction of the chiefs to the Bekwaihene was one of hostility. They regarded the action of the people of Bekwai as constituting a threat to their national unity, and they swore the oath to allay any suspicion of their complicity in it.

The system of land-tenure

The system of land-tenure we have described may be summarized as follows:

The living regarded themselves as having rights of usufruct in the land which they held from the ancestors. They in turn were to hand it on to posterity.

The chief who was the occupant of the stool of the ancestors was the custodian of the land. This gave him certain defined rights in the land, and also certain responsibilities. To enable him to discharge his responsibilities for the welfare of the community, the people provided him with the necessary services. They built him a house and gave him attendants and servants. He was expected to entertain generously; so he was given food and meat and drink, especially at the *Odwera* festival when he was expected to entertain most royally. For a funeral, a war, or stool paraphernalia, gold was needed, and special taxes were levied, with the concurrence of the elders.

The chief's rights coexisted with a cluster of other rights. Each lineage had the right to use a particular portion of the land. This portion was under the care of the head of the lineage for the use of its members. The heads of the lineages were the chief's elders and councillors who assisted him to rule over the community. The chief could not sell any land without their approval. Whenever a sale or mortgage did take place, the sanction of the ancestors was obtained by the sacrifice of a sheep.

As the lineage had jointly the right of usufruct over its land, no individual could alienate it, and thus deprive his lineage of its means of livelihood. The ties of kinship determined where an individual farmed.

An army was required to defend the land, and so every able-bodied member was liable for military service, and took his place

[1] From the Minutes of the Confederacy Council (1945).

when necessary in the army within his lineage group and under the head of his lineage. Military service was his obligation to his kindred and to the ancestors. It was taboo to shirk it.

A new situation arose when the different States (Divisions) combined under the Chief of Kumasi, who became Asantehene, in order to break the dominion of Denkyira.

Though the Chief of Kumasi became the head of the Union, the Divisional chiefs retained their rights over their lands, but incurred the obligation to military service. It was essential that all should observe this obligation and that no one should secede. An additional sanction to that of physical force was found in the concept of allegiance to the Golden Stool which symbolized their national unity. Secession became an offence against the gods.

The Asantehene's position was greatly enhanced as the Union grew stronger. He claimed and exercised certain rights. He had the right of first entry into the Salaga market,[1] and other chiefs had to wait till his kola had been sold; he was entitled to a share in large finds of treasure-trove in the Divisions; at *Odwera* ceremonies the Divisional chiefs brought him gifts of food, and meat and drink which he afterwards distributed to entertain the chiefs and their followers. In judicial affairs he claimed the exclusive right to exact or authorize the death penalty.

The whole Union was kept together in a pseudo-feudal organization operating under the sanctions of kinship, obedience to the ancestors, and allegiance to the Golden Stool.

Ashanti society not feudal

Rattray applied the concepts of English laws and medieval feudalism to the Ashanti system, and described it in terms of freehold, leasehold, vassals, fiefs, aids, levies, escheat.[2] 'The student of English Law of Real Property who comes to examine the Ashanti law relating to that subject, will at first be astonished to find that a system, which he had been taught to believe was peculiar to his own country, had an almost exact replica in West Africa among the Ashanti.'[3]

This approach was, I think, erroneous, for there were important differences between the Ashanti system and English medieval feudalism. 'Feudalism in both tenure and government was, so far

---

[1] A big trading centre in the Northern Territories of the Gold Coast.
[2] Rattray, *Ashanti*, chap. xxi; *Ashanti Law and Constitution*, chap. xxxiii.
[3] *Ashanti*, p. 223.

as it existed in England, brought full-grown from France.'[1] It developed in France as a result of the break-up of the Carolingian empire in the ninth century. Conditions were insecure, for the State failed to give protection to life and property. Kinship ties had weakened. Exchange was not entirely absent, but money payments were rare, and played a restricted role in the economic system. It was these conditions of general insecurity that led to the social relations to which the name of feudalism was later given.

A superior individual granted his protection and other material advantages to an inferior who pledged himself to give various services. In its fully developed form, the leading features of feudalism were the system of vassalage, and the institution of the fief. The relations of vassalage were established by the formal act of the homage. The future vassal placed his hands between the lord's joined hands, and promised to 'become your man for the tenement I hold of you, and bear faith to you of life and members and earthly honour against all other men, saving the faith I hold to the king'.

The lord in return promised to maintain his tenant in his tenement, rights, and custom, to warrant his tenure in law, and to defend him against all other men.

Homage is a bond of law by which one is holden and bound to warrant, defend, and acquit the tenant in his seisin against all men, in return for a fixed service named and expressed in the gift, and whereby the tenant is bound to keep faith with his lord and to perform the due service, and such is the relation of homage that the lord owes as much to the tenant as the tenant to the lord, save only reverence.[2]

The reciprocal relations of lord and vassal were defined by custom. The vassal owed the lord fidelity, obedience, and aid in all circumstances in which the lord might need it. This 'aid', became defined in England to include certain money payments on such occasions as when the lord's eldest son was knighted, or his eldest daughter was married, or to ransom him from captivity. Above all, the vassal owed his lord military service, and this came to predominate over all others.

In return, the lord owed his man protection. He defended him before the courts, avenged his wrongs, gave his vassal an assured livelihood, and cared for his orphans until they became of age.

In the absence of a salary system the master could either take

---

[1] Stubbs, *Constitutional History of England*, vol. i, p. 273.
[2] Joliffe, *The Constitutional History of Medieval England*, p. 153.

his vassal into his own home and give him food, clothing and shelter, or he could give him a piece of land to work himself. The latter was the more common. The land assigned carried with it certain clearly defined services that were performed for the grantor. The land became known as a fief. Its introduction brought with it the recognition of a perpetual right of one party in the lands of another.

An essential characteristic of this system was that it was contractual. As the system was developed in England, if either of the two contracting parties broke his pledges, he thereby freed the other party from all obligations. 'Being made for a certain tenement, and constituting a contract by which that tenement is held, it has a material guarantee in law.'[1] If the lord took away the fief, or deserted the vassal in mortal necessity, and refused him redress after legal complaint, the vassal could free himself of his homage. The law provided for this in the ceremony of diffidation. The ground of the loosing of homage was well put for Richard Marshal by Matthew Paris (about 1233):[2]

> I have done no treason against the King, for he has disseized me of my office of the Marshalsea unlawfully and without judgement of peers ... whereas I have ever been ready to appear in his court to fulfil the law and to stand to the judgement of my peers. So I was not his man (when I took arms against him) but stood absolved from his homage rightfully, and not by my own doing, but his.

In England William the Conqueror forfeited all the lands, and assumed universal overlordship over them. This was 'the great generalization which governs the whole scheme of Domesday Book'.[3] The king divided the whole country into military fiefs according to a system that prevailed in his Norman duchy. The tenants-in-chief were to furnish the king with a certain number of knights. To be able to do so, they distributed fiefs in their turn. But the king saw to it that the vassals' vassals swore the oath of fealty to him.

In Ashanti, as has been shown, the Divisional chiefs remained custodians of their lands. They owed their position to the fact of their having been elected by the elders and people of their Division to the stool of their ancestors. The chiefs as well as their people had the right to use the land which their ancestors had left

---

[1] Joliffe, op. cit., p. 153. [2] Ibid., p. 155 n.
[3] E. Pollock and Maitland, *History of English Law*, p. 69.

to them. The oath of allegiance sworn to the Asantehene, or by an elder to his chief did not confer rights in land. It was more like the English hold-oath. The hold-oath 'was a solemn promise, the breach of which incurred moral reprobation: the breaking of homage gave rise to an action at law, and made the tenant liable to lose his tenement'.[1] The sanction for the Ashanti oath was religious and military rather than legal.

In Ashanti security of tenure was provided by the kinship system upon which rights in land were based. The lineage structure of Ashanti society was different from the rigid class structure of king, lords, and vassals of English feudal society. Of the Ashanti system Rattray correctly wrote:

> There is in Ashanti no such thing as the individual ownership of land. Now something that could never belong to one person, but which was always in the hands of an interested group, was, from its very nature, not likely to be stolen, lost sight of, sold, seized, or given away. . . We have seen that this communal and family interest in land protected it from forfeiture, even when a clansman had committed some capital offence, and that the king, despotic as he was in many ways, did not dare to seize the offender's land, because he would have had opposition from the whole clan.[2]

Whereas kinship ties weakened in England and the individual was left to seek protection for himself, in Ashanti the individual was protected by his kindred.

The payments which the English vassal made to his lord on the marriage of his daughter or the knighthood of his son were unknown in Ashanti. Such payments as were made were levies for specific purposes approved by the councillors who were representatives of the people. Payments in kind were to enable the chief to fulfil his obligations of generosity to his subjects. The demand for military service was a common feature of both systems. But in Ashanti, kinship and not land-tenure was what decided where and for whom a man fought.

The system of land-tenure in Ashanti, as we have seen, was based on kinship solidarity, allegiance to tribal stools, and the supremacy of the ancestors. It was essentially different from the English feudal system of land-tenure based on the universal ownership of the king, individual tenancies and fiefs, and contractual relations of lord and vassal guaranteed by legal sanctions.

[1] Joliffe, op. cit., p. 153.   [2] *Ashanti*, pp. 230-31.

CHAPTER IV

ADMINISTRATION AND JUSTICE

A DIVISION in Ashanti consisted, as now, of an aggregation of units: the lineage, the village, the sub-division, and then the Division itself.

About 1900 the Mampong Division, for example, was made up as follows:

The Abirempon

There were five Abirempon in the Division. These were the Abirempon of Ejura, Jamasi, Effiduase, Apaa, and Beposo.

The Birempon of Ejura was also the Adɔntenhene[1] of the Division, and ranked as the most senior elder. In time of war he led the main body of the Divisional army. But he did not live in Mampong. He lived in his own capital at Ejura, twenty-five miles away. He had twelve villages under him in the Ejura sub-division: Abotang, Babaso, Bunyum, Asomen, Nkrease, Nkontase, Kukutia, Nkwantorodo, Nsuansu, Mensiedu, Oyon, and Yoko.

This Birempon had his queen-mother (*Ɔbaapanyin*) and his council of elders at Ejura, just as the chief had at Mampong. Ejura was a separate administrative unit. Some of the elders there were responsible for outlying villages. They and the Birempon managed all the affairs of the sub-division, judicial, administrative, financial, and ritual. The Birempon had his own court. He held his own *Adae* and *Odwera* ceremonies, which all his people attended, and he had his own treasury.

The chief at Mampong had no direct administrative contact with the subjects of the Birempon in the Ejura sub-division. He dealt only with the Birempon himself.

Besides being head of the sub-division of Ejura, the Birempon was one of the elders of the chief. As he did not live at Mampong he was not a regular member of the chief's council, but in all matters concerning the whole Division of Mampong or affecting Ejura he was summoned to the council to take part in its deliberations.

[1] See Chap. I.

The Birempon of Jamasi was also the *Benkumhene* (left wing) of the Division. Like the Birempon of Ejura, he and his council of elders managed all the affairs of Jamasi, which included the seven villages of Amenase, Dawu, Dome, Abanim, Yonso, Tabre, and Wono.

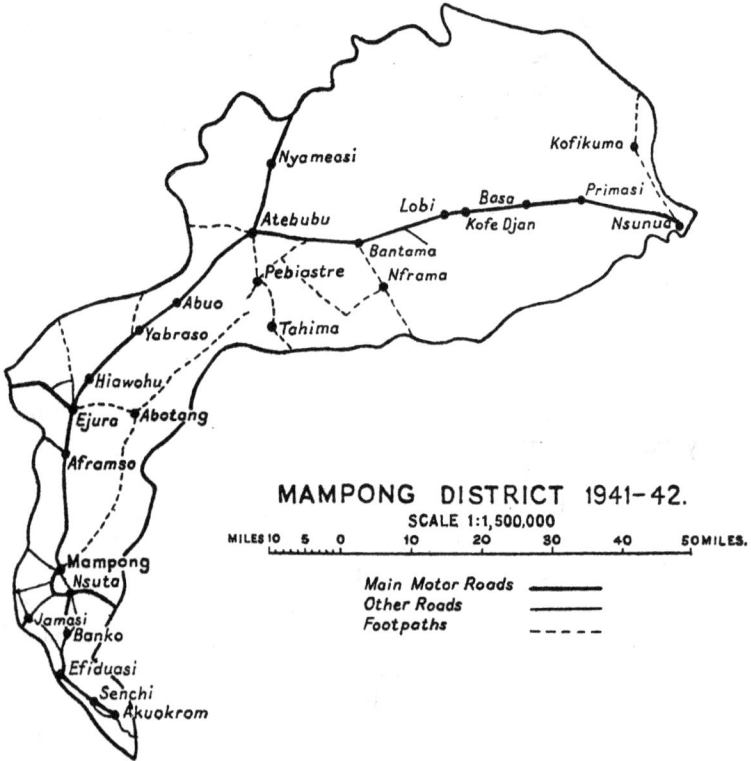

MAMPONG   DISTRICT   1941–42.

SCALE 1:1,500,000

MILES 10   5   0   10   20   30   40   50 MILES.

Main Motor Roads
Other Roads
Footpaths

The Birempon of Effiduase, who was also the *Nifahene* (right wing) of the Division, similarly managed the affairs of the Effiduase sub-division with his council of elders.

Both the Abirempon of Apaa and Beposo had only a few villages, but these villages were run as sub-divisions. The royal lineage of Apaa was a branch of the royal lineage of Mampong, and there is a close bond between the two stools, strengthened not only by the ties of kinship but also by their comradeship in arms. Apaa, according to tradition, played an important part in the wars of Mampong.

The Odekuro

Under these Abirempon were the *Adekurofo* (headmen) in charge of the various villages. Each village consisted of a number of lineages which formed a local political unit. The Odekuro was selected from one of the lineages as head of the village. He became its official representative or spokesman through whom the elder, or the chief, if the village came directly under him, transmitted his orders. He and the heads of the other lineages that formed his council discussed and managed the affairs of the village.

If any communal labour had to be performed, the villagers worked under the Odekuro. Some Adekurofo had their own lineage stools, and performed ritual sacrifices on behalf of the village. Their authority came to have ritual sanctions, but they were always obliged to act on the advice of their council of elders, consisting of the heads of the other lineages composing the village.

The elder

Both in the villages and in the capitals at Effiduase, Ejura, Apaa, Beposo, Jamasi, and Mampong, there were lineages each with its own elder, selected by the members of the lineage. The elder was the ritual and political head of his lineage. As occupant of the lineage stool he was the successor of the ancestors. He was also the intermediary between the ancestors and their living descendants, and performed ritual sacrifices on behalf of his kinsmen.

He was a member of the council of the Odekuro, or Birempon, or the chief, and watched over the interests of the members of his lineage, whom he represented. It was also his duty to see that his kinsmen carried out the orders of the chief or Odekuro, in so far as these affected them.

It was to the elder that the members of the lineage turned in all their troubles. He settled any disputes involving members of his lineage, and saw to it that amicable relations were maintained amongst them. If any of them offended someone outside the lineage, he turned to the elder for help and guidance.

The capital

In the capital at Mampong lived the chief, the queen-mother, the Kontihene, the Akwamuhene, the Kyidɔmhene, the Gyasehene, and the Ankobeahene. They were responsible for the administration of the capital, and the villages which came under them.

Three villages came directly under the chief: Nonkwarease, Kotobra, and Kodiekurom. These villages provided his personal attendants. The Kontihene, the Akwamuhene, and the Kyidɔm-hene had eight, ten, and eight villages, respectively, directly under them. The Gyasehene had charge of the chief's household. The Ankɔbeahene was not the representative of any lineage. His stool was filled by a nominee of the chief.

Ashanti administration

The following points may be noted concerning the administrative practice of the Ashanti.

The chief was the hub of unity for the separate lineages, villages, and sub-divisions. He held the whole together. Without him the elders and the Abirempon were isolated units.[1]

The work of administration was done by the heads and councillors of the administrative units—lineage, village, or sub-division. The chief dealt with the council of elders at the capital and, in matters affecting the whole Division, with the full council of elders and Abirempon. In each administrative unit the elder, Odekuro, Birempon, or chief acted with the advice and concurrence of his council.

The councils consisted of representatives who were expected to consult the groups they represented, and give effect to their wishes on the councils. If the lineage, village, or sub-division was not consulted or properly served, the group concerned could change its representative. In this way they were all subject to popular control.

Underlying all was the uniform principle that each unit had the right to manage all affairs which concerned itself alone. The authorities of the larger units interfered only when the affairs of the smaller unit touched the larger. This practice applied to administrative as well as judicial affairs.

Administrative functions

The administrative function of the officials—elders, Adekurofo, Abirempon, and chiefs—was to keep law and order in the community. This entailed defending the community from external attack, maintaining amicable relations among the persons and

---

[1] See Rattray, *Ashanti Law and Constitution*, pp. 96–7.

groups within the community and between the community and its ancestors and gods.

As regards the first objective, defence from external enemies, military service was based on kinship, which was also the basis of the political organization. Every elder, Odekuro, or Birempon was also the military head of the unit under his care. To fight to defend the land was a duty which one owed to one's kindred, and to the ancestors from whom the land was inherited.

With regard to maintaining amicable relations among persons and groups within the community, again the practice was to leave each unit to settle its own affairs. If an offence was committed within the circle of the domestic unit, or the lineage, the unit was expected to deal with it.

Two categories of offences

The Ashanti themselves divided offences into two categories. Those which did not concern the chief, that is, the central authority, but were household cases (*efisɛm*) and those which concerned the central authority because they were taboos or things hated by the tribe (*ɔman akyiwade*).[1]

All the old Ashanti declare that within traditional memory there was a time when war, in its modern sense, was unknown, and when capital punishment was unheard of. The chief sources of possible trouble in those days were (this we can safely surmise from the fact that they still are) women; sexual offences; disputes as to the possession of such trifling articles as alone could be held as personal property (i.e. weapons, tools, clothes, ornaments); sacrilege; violation of taboos; common assaults; witchcraft; and last, but perhaps most common of all, quarrels arising out of personal abuse.[2]

Following their own distinction, Rattray classified these offences in two categories as follows:[3]

1. *Sins or tribal taboos* (ɔman akyiwade)
    1. Murder (*awudie*).
    2. Suicide.
    3. Certain sexual offences.
    4. Certain forms of abuse.

---

[1] This subject has been ably treated by Rattray in *Ashanti Law and Constitution*, chaps. xxv–xxxvii.
[2] Ibid., p. 6.   [3] Ibid., chaps. xxvi–xxx.

5. Certain kinds of assault.
6. Certain kinds of stealing.
7. The invocation of a curse upon a chief.
8. Treason and cowardice.
9. Witchcraft.
10. The violation of any other recognized taboo.
11. Breaking a law or command enjoined by the swearing of an oath.

Some of these require explanation.

1. 'Murder' included homicide, as well as sexual connexion with a woman who was *enceinte* by another man, or with a girl before she had reached puberty.

2. 'Suicide' applied to one who had killed himself in order to avoid the consequence of some wrongful deed, or from unknown motives which the Ashanti therefore presumed to be evil. The suicide was tried, found guilty, and decapitated.

3. The sexual offences under this class were incest (*mogyadie*), that is, sexual connexion with one of the same blood or clan; sexual connexion with an 'unclean' woman, that is, with a woman during her menstrual period (*bratwɛ*); sexual connexion with a half-sister by one father, a father's brother's child, or anyone of the same *Ntorɔ* (*atwebɛnefie*); adultery with a chief's wife; or forcible seduction of a married woman in the bush (*ahahantwɛ*).

4. The forms of abuse which were tabooed were words of abuse against the chief which reflected on his ancestors.

5. Assaults which were tried by the chief's council were assaults on the chief himself, or any official of the stool, such as the soul-washer, stool-carrier, or custodians of the royal mausoleum.

6. Stealing was a tribal offence if it was the theft of regalia, or treasure-trove, or stool property (*akonwa agyapade*). Stealing from a tribal god, that is, the sword, stool, gold, or sacred things of a god, also came under this class.

8. Treason, especially on the part of an elder who had sworn the oath of allegiance to the chief, or cowardice on the part of a captain who before setting out to battle took the oath never to turn his back to the enemy, were crimes regarded as tribal sins.

The penalty for any of these crimes was originally death, though in all except murder the offender could be permitted to 'buy his head' by paying a fine. The fine imposed depended on the circumstances of the case.

2. *Household cases* (efisεm)

    Theft, which in Ashanti included adultery and certain sexual acts.
    Certain kinds of abuse, including slander and tale-bearing.
    Certain kinds of assault.
    Cases regarding property.
    Pawning, loans, suretyship, and recovery of debts.

'Private' and 'public' offences

The clearest way in which the distinction between these two classes may be drawn is in terms of 'private' and 'public' offences. 'Private' offences (*efisεm*) concerned the living only, and were deemed to affect only the social relations of persons or groups living in the community. 'Public' offences (*ɔman akyiwade*) affected the relationships between the community on the one hand and the chief's ancestors or the tribal gods on the other. Such offences were religious offences deemed to affect the weal of the whole tribe.

There were, however, certain cases which did not fall clearly into either category. Such were offences against the ancestors or gods of particular lineages. For example, swearing an elder's oath was a religious offence; but it was one against the ancestors of the particular elder, and was dealt with under the first category of offences (*efisεm*). On the other hand, certain offences against the ancestors of an elder could be dealt with under the second category. For example, in Ashanti every lineage had its graveyard in its native village where the ancestors were buried. The place was sacred, and no one might cut trees or collect faggots from the area. If one did this it was an offence against the ancestors of the lineage, whose burial-place had thus been desecrated. The offence could be treated as *efisεm*, or it could be brought before the chief under the second category. This was done especially if the offender belonged to a different lineage.

Private offences

There were two kinds of relationships in which private offences were committed. An offence committed by a member of a domestic unit or lineage against another of the same group, and an offence committed by a member of a lineage against a member of another.

If an offence was committed by a member of a lineage against another of the same lineage, it was settled within the lineage. The

injured person laid his complaint before any respected member of
the lineage. If the offence was of a serious nature, he brought it
before the head of his lineage by complaining direct to him, or by
swearing the household oath.[1] In either case the aim of the settlement was to reconcile the parties estranged by the commission of
the offence. The matter was, in effect, settled by arbitration. A
pacification or conciliation (*mpata*) was claimed from the offender
for the injured man, who was expected to accept it, not only as
proof that the injury had been annulled but also as a sign that
friendly relations had been restored between the parties. The
pacification was small: a fowl or a few eggs for the injured man
to 'wash his soul' (*dware ne kra*) so that his feelings might be
assuaged. In more serious offences gold-dust to the value of 7*s*.,
or at most 10*s*., was paid as pacification.

When the offence was committed by a person of one lineage
against another of a different lineage, it was still a private injury,
but two factors were now involved. The members of the offender's
lineage were expected to help their kinsman to put the matter
right. Similarly, the kinsmen of the injured man were expected to
see that his injury was repaired; so two lineage groups now became
concerned in the matter. Secondly, not only had reconciliation to
be effected, but justice had also to be done. An equivalent return
had to be made to the injured man for the injury he had suffered.
This was not expected between members of the same lineage, but
outside the lineage it was the collective responsibility of the
offender's lineage to see that an equivalent return was made in
satisfaction for the wrong done, and amicable relations restored
between the two groups.

The injured man had several courses open to him. He could
submit the matter for arbitration by any respected member of
the community. He did this especially if the offender was his
friend, and the offence not a grave one. He could waive his claim
to an equivalent satisfaction (i.e. damages or compensation) and
accept pacification instead. He could also submit his complaint to
the elder of his lineage. The latter then informed the head of the
offender's lineage. The elders of both lineages met to settle the
matter. They might decide to call in other elders to help, so that
the arbitration might be impartial. The elders decided who was in
the wrong and settled how much compensation was to be paid

---

[1] See below, under 'The oath', pp. 75 ff.

to the injured person. The one they found to be in the wrong apologized, and they then effected a reconciliation between the two parties. There was no ritual. The injured man accepted the compensation and the apology tendered through the elders. The elders who arbitrated accepted a gift (*aseda*) or *nsa* (palm-wine) for settling the dispute. This provided evidence of the settlement, and secured witnesses to the fact.

The respect in which the elders were held secured obedience to their judgements. So although their decisions could not be legally enforced they were generally accepted. The elders of a community were frequently engaged in this way, settling differences, determining the satisfaction to be paid, and reconciling estranged persons or groups so as to ensure order and amicable relations in the community.

Often an offender who was aware of his guilt took the initiative. He approached an elder, told him what he had done, and asked him to intercede with the injured party on his behalf (*Kɔma no dibem mame*: Go and give him the right or justice of his cause). In this case the elder's responsibility was to see that the apology was accepted, and the two parties brought together.

For offences committed between parties of different lineages there was a third course open—the matter could be submitted to the chief's court. This was done by the injured man swearing the chief's oath. If the offender also swore the chief's oath in defiance of the claim, or to maintain his innocence, the matter then came under the category of sins or tribal taboos. It was no longer an issue involving the two persons or parties only, but became one that concerned the relations between the community and the chief's ancestors. The swearing of an oath was the deliberate transgression of a taboo: that is, the commission of a religious offence involving the whole tribe.[1]

Public or tribal offences

We must now examine the offences listed under sins or taboos (*akyiwade*). This class of offences came before the chief because they were religious offences. By our definition, these were offences which estranged, or threatened to estrange, the ancestors or the gods from the community and so endangered its well-being.

---

[1] See below, under 'The oath'.

These offences may be classified under five heads, as follows:

Class I. Murder (*awudie*)

Suicide by hanging (*hyɛ akomfo*); by wounding oneself (*di wo ho awu*).

Class II. Sexual offences which were tabooed. These were:

Intercourse with one of the same blood or clan (*mogyadie*); with a woman during her menstrual period (*bratwɛ*); with a woman who was *enceinte* by another man (*mogyafra*); with a girl before she had reached puberty (*kyiri-bra*); with a half-sister by one father, or a father's brother's daughter (*atwɛbenefie*); with a woman in the bush (*ahahantwɛ*).

Class III. Offences against the chief

Adultery with the chief's wife.

Assault on the chief, his soul-washer, stool-carrier, or keeper of his mausoleum.

Stealing from the chief (*krono kɛse*).

Invoking a curse on the chief (*hyira ohene: bo hene dua*).

Abusing the chief.

Class IV. Oaths

Treason (*ɛpo*).

Cowardice (*dwane dom*: flee from the enemy).

Commands enjoined with the chief's oath.

Class V. Supernatural powers

Stealing from the gods.

Witchcraft (*bayie*).

Other taboos.

Murder and suicide were regarded as cases which should be submitted to the central authority for hearing, so that justice could be done. It was feared that the ghost of a murdered man would disturb the chief until a judicial investigation had been held, and blood exacted for blood. The Ashanti maxim on this is: *Yɛde mogya na tene mogya* (blood is righted with blood). It was the chief's duty to prevent any supernatural reprisal by trying the murderer.

The religious element of murder is more clearly seen in cases of unintentional homicide, such as occurred when a hunter unintentionally shot a man whom he saw disturbing the bush and mistook for a beast. If the elders found that this was in fact an accident, the man who was responsible for the misadventure was asked to give a sheep, which was sacrificed on the ancestral stools of the chief, the Ɔkyeame addressing the spirits :[1]

Obi na wato tuo bone, na yɛahwehwɛ asɛm no mu. Ɔmmoapa na yɛse ɔnkosie nipa no. Yɛserɛmo, momma asɛmmone sɛ eyi bi mma bio.

Someone has fired a bad gun; we have investigated the matter, he did not do it intentionally, and we say he should go and bury the man. We pray you not to let such a misfortune (bad thing) happen again.

As regards the suicide, the presumption was that he had killed himself because he had committed a sin which was a taboo and, instead of waiting to be tried by the central authority, had taken his own life. The dead body was tried again and found guilty. Where the motive was not known the sentence was: 'Whatever evil you did, since you did not bring it before the chief to be inquired into with a good hearing . . . then have we found you guilty.' The relatives, on behalf of the suicide, acknowledged the evil he had done. A sentence of death was duly passed and the dead body was beheaded. This put the community right again with the ancestors, and the evil spirit of the suicide (*tɔfo sasa*) would no longer disturb the living.

The commission of the sexual offences under Class II was regarded as something which defiled the Earth and offended the gods and the ancestors. Unless the offenders were tried and punished, the Earth purified, and the ancestors appeased by sacrifices, the community would suffer. Informants confirmed that what Rattray wrote of incest (*mogyadie*) was believed to be true of all the sexual offences in this class. Had such an act been allowed to go unpunished, then, in the words of my informants, 'hunters would have ceased to kill the animals in the forest, the crops would have refused to bear fruit, the *samanfo* (spirits of dead ancestors) would have been infuriated, the gods would have been angered, *abusua* (clans) would have ceased to exist, and all would have been chaos in the world'.

[1] See Rattray, *Ashanti Law and Constitution*, p. 296. I checked his statements on sin and tribal taboos at Mampong. The elders agreed that he was correct in every particular. Two of them were among Rattray's original informants.

Before these offences—sexual intercourse with one of the same blood or clan, with a woman in the bush, even with one's own wife, with a woman who was *enceinte*, with a girl who had not reached puberty, or with a woman during her menstrual period—were tried, the male offender was asked to bring a sheep, which was sacrificed in the open space where the court sat. This was to appease the ancestors and the gods and to cleanse the Earth, which was believed to have been defiled.

The Ashanti regarded a woman in her menses as unclean. She left the house and lived in a hut outside for six days. On the sixth day, before she returned to the house, she went to the river and washed all her things—clothing, utensils, stools—before she came back home. It was taboo for a woman in her menses to enter a chief's house. Bowdich observed this practice during his stay in Kumasi in 1817. 'During the menses, the women of the capital retire to the plantations or crooms in the bush.'[1]

The custom is still observed in many villages to-day, although owing to the influence of Christianity and, in the large towns, to housing difficulties, very many people do not observe it.

But the offences are still treated with the same reprobation. In a case which came before a chief in 1934 at a place twenty-four miles from Kumasi, a girl was found pregnant although her puberty rites had not been performed. The man concerned was sent for and asked to bring a sheep. The sheep was killed and some of its blood was sprinkled on the two offenders. They were then driven out of the town amidst shouts of derision. They lived in a hut away from the town, and were not allowed to return until forty days after the baby had been born.

A similar incident happened in 1935 in another town, also close to Kumasi. A young man had sexual connexion with a girl whose puberty rites had not been performed. In this instance she was not pregnant. The young man provided a sheep, which was sacrificed to the Earth and the ancestors, with the prayer that they might accept the sheep and avert any misfortune which the crime might have occasioned. The young man was then beaten severely, the elders having decided that this was a more effective way than imposing a fine on him.

The offences in Class III show the close social identification that existed in the mind of the Ashanti between the ancestors and the

[1] Bowdich, op. cit., p. 303.

chief who was their appointed successor.[1] The chief's wives were stool wives. When he died or was destooled the wives remained. Adultery with any of them was therefore a grave offence. It was taking the wife of the ancestors. In the same way assaulting the chief, invoking a curse upon him, stealing the stool property entrusted to his care, were offences against the ancestors and were believed to anger the ancestors and alienate them from the community. The trial of these offences commenced with the sacrifice of a sheep to the ancestors who had thus been wronged. The central authority had to see that the danger of forfeiting the favour of the ancestors, with all the consequent evils that were dreaded, was averted.

This fact of the social identification between the chief and the ancestors is still one of the difficulties of Ashanti law. It is very difficult to distinguish between offences committed against the chief personally, and offences against the stool or the ancestors. The Ashanti themselves appear to make no such distinction, for as long as a chief remains on the stool he is a sacred person in a special relationship with the ancestors. Treason, cowardice, the breaking of a command enjoined by an oath were all regarded as offences against the ancestors or the stool.

Only two informants remembered trials for treason before the time of the British Administration. In both instances the offenders charged were elders who had taken the oath of allegiance on their enstoolment to be loyal to their respective chiefs. This required of them that they should advise the chief if they found him doing wrong. Both men were charged with joining in plots to destool their respective chiefs when they had not advised the chiefs of the wrongs complained of. Both elders lost their stools, and were fined in the one case £16 (*ntanu*) and two sheep, in the other £24 (*ntansa*) and two sheep.

Even to-day, if an elder knows that there is reason for his being suspected of complicity in a plot, he takes the oath to his chief, as the Kokofuhene and the other chiefs did in the Bekwai case that has already been referred to.[2] Or the chief might ask an elder whom he has cause to suspect to 'drink fetish' (*nom abosom*) to testify that he has not broken his oath.

[1] Cf. the position of the Bemba chief in 'The Political System of the Bemba Tribe' by Audrey Richards, in *African Political Systems*, ed. M. Fortes and E. E. Evans-Pritchard. [2] See p. 55.

Sometimes an urgent order was made asking the subjects of a chief to perform a service. One such instance occurred in 1920 when a chief was fined £25 by the District Commissioner because he had not cleared his road. He was allowed three days in which to have the work completed. There were about ten miles of road to be cleared. The chief caused a gong to be beaten, declaring that all his men should turn out, and that anyone who failed to do so was guilty of the oath *Yaora* (Thursday). Anyone who disobeyed such an order offended the ancestors whose oath had been used.

It must be added that it was rare for a chief's order to be enjoined by the chief himself swearing an oath. He could only do so in respect of an order that had been made with the consent of his councillors. If he used it merely to get his subjects to fulfil his own wishes he was liable to be called to question by the Divisional Council. A chief who was found guilty of misusing the oath was liable to be destooled.

Stealing from the house of a god (*ɔbosom*) was an offence against the *ɔbosom*, and the chief tried the case, as it was classified as a national taboo. It threatened the relationship between the community and the god.

Witchcraft was in a class by itself. The witch was in a sense a murderer. The connexion with the gods and the ancestors, as informants explained, was that they tabooed witchcraft (*Yekyi kɔkɔkɔkɔ*: They taboo it utterly: a red taboo). There was also the fear that unless the victim of the witch was avenged his ghost would disturb the community.

The other taboos varied from town to town. But in every case the keeping of them was enjoined because they 'came from long ago' (*efiri tete*). It was the ancestors who decreed them (*nananom na hyehyee*). Of many of their traditional laws and taboos the chiefs say, 'They are Kɔmfo Anɔkye's Laws' (*Kɔmfo Anɔkye mmera*). That is regarded as the sanction for the observance of these laws.[1]

Every case which came before the chief involved the ancestors and the gods, some more obviously so than others. There was

[1] Kɔmfo Anɔkye was the priest and counsellor of Osei Tutu. Tradition says it was he who by his magic powers brought the Golden Stool down from the skies, and told the Ashanti it was the symbol of their unity, and was never to be lost. The Ashanti Union owed much to his genius, and tradition has endowed him with many magical powers.

always present the fear that some misfortune would befall the community unless the transgressors were tried and punished, and the laws of Kɔmfo Anɔkye and the ancestors were obeyed.

The oath[1]

We have alluded to the oath as a method whereby a private injury was brought before the chief.

Every elder, Odekuro, Birempon, or chief has his oath. Oaths in Ashanti have reference to some misfortune or disaster that, according to tradition, occurred in the past. In the case of an elder of a lineage, it was usually the death, or disease, or bodily deformity, or mutilation of an ancestor. The oaths of chiefs and Abirempon refer either to a similar misfortune of an ancestor, or more often to defeat in war. The important thing is that the oaths allude to distasteful incidents or tribal disasters connected with the ancestors. It is taboo to allude to these misfortunes, because the ancestors are either annoyed or aggrieved by the recollection of their disaster, and this estranges them from the community. There is also the fear that the use of the oath may cause a repetition of the misfortune to fall on the successors of the ancestors. The elder, Odekuro, Birempon, or chief whose oath is used has therefore to inquire into any matter in connexion with which it is used.

The oath is a set formula alluding very obscurely to the tragic incident. The usual form is merely to mention the day of the week on which the incident is alleged to have occurred. For example, the Mamponghene's oath is '*Meka Yaora*' (I say (the forbidden) Thursday). There are less obscure forms of every chief's oath, but they are regarded as more serious. The Asantehene's oath is merely to say, 'I say the Great Oath' (*Meka Ntam Kɛse*). To say '*Meka Kormante ne Memenada*' (I say *Kormante* and Saturday) is to allude less obscurely to the incident, and to incur heavier penalties —in this case, death.

The incidents to which these oaths refer are handed down by tradition in various forms. Rattray was informed[2] that the Mampong oath 'owed its origin to the defeat of the Ashanti by Kakari Apao in the war against Akyim, when Osei Tutu died or was killed and Mampong Akuamoa Panyin was wounded'.

---

[1] See Rattray, *Religion and Art in Ashanti*, chap. xxii.
[2] *Ashanti Law and Constitution*, p. 247.

In the presence of the Mamponghene, informants narrated a different tradition as follows:

'Baa Panyin (Chief of Mampong) married the queen-mother of Amanten. The queen-mother sent a message to tell the people of Amanten that they should come and make war on Mampong, because her husband's fighting men had decreased as a result of his wars against Adwera (Ejura). So the people of Amanten came and fought against Mampong. Baa Panyin, the Chief of Mampong, was left with his Gyase and the people of his household (*fiefo*) alone. These were the people of Nenten and Kyekyewere. During that battle we installed seven chiefs in Apaa on that one day (i.e. they were killed in succession). Baa Kumaa pushed the army from behind, saying to those who tried to turn back, "Go forward; go forward". Hence he earned the name Baaye-Sii-Akwan (Baa who closes paths). That day was a Thursday (*Yaora*). Baa Panyin fell in this battle. It was on that day that the Mamponghene's oath became Thursday. For the Apaahene's part in this war, the Mamponghene allowed him to hear *Yaora* oath cases.'

The traditional account of the Wenchihene's oath, which is also *Yaora*, is as follows:

During the reign of Anye Amoampon the Asantehene fought against Dormaa (about 1746).[1] The people of Wenchi then lived at Ahwene. The advance guard of the Asantehene's army took the wrong path and attacked Wenchi by mistake. Many of the unprepared people were killed before the error was discovered. The treasures of the Wenchi stool were hurriedly hidden in the bed of the River Tain. This tragic incident occurred on a Thursday, which is the Wenchihene's oath.

The most serious oath an Ashanti can use is the Asantehene's Great Oath. The tradition generally believed is that Osei Tutu, the greatest Asantehene, was killed on a Saturday at a place called Koromante when he and his party were crossing the River Pra to fight against the Akims.[2] No one is held in greater veneration than Osei Tutu, and this oath associated with him is the most solemn in Ashanti.

Rattray records similar traditions in *Ashanti Law and Constitution*. The significance of these oaths is that they are connected with the ancestors, who are offended when they are used. Those who

---

[1] Ward, op. cit., chap. v.
[2] Claridge, op. cit., vol. i, p. 199; Bowdich, op. cit., p. 233.

submit their private injury to the chief's court by using an oath appear there as guilty men who have broken a taboo, and the guiltier stood in peril of his life. But it was the only means of having a private injury inquired into by the central authority.

The procedure was for the one who desired his cause to be inquired into to swear the oath in the presence of a third person. If the other also 'responded' by swearing the oath in defence of his claim, the third person arrested them both. Anyone who heard the chief's oath sworn and responded to had to arrest the offenders and report the matter to the chief. If he failed to do this he would himself be guilty of an offence. Whoever arrested the offenders and reported to the chief became entitled to a fee of 13s., which the offenders paid. If the defendant did not respond, the fact had to be reported to the chief.

The private issue, which thus became a public matter, was inquired into. The one found not guilty paid *aseda* (thanking fee); the one who was found guilty apologized to the chief through an elder (*medwane toa ma Nana dibem*: I run to you to give the chief the justice of his cause). This was a public acknowledgement of his guilt in using the oath, and so transgressing the taboo. The apology was accepted, but he had to pay the oath fee and any fines decided by the court according to the nature of the case. Private issues like adultery, theft, abuse, slander, debt, and assault could be made public issues by the use of the oath. It was possible by that means to get the chief and the elders to inquire into a private cause. By arbitration, as well as by the formal tribunal, provision was made for settling disputes in the community. The chief and the elders maintained amicable relations in the community, and saw to it that those who transgressed the laws and customs of the tribe were punished.

Examples may be given of other occasions on which the oath was used for various other purposes:

(i) Captains going to war swore that they would never turn their back to the enemy. In Ashanti, the penalty for transgressing this oath was death.
(ii) A captain swore an oath ordering that none of his men should retreat from an enemy.
(iii) A chief might swear an oath enjoining his men to observe a certain custom.

(iv) A chief or an elder might swear an oath ordering all present to assist in quenching a fire.

(v) A man might swear an oath to restrain others from stealing crops from his farm.

(vi) A man might swear an oath to prevent another from doing him bodily harm.

(vii) A chief might swear an oath ordering the cleaning of the path to the village stream.

(viii) A chief might swear an oath ordering all his men to help in the search for or apprehension of a murderer.

(ix) A chief might swear an oath asking his men to rescue the dead or dying from a fallen house or tree.

(x) A chief might enforce the accepted rules of conduct by oath, e.g. restraining young women from loose sexual morality or young men from riotous living.

(xi) A man might swear an oath to retrieve his lost property from another.

(xii) On the dissolution of a marriage a divorced husband may swear an oath restraining his divorced wife from associating with a paramour suspected to have been instrumental in disrupting the marriage.

In these and other ways the oath was used to secure the backing of the central authority in the settlement of the issue involved.

The treasury system

Financial matters did not bulk large in administration, for there was no wage-earning system. The chief function of the administration, as has been emphasized, was to ensure harmony in the society rather than to provide services requiring expenditure.

There were what can be described as public services, provided by communal labour. The women kept the village clean, each one sweeping the area round her house. The men provided the place of public convenience by digging pits a few yards from the village and building huts over them. They also cleaned the roads and paths. It was left to each village to provide its own services under the direction of the Odekuro and his council.

The chief's house was built and kept in repair by the various elders and their subjects and slaves. To feed his household there were stool farms managed by the subjects who came directly under the chief. As Bowdich noted of Kumasi, 'the higher class could not support their numerous followers, or the lower their large families, in the city, and therefore employed them in plantations, (in which small crooms were situated) generally within two or three miles of the capital, where their labours not only feed themselves, but supply the wants of the chief, his family, and more immediate suite.'[1]

But some money was required by the chief, and a treasury system was evolved to meet the need.[2]

The currency used in Ashanti was gold-dust, for which standard weights were adopted throughout the country.[3] For the purpose of exchange the commonest weights were:

Name in Ashanti	Equivalent in English currency
Soaafa	3s.
Dommafa	3s. 6d.
Soaa	6s.
Fiaso	6s. 6d.
Domma	7s.
Nsaanu	13s.
Surupa	£1.
Dwoa	£1. 10s.
Asoaanu	£4.
Peredwan	£8.
Peredwan asia	£9. 6s.
Ntanu	£16.
Ntansa	£24.

In each Division the chiefs, the Abirempon, and some of the more important elders had their own local treasuries. They required money for buying gunpowder and arms, for paying funeral expenses, for sacrifices, for buying regalia, and for entertaining.

The gold-dust for the treasuries was raised from various sources. One source was trade (batadie). Every chief or Birempon had men among his gyase subjects who traded for him. There were two trade routes, one between Ashanti and the Northern Territories and the other between Ashanti and the coast. To the north the Ashanti took kola, and brought back slaves, shea-butter, blankets, and livestock. To the south they took ivory, gold-dust,

---

[1] Bowdich, op. cit., p. 323.
[2] Rattray, *Ashanti Law and Constitution* (chap. xiv) gives a correct and detailed account of the Ashanti treasury system.
[3] Rattray, *Ashanti*, chap. xxv.

and slaves, and returned with metal rods (*ntwea*), rum, guns and gunpowder, salt, and cloth.

By the end of the nineteenth century the trade had become considerable, as may be judged from Casely Hayford's account:

In the olden times a most active trade was carried on between this country and the hinterland through Ashanti. There were merchant princes in those days, when such men as the Hon. Samuel Collins Brew, the Hon. George Blankson, the Hon. James Bannerman, Samuel Ferguson, Esq., the Smiths, the Hansens, and others flourished....

The King of Ashanti knew most of these merchant princes, and His Majesty, at stated times in the commercial year, sent some of his head tradesmen with gold dust, ivory, and other products to the coast to his merchant friends in exchange for Manchester goods and other articles of European manufacture. In one visit the caravan cleared off several hundred bales of cotton goods, which found their way into the uttermost parts of Soudan.

It was part of the State System of Ashanti to encourage trade. The King once in every forty days, at the *Adai* custom, distributed among a number of chiefs various sums of gold dust with a charge to turn the same to good account. These chiefs then sent down to the coast caravans of tradesmen, some of whom would be their slaves, sometimes some two to three hundred strong, to barter ivory for European goods, or buy such goods with gold dust, which the King obtained from the royal alluvial workings. Down to 1873 a constant stream of Ashanti traders might be seen daily wending their way to the coast and back again, yielding more certain wealth and prosperity to the merchants of the Gold Coast and Great Britain than may be expected for some time yet to come from the mining industry and railway development put together. The trade Chiefs would, in due course, render a faithful account to the King's stewards, being allowed to retain a fair portion of the profit.... Important Chiefs carried on the same system of trading with the coast as did the King. Thus every member of the State, from the King downwards, took an active interest in the promotion of trade and in the keeping open of the trade routes into the interior.[1]

This corroborates Bowdich's earlier observations:

It is a frequent practice of the King's, to consign sums of gold to the care of rising captains, without requiring them from them for two or three years, at the end of which time he expects the captain not only to restore the principal, but to prove that he has acquired sufficient of his own, from the use of it, to support the greater dignity the King

[1] Casely Hayford, *Gold Coast Native Institutions* (1903), pp. 95–6.

would confer on him. If he has not, his talent is thought too mean for further elevation.[1]

A second source was from *atitɔde*. This was what transgressors who had been found guilty by the court paid 'to buy their heads'. It was a fine in lieu of the death sentence. The whole amount of such fines was paid into the chief's treasury. Also accruing from court cases was the *aseda* (thanksgiving money) from those whom the court had found innocent. The *aseda* was distributed among the chief, his *Abusuapanyin* (elder of the royal lineage), the queen-mother, the Ɔkyeame, the elders, females of the royal lineage, stool-carriers and keepers of the mausoleum, the sword-bearers, the treasurers, children and grandchildren of the chief, gun-carriers, and even strangers of the public who happened to be present at the trial.[2]

The Ɔkyeame at Wenchi gave me an example of the distribution from a case heard at Wenchi in 1934. The new treasury system has changed this practice. The *aseda* charged in this case was £2. 7s. It was distributed as follows:

7s. to the Akyeame (three of them).
2s. to the queen-mother.
1s. to the chief's mother and her sister.
1s. to stool-carriers.
1s. to sword-bearers.
2s. to the *Sanaahene* (treasurer).
1s. to the children of chiefs (*ahenemma*).
2s. to four elderly strangers who had helped to settle the case.
14s. to the chief.
16s. to the elders.

The chief also received revenue from gold-mining. Two-thirds of all gold mined in his Division was paid into the chief's treasury, the remaining third being retained by the elder or Birempon in direct charge of the area in which it was mined.

Direct levies were also imposed for the specific purposes indicated above: for funerals, regalia, war, ceremonial, or hospitality. Sometimes a special levy was collected for the chief's treasury when a new chief was installed (*Yedi tɔɔ bɔ Ɔhene fotoɔ*: We raise a levy for the chief's treasury).

The chief's council or the Birempon's council had first to

[1] Bowdich, op. cit., p. 295.
[2] See Rattray, *Ashanti Law and Constitution*, p. 115.

approve of the levy, and also of the amount to be collected. The collection was then made through the different units of the Division. The Birempon, elder, Odekuro, or head of a lineage each collected from those under his direct control and paid the lump sum to his next immediate superior. The elders and Abirempon then paid the money into the chief's treasury. An elder or Birempon who had a treasury was allowed to collect more than was due from him so that he might replenish his own local treasury.

There was a strict control of public funds. The chief had his treasurer, Sannaahene (head of the leather bag), as did the Birempon whose treasury officer was the *Fotosanfo* (he who unlooses the bag). It was to the treasurer of the chief or Birempon that all revenue was paid. It was also the treasurer who paid out any money required, and the Ɔkyeame (spokesman) or *Daberehene* (chamberlain) witnessed all such transactions. The chief or Birempon himself might not hold the scales used for weighing out the gold, nor might he open the leather bag in which it was kept. For the *Adae* and other ceremonies it was the Sannaahene who saw to the purchase of all the things that were required. If a levy was raised for a specific purpose, the Sannaahene's duty was to see that the levy was used for that purpose.

That the system worked well may be judged from the fact that the destooling of chiefs for 'misappropriating stool funds' was of very rare occurrence before the period of the British Administration of Ashanti.[1]

Bowdich's description of Opoku, the Asantehene's Sannaahene, is evidence of the importance of this officer:

Apokoo is the keeper of the royal treasury, and has the care of all the tributes, which are deposited, separately, in a large apartment of the palace, of which he only has the key. Numerous and various as the sums are, he disposes of them by a local association which is said to be infallible with him, for the Moorish secretary, . . . only records the greater political events. Apokoo holds a sort of exchequer court at his own house daily, (when he is attended by two of the King's linguists, and various state insignia,) to decide all cases affecting tribute or revenue, and the appeal to the King is seldom resorted to. He generally reclined on his lofty bed, (of accumulated cushions, and covered with a large rich cloth or piece of silk,) with two or three of his handsomest wives near him, whilst the pleadings were going forward. He was always much gratified when I attended, and rose to seat me beside him. I observed

[1] See Chap. IX.

that all calculations were made, explained, and recorded, by cowries. In one instance, after being convinced ... that a public debtor was unable to pay gold, he commuted sixteen ounces of gold, for twenty men slaves. Several captains, who were his followers, attended this court daily with large suites, and it was not only a crowded, but frequently a splendid scene. Before the footoorh or treasury bag is unlocked by the weigher, though it be by the King's order, Apokoo must strike it with his hand in sanction.[1]

The system of accounting was in the following manner. For revenue, there were two boxes. One box, the *adaka kɛse*, had three separate compartments, each containing gold-dust made up in £8 packets (*peredwan*). The box was kept in the chief's sleeping-room, and the chief, the Sannaahene, and the head chamberlain witnessed withdrawals from it. A cowrie shell was put into the box whenever a packet was withdrawn.

The Sannaahene had another box in which smaller sums were kept. When he had enough to make a *peredwan* (£8), it was weighed out and put into the larger box.

For expenditure there was a third box, the *apem adaka* (box of a thousand). This was replenished by £8 packets taken out of the large revenue box (*adaka kɛse*). The money was weighed out in small packets (3s., 3s. 6d., 7s., 13s.) which the Sannaahene used for his purchases. The payments were recorded by replacing each packet taken out with a cowrie shell.

Bowdich records a way in which the Asantehene's busy officials were probably remunerated:

It is to be observed that the King's weights are one-third heavier than the current weights of the country; and all the gold expended in provision being weighed out in the former, and laid out in the latter, the difference enriches the chamberlain, cook, and chief domestic officers of the palace, as it is thought derogatory to a King avowedly to pay his subjects for their services.[2]

This was probably so, but I was unable to obtain confirmation of it. What was confirmed was Rattray's more recent observation:

The first point to notice in connexion with the sums formerly imposed by Native Tribunals (which we wrongly translate by 'fines') was that the sum demanded and paid was always some odd amount. 12s., 23s. 6d., £4. 13s., £9. 6s., and so on, i.e. in the gold-dust currency was made up of two weights—10s. and 2s., £1 and 3s. 6d, £4

---

[1] Bowdich, op. cit., p. 296.   [2] Ibid., p. 293.

and 13*s*., £8 and £1. 6*s*. The odd amounts were known in Ashanti as *mataho* or *kyekyerekon* (i.e., something stuck or tied 'on the neck' of the larger packet of gold-dust). *Sika kuntunsin nko ahen fie* (A headless packet of gold-dust does not go to the Chief's palace). These little extra bundles were invariably the perquisites of the *Okyeame* (or *Akyeame*), upon whom fell by far the most onerous duties in a Native Tribunal.[1]

In financial matters, as we have already noted in other administrative and judicial affairs, 'every section managed its own finance with a minimum of interference from the central authority, which all, however, acknowledged and to whose maintenance all contributed'.[2]

To sum up then, the administrative system of Ashanti was based on the political units : the lineage, the village, the sub-division, and the Division. The chief administrative function was the maintenance of amicable relations among the members of the community and between the community and its ancestors and gods. Each unit was left to manage its own affairs under its own head and council, and to provide its public services by communal labour. But in judicial matters the central authority stepped in whenever the welfare of the community was threatened by an offence which might affect the relationship between the community and the royal ancestors and the gods that protected it. In other administrative affairs the chief worked through the Abirempon, elders, and Adekurofo, he himself being the hub integrating the respective units of the administrative system.

[1] Rattray, *Ashanti Law and Constitution*, p. 114.
[2] Ibid., p. 118.

CHAPTER V

THE ASHANTI UNION

Character and purpose of the Union

THE tradition is that the Ashanti States formed a Union in order to fight for their independence against Denkyira, to which they were tributary.

At that time the States lived close to one another near Sante-manso, whence they subsequently moved into other areas. The picture presented is that of a segmentary political system in which the segments or States, possessing similar social and political institutions, a common language and religion, and bound by ties of clanship, were welded into a Union under the Asantehene, whose capital was Kumasi. The six leading States were Kumasi, Juaben, Mampong, Kokofu, Nsuta, and Bekwai. With the exception of Mampong all these States belonged to the same clan—the Oyoko clan.

The clan

In theory members of the same clan are believed to be descendants of a remote common ancestress.[1] Marriage between members of the same clan is taboo, as they are believed to be maternal kinsmen.

The clan is spread all over Ashanti, and in fact over the whole of the Akan tribes—Fanti, Ashanti, Akwapem, Akwamu, and Warsaw:

One curious evidence however may be added of the former identity of the Ashantee, Warsaw, Fantee, Akim, Assin, Aquamboe, and part of the Ahanta nations; which is a tradition that the whole of these people were originally comprehended in twelve tribes or families . . . in which they class themselves still, without any regard to national distinction.

[1] See App. I. The clan is composed of a number of lineages, the latter being localized, and more closely knit. The lineage can usually trace descent in the matrilineal line to a common ancestress, and give the name. The clan is scattered all over Ashanti, and no clan can give accurately the list that will embrace all the people that claim membership within it. The clearest link now is the name: it is enough for one to say that he belongs to the Oyoko or Bretuo or Asenie or Aduana or Asona clan, &c., and he is accepted as a 'brother', i.e. kinsman, by other members of the same clan.

For instance, Ashantees, Warsaws, Akims, Ahantas, or men of any of the nations before mentioned will severally declare that they belong to the Annŏna family; other individuals of the different countries that they are of the Tchweedam family; and when this is announced on meeting, they salute each other as brothers.[1]

Membership in the same clan still creates feelings of belonging together, and of spontaneous goodwill towards one another. In 1942, for example, a stranger from Akim Abuakwa arrived in Mampong on a visit. He called on the chief, and in conversation it was discovered that he was a member of the chief's clan— Bretuo. The stranger was thereupon accorded liberal hospitality. This is quite common; strangers travelling from one place to another in Ashanti claim and receive hospitality on the strength of membership in the same clan. Many cannot name the ancestress of their clan, yet the discovery that anyone belongs to the same clan as another rouses feelings of fraternity between them.

Members of a clan are not a political unit, but are spread over all the Divisions or States of Ashanti in separate lineages, yet the clan has political significance in that chiefs of the same clan treat one another with special cordiality and tend to draw together. There is, for example, a close bond between the chiefs of Kumasi, Juaben, Kokofu, and Bekwai, who are members of the Oyoko clan. They treat one another as brothers, of whom the Asantehene is the senior brother. There is a similar bond between chiefs of the Bretuo clan, of whom the Mamponghene is the senior brother. Every chief belongs to one or other of the seven major clans of Ashanti.[2] The ties of clanship helped to strengthen the Ashanti Union.

An example of its influence occured in 1945, when the Bekwaihene refused to attend a meeting of the Confederacy Council. There was a long discussion as to what steps should be taken. The Juabenhene said: 'The Bekwaihene is my younger brother, according to our Constitution[3], and if the Council will entrust the matter to me, I will see to it that he joins us at our next sitting.' So it was agreed that the matter should be left to the Juabenhene as, 'constitutionally, he is the right man for it.'[4]

---

[1] Bowdich, op. cit., pp. 229–30.
[2] See App. I.
[3] They belong to the same Oyoko clan.
[4] Minutes of the Confederacy Council (1945).

The Union a loose confederation

In spite of the bonds of clanship and the possession of common social and political institutions, language, and religion, the Ashanti Union was, as far as can be ascertained, a loose confederation.

Each of the segments had had a previous existence as a distinct community before the Union, and had developed in its own region a well-established form of government through the lineage, village, and sub-division, which enabled it to manage its own affairs.

Without rail or road transport or other means of communication even the short distances which separated the States isolated them, and each State developed a regional consciousness and a strong tendency towards independence.

This desire persisted throughout the period of the Union. For example, the States of Kumawu and Mampong claim that according to tradition they did not surrender the spoils they took in war to the Asantehene. There are stronger proofs of the loose nature of the Union.

About 1800 Mampong was suspected of designs to attack Kumasi, as is evidenced by the following tradition told me by the Mampong elders. 'Then came the reign of Nana Owusu Sekyerɛ Panyin (the First). He was the son of Nana Sei Kwame. He it was who fought across the Volta, and conquered many tribes. He was away for three years. When he was about to return to Mampong, some of the elders he had left behind there went and told the Asantehene that if Nana Sei Kwame returned he would dominate Ashanti; he might even fight against him, the Asantehene; so at their request the Asantehene collected an army and placed the Ankaasehene over it. This army was joined by people left behind in Mampong. The Asantehene did not go to fight himself, because it was taboo that the Golden Stool (Kumasi) and the Silver Stool (Mampong) should fight against each other. Owusu Sekyerɛ had only his *gyase* (bodyguard) and his *kyidɔm* (rear) with him. The battle was fought near the River Volta. The army sent against the Mamponghene was routed, and he pursued it as far as the Daho cross-roads. There, a captive, on being questioned, said that he came from Kumasi. "Is my father (i.e. Asantehene) fighting against me, then?" declared the Mamponghene. "The Golden Stool and the Silver Stool should not fight." So the Mamponghene stopped fighting, turned back, and was not seen again.'

There are less remote accounts which point to the same tendency. As late as 1817, over 100 years after the death of Osei Tutu, the founder of the Union, Bowdich gives the following eyewitness account:

It is clear, that the King of Ashantee contemplates the reduction of the King of Dwabin from an independent ally to a tributary. We witnessed one circumstance to the point. A messenger being sent to require gold of Dwabin, the King of which is a very weak young man, a captain of the royal family replied, that there was no war on foot to require gold, and as it could only be for the individual benefit of Ashantee, the government must be reminded that Dwabin had formerly exacted gold, and was not now to be subjected to imposition, because the right had been yielded from respect to the sister kingdom. This being reported to the King, he suppressed his anger, and sent a gold headed sword, with other marks of dignity and favour to this man, who, to his surprise refused them, alleging, that the honours he already possessed at home became him better.[1]

These were not mere sporadic incidents but were symptomatic of the Union, especially during the nineteenth century. Banda, Techiman, and Gyaman frequently revolted against Kumasi. In 1875 Juaben revolted and fought to secure her independence.[2] Not only Juaben, but Kumawu, Mampong, Nsuta, Bekwai, and Kokofu also broke away from Kumasi. Even the small division of Mansu-Nkwanta revolted against Kumasi during the reign of Mensa Bonsu (1875–83) and was successful because none of the other chiefs would join in the war.[3] In 1895 the chiefs of Bekwai and Abodom signed formal treaties with the British Government without the permission of the Asantehene.[2] The history of the Ashanti Union in the nineteenth century gives the impression that the Union was a loose one in which the separate States exercised a wide degree of autonomy, and showed a tendency towards complete independence.[4]

Local loyalties were also strengthened by the fact that each village was economically self-sufficient. It grew its own food and hunted its meat in its own forests. The women practised pottery

[1] Bowdich, op. cit., pp. 245–6.
[2] Claridge, op. cit., vol. ii; Ward, op. cit., chap. xv.
[3] Rattray, *Ashanti Law and Constitution*, p. 15.
[4] Also, see Fuller, *A Vanished Dynasty—Ashanti*, for similar examples supporting this view.

and spinning, and there were weavers, wood-carvers, and smiths amongst the men. In this way each State provided for its own needs. There was little trade or other economic bond between the States. Their previous existence as separate, autonomous States, their isolation through geographical factors, and the economic self-sufficiency of each village produced a tendency to resist a centralized administration. This is borne out by tradition and practice. Within the Union each State maintained its own treasury, held its own *Adae* and *Odwera* festivals, and managed its own internal affairs.

The achievement of the kings of Kumasi was the building up of this loose political system into a strong military power. By the end of the nineteenth century, partly by migrations and partly by the conquest and absorption of other tribes, the Union included the States of Kumasi (which included Nkwanta and Berekum), Mampong, Juaben, Bekwai, Kokofu, Nsuta, Asumegya, Kumawu, Adansi, Offinsu, Agona, Wam-Pamu, Nkoranza, Techiman, and Banda. The States which were conquered and absorbed were left in possession of their lands and they managed their own internal affairs. The bond between the States was their common allegiance to the Asantehene.

Although the formation of the Union was impelled by the need for common defence, no permanent Union Army was established. The constituent States supplied the men required for defence or external aggression as the need arose. All able-bodied men of each State were liable for military service, and their chief was responsible for providing them with powder and ammunition. For a major war the Asantehene collected the necessary powder and ammunition together. Sometimes this took several years, as the powder and ammunition were purchased from the coast and carried to Kumasi. When he had collected enough the Asantehene distributed it to the chiefs, who paid for it by a levy on their own people. This was the war tax (*apea-too*).

As it was the chiefs who provided the fighting men, they were consulted in all matters relating to war and their consent was gained for every action. Foreign policy was the joint responsibility of all the chiefs. Bowdich found that his mission was protracted because the chiefs were called together from the different States to consider every proposal he put before the Asantehene. At such meetings each chief had an equal voice, and the weight of his opinion depended on his rank and status rather than on the size of his State.

The Union enabled adequate and effective measures for defence or attack to be taken. This was achieved by all the States combining their forces. The Union military organization was the same as for a State. It consisted of an advance guard (*twafo*), a main body (*adɔnten*), and rearguard (*kyidɔm*), and two wings, left (*benkum*), and right (*nifa*). In the case of the national army each wing had two formations: right and right-half (*nifa noase*), left and left-half (*benkum noase*). Each State was assigned its place in this organization, and one of the chiefs of the more important States commanded each section. The positions of the major units were:

The main body (including the scouts and the advance guard):
   The Konti and Adɔnten clans of Kumasi.
The right-half wing: Juaben, Kokofu, Bekwai.
The right wing: Mampong, Adansi, Nkoranza, Offinso, Ejisu.
The left-half wing: Nsuta, Dormaa.
The left wing: Asumegya, Kumawu.
The reaguard: *Kyidɔm* of Kumasi, Ankaase, Domakwai.

The Asantehene, who was in command of the whole army, after the usages of Ashanti warfare directed operations from behind. That the united forces did provide the effective defence or attack expected of it may be judged not only from the successive victories of Ashanti over neighbouring tribes, but also from the fact that it withstood eight wars against the British (1806, 1811, 1814–15, 1823–6, 1863, 1873–4, 1895, 1900) before Ashanti was finally occupied.[1]

In order that the Union might provide permanent security, any attempt at secession by a member State was followed by reprisals designed to prevent it. If this resulted in a war, Kumasi could count on the support of some of the other States against the seceding State. Thus, when Juaben revolted in 1875, Kumasi was assisted by Asumegya, Mampong, Nsuta, Kokofu, and Bekwai. Kumasi was similarly supported in its wars against Jaman, Banda, and Techiman whenever these States revolted. Physical force was one of the sanctions of the Union.

The existence of other potentially hostile States to the north and

---

[1] Claridge, op. cit., vol. ii.

south of Ashanti also gave unity and solidarity to the segmentary organization of Ashanti. To the north were the Gonjas and Dagombas, and to the south the Assins, Denkyeras, Akims, Akwapems, and Fantis.

The Union was maintained not only by physical force or the threat of attack from a neighbouring tribe, but also, as we have shown, by religious sanctions. Sentiments of loyalty to the Golden Stool and reverence for the ancestors who had originated the Union were effective in ensuring the maintenance of unity. These sentiments of loyalty and solidarity were kept alive by the periodic ritual *Odwera* ceremonies which were held in Kumasi. The Durbar held in 1935, at the restoration of the Union under the name of the Ashanti Confederacy, demonstrated how effective these ceremonies must have been in rousing the sentiments of solidarity and patriotism of Ashanti. The ceremonies were marked by deep feelings of exaltation and expressions of loyalty to the Golden Stool. One of the Kumasi royals who watched the ceremony said movingly: 'I see now why the ancestors instituted the *Odwera* ceremonies. It was to bring the chiefs together to warm themselves (*ka yɛn ho hye*), so that they may be mindful of the Union.'

The Kumasi Division

We have shown that in the other States the military organization was built up on the lineage system. In war each elder was the leader of his lineage, which fought in the front, rear, centre, wing, or main body according to its traditional place in the military organization.

In Kumasi the lineage system gave way to groupings which appear to have been based entirely on military considerations. In the place of lineages we find military units or companies (*fekuo*) composed of people of different clans placed under captains (*Safohene*).

This arrangement is accounted for in tradition as follows:[1]

When Osei Tutu came to succeed Obiri Yeboa, there was already in Kumasi an elder who was known as the Soaduhene. This office was held by one Awere. There was also the Yokohene, who was the Chief of Juaben. He was the head of the Oyoko lineage (*Abusua Panyin*).

---

[1] I translate the words of Ɔkyeame Amoaten, the Asantehene's spokesman, and a recognized authority on Ashanti traditions and customs.

Then the King of Ashanti went to war against Dormaa[1] and defeated her. Dormaa Kusi was then Chief of Dormaa. After the war Osei Tutu said to the Chiefs of Juaben, Nsuta, Mampong, Asumegya, Kumawu, and Bekwai: 'I have now plenty of war captives (*nnomum*). I shall create war captains (*Asafohene*) so that when you go back to your capitals I shall be able, with their help, to protect Kumasi.

So he first created Amankwatia a war captain. He said, 'it is because of war that I have made you captain' (*ɔko nti na mabɔ wo*). He became Kontihene. Under him he placed six units, each with its own captain. These consisted of captives he had taken in the war from Banda, Berekum, Suatre, and Dormaa.

Then he said to the Juabenhene: 'You are the head of the Oyoko lineage. Give me someone in your place so that when you go to your capital he will help me to watch over Kumasi.' So the Juabenhene appointed Kwapon-Di-Awuo, and he was made the Oyokohene. This man originally came to Juaben from Akyem Abirim. He told the Juabenhene that he belonged to the Oyoko clan, so the Juabenhene received him.

At one stage in the war against Dormaa news reached Osei Tutu that 'the shields had turned' (*kyɛm ani adane*), that is, the Ashantis were fleeing from the enemy—the shields were facing in the wrong direction. Osei Tutu replied that the shields had only clashed (*kyɛm apem*), but not turned, and he pressed the people on to victory. So after the war he created a new company to commemorate the event. The new company was called Akyɛmpem, and Kra Amponsem, a Denkyira man, was its first captain.

Then he changed the title of the Soaduhene to Akwamuhene. He augmented the company. Adum Asamoa, who was captain of seven units (*atuo nson*: literally, seven guns), was placed in the Akwamu Company. So also was Asumen, a newly made captain (*Twafohene*: leader of the advance guard). The *Akrafohene*, another captain, was also placed in the Akwamu Company. The new company was named Akwamu because Akwamu was the place where Osei Tutu took refuge when he fled from Ashanti.

So Osei Tutu created the Konti, Kyidɔm, Akwamu, and Oyoko Companies. Each of these included people from different clans. Only the Oyoko contained members of the same clan.

The traditional account goes on to narrate that each of Osei Tutu's successors created a new captain or enlarged an existing company after a successful war. Only a few more examples need be given here. Poku Ware, after his victory in Banda, formed a new

---

[1] About 1700. The Dormaas then lived about two miles north of where Kumasi now is.

company under Fosu, who became Anantahene. He was placed in the Gyase Company. Sei Kwadwo further augmented the Gyase by the addition of a new unit under the Hiawuhene. Sei Kwame enlarged the Ankɔbea Company, which Poku Ware had created, by the addition of two units whose captains were the Atipinhene and the Apagyahene. Poku Fofie also augmented the Ankɔbea *fekuo* by the addition of a new unit under the Apeasemakahene. After Bonsu's victory over Adinkra in 1818 he also created a new captain, the Anamanakohene, who was also placed in the Ankɔbea Company.

The tradition is that the companies were created to commemorate victories. The practice was for captives to be grouped in companies and placed under captains who were given titles by which their company or military unit was distinguished.

According to this tradition the organization in Kumasi was purposely designed for military efficiency. There were eight companies: Konti, Akwamu, Adɔnten, Benkum, Oyoko, Kyidɔm, Gyase, and Ankɔbea. The present Asantehene has made a new company, Manwere, thus raising the number to nine. Of these the Oyoko and Adɔnten are clans.[1] The former consists of members of the Oyoko clan, to which the Kumasi royals belong, and the latter of members of the Asenie clan. So the Oyokohene and Adɔntenhene are *Abusuatire* (heads of clans) as distinct from the others, who are captains (*Safohene*) in charge of groups which contain people of different clans.[2]

The military organization was made the basis of the civil administration of Kumasi. The heads of the companies became the Asantehene's councillors. These captains were not only military leaders and civil advisers, but they were also responsible to the Asantehene for the administration of the areas and the people placed under them. A peculiar feature of the Kumasi Division was that some of the captains were appointed not only over groups and villages near Kumasi where they lived, but also over distant villages or people. The captains stayed in Kumasi, and left the

---

[1] i.e. consist of lineages claiming descent from a remote common ancestress, as opposed to the others which consist of people of many clans formed into a group.

[2] See App. II giving list of the nine companies, the units in each company (*fekuo*) and the clan of each unit. The Government refers to these heterogeneous companies as 'clans', and terms the captains Kumasi clan chiefs. This use results in some confusion, for the 'clan chiefs' are not heads of clans, that is, of lineages claiming descent from a common ancestress, but of people of many clans formed into a company.

distant villages or people to manage their own affairs under their headmen. Some of the distant villages placed under captains who lived in Kumasi were the following:

Under the Adɔntenhene
Abenkyim, Abuoso, and Asamang, all in the present Bekwai administrative District.[1]

Under the Akwamuhene
Abiram and Mansu-Nkwanta, in the Bekwai District.
Bechem, in the Sunyami District.
Bompata, in the Ashanti–Akim District.
Nsawkaw, in the Wenchi District.

Under the Ankɔbeahene
Anamaku (including Asamama and Atwere) in the Bekwai District.
Domiabra, in the Ashanti–Akim District.

Under the Benkumhene (Benkum wing)
Abodom, Amoaful, Assechere, Denyease, all in the Bekwai District.

Under the Gyasehene
Adomge, Morso, Patriensa, Prah river, Agogo, Bansu, Bankami, Juansa, Obogu, all in the Ashanti–Akim District.
Afworewa, Esase, Mansu–Abodom, Pekyi, Wirempe, in the Bekwai District.
Branam, Subinsu Awisa, Nchiraa, in the Wenchi District.
Kokobin, in the Obuasi District.
Mabang, in the Sunyami District.

Under the Kyidɔmhene
Whidiem, Krofah, in the Ashanti–Akim District.
Menji, Badu, Seikwa, in the Wenchi District.
Banko, in the Mampong District.
Offuasi, in the Bekwai District.

Under the Kontihene
Asuowin, Mosiaso, Pekyi II, in the Bekwai District.
Nkwanta, Nsoatre, Odumase, in the Sunyani District.
Seketia, in the Wenchi District.

Under the Manwerehene
Drobonsu, in the Ashanti–Akim District.

---

[1] District means an administrative area under a District Commissioner. See Chap. VI.

Under the Nifahene (Nifa wing of Kumasi)
Adankranja, in the Bekwai District.
Asokori and Beposo, in the Mampong District.

Under the Oyokohene
Tanoso, in the Wenchi District.

It is clear from the above that considerations other than administrative control dictated the grouping of villages so widely scattered. It gives support to the tradition about the organization of Kumasi. The important thing was the fact that the people who lived in these villages were available to serve under their respective captains in time of war.

The captains had judicial functions as well. They were members of the Asantehene's court, and they also settled disputes amongst their own subjects. But the distant villages were administered by their respective headmen.

In addition some of them had special duties at the Asantehene's court. The Gyasehene was in charge of the palace attendants who were responsible for all the household duties and for looking after the Asantehene's personal belongings—his trinkets, clothes, sandals, ceremonial swords, and the like. The Gyase Company was very large because its members were the personal subjects of the Asantehene.

Some of the captaincies became offices which were filled only by the sons of an Asantehene. The Kyidɔm or Akyɛmpem, Atipin, and Anamako stools belong to this class. This not only made it possible to raise the sons to positions of honour, but it also ensured that the Asantehene was loyally served by captains who besides owing their elevation to him were bound to him by filial ties. These captains had special duties. The Akyɛmpemhene was responsible for the welfare of the sons and grandsons of the Asantehene. Any deaths amongst them were first reported to him; he then reported to the Asantehene, and caused his drums to be beaten to announce the death to all. The Atipinhene superintended the duties of some of the palace attendants—the ceremonial sword-bearers (*afonasoafo*), soul-washers (*akradwarefo*), gun-bearers (*tumtufo*) and bathroom attendants (*adwareyefo*). The Anamakohene had special duties at the funeral rites of captains or royals. He led those who discharged volleys of guns (*atrane*) at the ceremony. In view of the very wide distribution of this practice, I may add that all my authoritative informants agreed that the discharge of guns at funerals was prompted by ostentation. It impressed people with the esteem in which the dead person was held, and with the piety of his kinsfolk.

The Asantehene

The Asantehene was the point of common contact for the separate companies and captains of the Kumasi Division. He was also the centre to which all the chiefs of the Union were connected. Within the Union he held a unique position.

It was by the prowess of Osei Tutu and the genius of Kɔmfo Anɔkye that the separate States were welded into the Union which secured them their independence of Denkyira and their later victories. No memories are more revered in Ashanti than those of Osei Tutu and Kɔmfo Anɔkye. The reverence in which Osei Tutu and Kɔmfo Anɔkye are held is accorded to their successors. The Asantehene is the most venerated living person in Ashanti. This gains significance from the fact that the religion of Ashanti consists for the most part in the worship of ancestors. In a previous chapter[1] it has been shown that it is as successors of the ancestors, and the principal actors in those rites by which the Ashantis symbolically express their sense of dependence on them, that Ashanti chiefs have the most potent sanctions for their authority. This gives the successor of Osei Tutu and the occupant of the Golden Stool, the sacred shrine which symbolizes the unity of the Ashanti, an immense power over the minds of his people. To them, an awe-inspiring aura of divinity surrounds him. The Ashanti do not like to speak of the Asantehene, still less to be questioned about him. When they have to talk about him they do so in low tones, modulating gradually into whispers.

A recent incident gave a good illustration of the unique position which the Asantehene occupies. On 26 September 1941 a meeting was held in Kumasi at which the Asantehene appeared in state. The chiefs, who had come from their Divisions to attend a meeting of the Confederacy, were present. One of them, the Dormaahene, had a chair (*asipim*) which had gold bands on it. No one in Ashanti apart from the Asantehene is allowed to have his stool adorned with gold. In the old days this would have led to a war. It was the ostensible cause of a war against Adinkra, King of Jaman, in

---

[1] Chap. II, 'The Religious Aspect of Chiefship'.

1818. The Dormaahene apologized through the Kokofuhene. Although he was forgiven he was asked to slaughter twelve sheep. The offence was considered an offence against the ancestors and the sheep had to be sacrificed to appease them. No one should make himself equal to the Asantehene, who is the successor of his royal ancestors.

The Asantehene was revered as the successor of Osei Tutu, but his authority had also the sanction of force. As we have seen, Kumasi was designed to be a strong State under specially selected and tried captains. Against other States in the Union the Asantehene could lead stronger forces; against other tribes he could muster the whole man-power of the Union.

Although the prestige of the Asantehene was high he was not an autocrat, but was subject to constitutional checks. There is a definite procedure regarding his election, installation, and destoolment.

When the Golden Stool becomes vacant, the Kontihene requests the Gyasehene to approach the queen-mother and ask her to nominate a candidate. The Gyasehene summons a meeting of the Kumasi clan chiefs and captains to discuss the matter. The clan chiefs and captains then send a deputation, headed by the Gyasehene and composed of some of the chiefs and a number of their spokesmen, to ask the queen-mother formally for a candidate. The queen-mother meets the members of the stool family, that is, the Oyoko lineage of Kumasi, and they discuss the matter and nominate a candidate. If her first nominee is not acceptable to the majority of the electors she may nominate a second, and then a third; after which the electors will choose their own candidate.

If the queen-mother's nominee is accepted or, failing that, if agreement is reached between her and the electors as to a candidate, a day is fixed for him to be publicly nominated and accepted. The Divisional chiefs are informed of the candidate, and of the day appointed for the public nomination. On the day appointed, the Divisional chiefs do not attend in person, but send their spokesmen to represent them. The occasion is only for the public nomination of the candidate. As the matter will have been already discussed, the meeting approves the candidate formally and publicly.

A day is then fixed for the election of the candidate. On this occasion the Divisional chiefs attend in person. The full meeting of the electorate consists of the Divisional chiefs and the Kumasi clan chiefs and captains. The candidate is formally introduced to the electorate. The head spokesman, on behalf of the electorate, presents the stool to him, and repeats to him the same admonitions which are repeated to every Divisional chief on his election.[1] The candidate thanks them, and customarily acknowledges the gift. This acknowledgement takes the form of a gift of about £93, formerly in gold (*mperedwan du*), to the electorate. The candidate-elect then publicly takes his oath, promising to administer the nation well, and to act in accordance with the advice of his councillors. The chiefs also swear the oath of allegiance to him.

The candidate-elect does not go to live in the palace until he has been installed. There is a public ceremony of installation, when all the Divisional chiefs are again present. The formalities are the same as have been described for a Divisional chief. On the night of the installation the Asantehene is taken to the stool-room. The Mamponghene holds his right hand, the Essumjahene his left, and the Kyidomhene of Kumasi his waist. He is then lowered and raised three times over the Golden Stool. After this the candidate-elect assumes the power and dignity of a successor of Osei Tutu.

Thus the same constitutional practice which governed the election of a chief applied to the Asantehene also. He had to be duly elected from the Oyoko lineage of Kumasi, which, like other royal lineages, had several branches. The election of the Asantehene was not only the concern of the queen-mother and the captains and clan chiefs of Kumasi, but also of all the chiefs of the Union. They were all members of the electoral body.

That the electors took their duty seriously is shown by the fact that there were two civil wars over elections during the latter half of the nineteenth century.[2] The first occasion was in 1884, over the election of Kwaku Dua. At first the chiefs of Mampong, Nsuta, Agona, Kokofu, and Nkoranza supported a rival candidate, Kofi Kakari, who had been deposed before. The Kumasi electors supported Kwaku Dua. After two years of wrangling and civil war the queen-mother invited the electors to Kumasi, where they agreed to elect Kwaku Dua.

Four years later there was a similar situation. There were two claimants to the Golden Stool, Atwereboanna and Prempeh. The former was supported by the chiefs of Kokofu, Mampong, and

---

[1] See Chap. I, 'Constitutional Aspect of Chiefship'.
[2] Claridge, op. cit., vol. ii.

Nsuta, the latter by the Kumasi electors and the chiefs of Juaben and Bekwai. Again civil war broke out, and the crisis was not resolved till a year later, when the electors met in Kumasi and agreed to elect Prempeh.

Like other Divisional chiefs the Asantehene promised to rule with the help and advice of his council. In the management of the affairs of Kumasi he had to consult the council of eight clan chiefs and captains, and act on their advice. In matters affecting the Union he was subject to similar checks from the chiefs of the constituent States.

The cardinal principle of the Ashanti Constitution—that those who elected a chief could also depose him—applied to the Asantehene also. Not only were the electors particular in electing a suitable man, but they were also particular that he should rule constitutionally. Again the history of Ashanti in the latter half of the nineteenth century provides examples.[1]

In 1874 Kofi Kakari, then Asantehene, took some gold trinkets and other valuable treasures from the royal mausoleum at Bantama. He did not consult his councillors in Kumasi or the chiefs about this. It might have been permitted in a case of national peril, but only with the consent of the Kumasi councillors and the chiefs of the Union. When the action was discovered, the chiefs of Juaben, Nsuta, Bekwai, and Kokofu joined the Kumasi councillors in denouncing it as unconstitutional and sacrilegious, and Kakari was deposed.

His successor, Mensa Bonsu, became unpopular, for in his effort to replenish the royal exchequer he imposed heavy fines on his people for trifling offences. It was even suspected that he designedly got his rich subjects into trouble so that he might fine them heavily. At this time it was found out that he had had an intrigue with the wife of the Kontihene's brother. This was one of the things a chief was admonished on his enstoolment not to do. The unconstitutional act, and the fact that the people were dissatisfied with his extortionate rule, caused a rebellion against him and he fled from Kumasi.

So although the Asantehene's sacred position was such that it gave him immense power, he was subject to clearly defined constitutional checks, and the popular will could be effectively exercised upon him through the electors.

[1] Claridge, op. cit., vol. ii.

The Union as an administrative machinery

It has been emphasized that the Union was military in purpose and character; but there were the beginnings of civil administration.

An instance of this is seen in the constitutional practice evolved for the election, enstoolment, control, and, when necessary, the deposition of the Asantehene.

There were other developments. The court etiquette of Ashanti demanded that a chief should not be approached directly but only through a spokesman. Conforming to this, each of the Divisional chiefs had as court friend (*adamfo*) one of the captains who lived in Kumasi to act as a liaison between himself and the Asantehene. For example, the court friends of the chiefs of Mampong, Juaben, and Nsuta were, respectively, the Kontihene, Oyokohene, and Tafohene. These captains, who lived in Kumasi, kept their friends informed of events in Kumasi. When any of the chiefs visited Kumasi they saw their court friends first and received an account of all that had happened in Kumasi since their last visit. If anything occurred which concerned the chiefs or required their presence in Kumasi, messengers were sent to them by their court friends. The Juabenhene's link with Kumasi was through the Oyokohene, the Mamponghene through the Kontihene, the Nsutahene through the Tafohene, the Asumegyahene and Adansehene through the Domakwaihene. Every Divisional chief had his court friend (*adamfo*) who referred to the chief as his man (*barima*).

These court friends were not representatives in Kumasi appointed by the chiefs themselves. The traditional account is that the captains were appointed to act as court friends for the Divisional chiefs at different times by successive Asantehene. It was a development which recognized the need of some contact between Kumasi and the outlying States in the period between the intermittent meetings of the Union Council.

The furthest advance in civil administration was in the judicial sphere. The Asantehene's Court was a Court of Appeal for all cases arising within the Union. Thus, a man tried in Mampong could appeal to the Asantehene's court by swearing the Great Oath on the Mamponghene's spokesman, the official who pronounced the judgement of the court. The spokesman became the defendant at the Court of Appeal. Certain cases came before a national tribunal consisting of the Divisional chiefs and the Kumasi chiefs and presided over by the Asantehene. This was the highest tribunal. It was not a regular court, but was summoned if the nature of a particular case was such that it could only be properly heard by this national tribunal. The types of case which came before it were cases between two Divisional chiefs, or crimes which were specially grave, such as treason.

The Council of the Ashanti Union had four main functions. It met to discuss war; this was its primary function. Later, the periodic *Odwera* ceremonies were instituted, when the chiefs met to participate in those rites which rekindled their sentiments of solidarity and nationhood. Thirdly, it met as a national tribunal before which even the Asantehene himself could be tried. And, finally, it met for the enstoolment or destoolment of an Asantehene.

Such was the Union, at the head of which was the Asantehene, who had religious and physical sanctions for his authority, but was subject to constitutional checks. As an administrative machinery the Union was only incipient. It was primarily a military council, and throughout the period of its existence, from the latter part of the seventeenth century to the beginning of the twentieth, Ashanti was engaged in warfare.

The effect of the banishment of Prempeh to the Seychelles Islands in 1896 on the administration of the States was not as serious as its effect on the Kumasi Division. As has been shown, the States possessed a great degree of autonomy within the Union. As far as they were concerned the effect of the Asantehene's removal was to destroy any contacts they had with each other, for the Asantehene was the hub to which they were all joined. Without him they became isolated units again, and reverted to the position they were in before the formation of the Union. But the internal administration of their affairs was not affected.

In the Kumasi State, however, the effect was a complete disorganization of its political life, for it could not function as a State without the chief, who was the link between the different companies and captains.

The British occupation of 1900 disintegrated the Ashanti Union.

CHAPTER VI

BRITISH RULE AND THE CHIEF

I. SOCIAL CHANGE

1. *Territorial organization*

THE British occupation implied the abolition of the military and political sovereignty of Ashanti. The first task of the new régime was to establish the *Pax Britannica* over the territory it had occupied.

In 1902 Ashanti was divided for administrative purposes into four Districts: North-eastern, North-western, Southern, and Central. A District Commissioner was placed in charge of each of the first three Districts, but the Central District came directly under the control of the Chief Commissioner.

This District included Kumasi, Ejisu, Juaben, Bompata, Obogu, Kumawu, Mampong, Nsuta, Agona, and Offinsu. It extended over an area of about 2,700 square miles.

The North-western District included Jaman, Wenchi, Techiman, Berekum, Wam, and Asafo, covering an area of 5,000 square miles. The headquarters of this District was first established at Sikassiko, then at Odumase, and, in 1906, at Sunyani.

The North-eastern District included Nkoranza, Atebubu, Abease, and Kratchi, an area of some 4,000 square miles. The District headquarters was first established at Atebubu, and later at Nkoranza.

The Southern District included Bekwai, Obuasi (headquarters), Kokofu, Adansi, and Mansu–Nkwanta, an area of 2,300 square miles.

In 1907 the territorial Divisions were renamed 'Provinces', and a few changes were made in the grouping of certain areas. The North-eastern District became the Northern Province, the North-western District the Western Province, and the Central and Southern Districts became the Central and Southern Provinces, respectively.

The Central Province included Kumasi, Juaben, Mampong, Kumawu, Nsuta, Agona, Ejisu, Bompata (including Agogo), and Obogu.

The Northern Province included Banda, Mo, Kintampo, Nkoranza, Abease, Atebubu, and Kratchi.

The Western Province included Jaman, Wenchi, Techiman, Berekum (including Ahafo), and Wam; and the Southern Province Bekwai (with the sub-districts of Essumeja and Abodom), Kokofu, Adansi, and Mansu-Nkwanta.

NORTHERN   TERRITORIES

W E N C H I
  ₒWenchi

M A M P·O N G

SUNYANI
  ₒ
  Sunyani

ASHANTI — AKIM

  ₒMampong

K U M A S I
ₒAhafo Goaso
    KUMASI ₒ
         Juaso ₒ

      ₒBekwai

ASHANTI
SHOWING DISTRICT BOUNDARIES
1941—42.
SCALE 1:3,000,000
MILES 10 5 0   10   20 30 40   50 MILES

BEKWAI
  ₒObuasi
    OBUASI

G O L D   C O A S T   C O L O N Y

In 1913 these administrative Provinces were sub-divided into Districts, and a Commissioner was put in charge of each District.

The Central Province was divided into three Districts:

(1) Kumasi (headquarters), Ejisu, Offinsu, and Agona; (2) The Ashanti-Akim District, which included Bompata, Juaben, Kumawu, and Obogu, with its headquarters at Juaso; (3) The Ejura District, which included Mampong, Nsuta, and Atebubu (removed from the Northern Province) with headquarters at Mampong.

The Western Province was divided into two sub-districts: (1) The Wenchi District, which included Jaman and Techiman, with the headquarters at Wenchi; and (2) Ahafo, with its head-quarters at Goaso.

The Southern and Northern Provinces remained the same, except that Atebubu, which was formerly in the Northern Province, was now included in the Central Province.

Several reorganizations have been made since. In 1921 the four Provinces were merged into two; and since 1934 Ashanti has been administered in seven Districts as follows: the Districts of Kumasi, Bekwai, Obuasi, Mampong, Ashanti–Akim (headquarters Juaso), Sunyani, and Wenchi. Another reorganization was proposed in 1944, and arrangements are being made for the amalgamation of the seven Districts into four (1947).

These reshuffles have been made for administrative convenience, but the changes of administrative headquarters have affected the fortunes of the people in the different areas. When a place is made the headquarters of a District its trade becomes brisker, it attracts immigrants from other places, it receives more attention from the District Commissioner, and its prestige rises higher in the estimation of the people.

When the District headquarters change, the towns affected decline in importance and wealth. The towns of Kintampo, Odumase, and Goaso all declined in prosperity when they ceased to be District headquarters.

The chiefs are aware of this and there is much rivalry amongst them for the District headquarters to be established in their respective Divisions. When the reorganization at present (1947) being carried out was first publicly announced in 1945, Wenchi was mentioned as the headquarters for what would be an amalgamation of the two districts of Sunyani and Wenchi. This was later confirmed by the Chief Commissioner and also by the District Commissioner of Wenchi (1946). It raised expectations regarding improvement in the trade and the development of the amenities of the town. People of the surrounding Divisions began applying for building plots in Wenchi. A few months later Government changed its plans and the Wenchihene was informed that Sunyani would be the headquarters of the new District. This has caused a general disappointment.

Petitions have been sent to Government by the various chiefs affected, some supporting Wenchi, others Sunyani, as the District headquarters, according to its proximity to them. At the Durbar held in Kumasi on 12 December 1946 the Governor announced: 'I understand that anxiety has been caused by Government's proposals for the amalgamation of Districts. Any representations made to me regarding the headquarters of any District will be carefully considered, but I am convinced that the reorganization will be of considerable benefit to Ashanti.'

In this matter there is a difference of outlook between the chiefs and the Government. The latter thinks in terms of large territorial administrative units (Districts), and the chiefs in terms of the tribal groups (Divisions) they represent. Since the British took over the administration of Ashanti the two units have existed side by side, a District usually including several Divisions. While the tribal units have been preserved, the chiefs have become accustomed to a new and larger unit of administration.

Government supports the Chief

Ashanti has been administered on the system of indirect rule which is 'the system by which the tutelary power recognizes existing African societies and assists them to adapt themselves to the functions of local government'.[1] Dr. Lucy Mair has defined indirect rule more comprehensively as 'the progressive adaptation of native institutions to modern conditions'.[2]

In Ashanti a characteristic of the system has been the support which Government has given to the chiefs.

Soon after the British had taken over the administration of Ashanti there was a rising, in 1900, occasioned by Governor Hodgson's demand for the Ashanti Golden Stool.[3] After the rising the candidates who were known to have been loyal to Government were elected as chiefs even though they had no title in native law and custom to the offices. Confident of Government support and scornful of the traditional checks on the chief, these men ruled badly, and in many places there was a move to get rid of them so that they might be replaced by men elected from the authentic lineages.

The movement to destool the government-sponsored chiefs started at Agona, where in 1905 the people refused to serve their chief, Kwame Boakye; but Government backed the chief, and

[1] Hailey, *African Survey*, p. 413.
[2] L. P. Mair, *Native Policies in Africa*, 1936, p. 56.
[3] Claridge, op. cit., vol. ii, part iv, p. 438.

ordered the people of Agona to continue their allegiance to him. The rebellion subsided for a few months, but burst out again in September 1906. The Acting Chief Commissioner investigated the matter, upheld the chief, and punished the ringleaders of the malcontents. Rebellions occurred in the same year at Ejisu, Akropong, Ahinkuro, and Nsuatre, where chiefs had been similarly appointed. In each case the Government backed the chief and kept him on the stool.

A constitutional case occurred at Juaben in 1907 in which Government followed the same policy. The Chief of Juaben, Yaw Sapong, had died in November 1906. His younger brother succeeded him in 1908. The queen-mother of Juaben and members of the royal lineage opposed the election, and they were supported in this by some of the elders. The Chief Commissioner who investigated the matter not only retained the chief on the stool, but deposed the queen-mother, Amma Sewaa, detained her in Kumasi, and inflicted fines on the elders who opposed the chief's election.[1] The constitutional custom which governed the election of chiefs did not now depend solely on the will of the people, but also on the will of Government.

Government policy in the constitutional struggle declared

In an earlier chapter[2] we drew attention to the fact that the commoners in Ashanti did have a recognized way in which they expressed their wishes in political matters, and that their opinions were considered. They kept careful watch on the way the chief and his council exercised their authority. The struggle between the commoners and the traditional authority took a new turn under British rule. As the examples given above have shown, the commoners had now to reckon with the new Government as well. As early as 1909 the Chief Commissioner stated the official policy regarding constitutional disputes.

The Ashanti organization so powerful in olden days still maintains many elements of cohesion, but with the spread of Western Civilization and more liberal ideas, the inevitable conflict between youth and authority has already commenced. In so radical and, so to speak, brusque a change of conduct, custom and condition as has been experienced by this country of late years, it is, perhaps, but natural that

---

[1] *Colonial Reports: Ashanti*, 1908.
[2] Chap. I, 'The Constitutional Aspect of Chiefship'.

the younger members of the community should wish to throw off an irksome and restraining, albeit legitimate authority.

It is the duty of the Administration to check this tendency when it oversteps the bounds of prudence and reason, or the country would experience a convulsive collapse of a tribal system which, when purged of certain repugnant features, has proved worthy of admiration and support, and one which has been of the utmost assistance in carrying out a succession of constant and rapid reforms.[1]

In the Report for 1910 the Acting Chief Commissioner had this to say:[2] 'Referring to the contest between youth and authority mentioned in the concluding observations of the 1909 Report, the Administration continued throughout the year to watch and guide the inevitable change, maintaining the rightful authority of the chiefs, but discouraging retrogression and superstition.'

The report of a destoolment case which occurred at Bekwai in 1920 confirms the view that in these political disputes the commoners were exercising a recognized constitutional right. The Commissioner who investigated the dispute reported:[3]

In the case of Bekwai, for instance, the 'youngmen', that is to say the lower classes, those who were not Elders, complained that they were not consulted in the choice of the Headchief, that they did not regard him as a credit to the Stool, that people did not respect him in Bekwai itself, or when he visited the villages, and to a man they refused to serve him. The Elders remarked that 'One cannot be a chief without subjects. If we support the Headchief we shall be alone. The whole of the youngmen refuse to serve the Headchief and we support them.'

There was no dispute about the legitimacy of the youngmen's action in accordance with native custom.

The policy of supporting the chief has been consistently followed, and many examples could be given.

In 1915 the commoners of Kumawu rebelled against the chief. One of the reasons for this was that the chief had kept for himself money which had been collected for the War Fund. This was found to be true on investigation, but Government retained the chief on the stool. He was made to refund all the money he had collected and pay a personal contribution to the War Fund. The Chief Commissioner who settled this matter reported: 'The youngmen of this Division have become rich through their cocoa farms,

---

[1] *Colonial Reports: Ashanti*, 1909.   [2] Ibid., 1910.   [3] Ibid., 1920.

and are of a rather turbulent nature.'[1] The following year the commoners again rebelled against their chief, and this time he was destooled. The Chief Commissioner, recording the destoolment in the Annual Report for 1916, explained: 'Kwame Afram, Oman-hene of Kumawu was destooled. He had become tyrannical and harsh in his conduct towards his subjects, and the only solution of the difficulty was destoolment.'

In 1915 the Chief Commissioner had reported: 'The growing importance of the youngmen class through better education and increased wealth is a factor that has to be taken into serious consideration.' The warning was justified. In 1918 there were political disputes between the youngmen and the chiefs at Ejisu, Juaben, Bompata, Obogu, as well as in other Divisions. There was a common element in these disputes: the youngmen petitioned for the reduction of the 'oath fees' charged by the chiefs and elders at the hearing of cases which came before them. Government agreed that the fees should be reduced, but no destoolments were permitted.

During 1920 there were widespread political disputes and dissensions all over Ashanti. Many chiefs were involved, amongst them the headchiefs of Bekwai, Offinsu, Kumawu, Agogo, Agona, and Wenchi. In the case of Offinsu and Kumawu, the chiefs were mobbed and wounded. Government recognized the destoolment of the chiefs of Bekwai, Offinsu, and Kumawu, but punished the rioters. The other chiefs were retained on their stools.

Since the British Administration, Government support for the chiefs has been a new and important factor in the constitutional development of Ashanti. On the one side, the commoners have been struggling to keep the chiefs in check so that they may have regard to the popular will in the government of their tribes; on the other, the Government has protected the chiefs from excessive restraint by the people. Such constitutional changes as have been made have therefore resulted not solely from the sensitivity of the political organization to the popular will, but also from Government control and policy. This has been an underlying factor in constitutional disputes down to the present day. The efforts to restrain chiefs have resulted in frequent political disputes and destoolments.

The consistency of Government policy is illustrated by the following extract from the first address delivered by the present

[1] *Colonial Reports: Ashanti*, 1915.

Governor, Sir Alan Burns, to the Legislative Council of the Gold Coast at its session in 1942 :

As a newcomer to this country I have been struck—and struck with dismay—by the large number of interminable Stool disputes which disturb the peaceful life of the community. From enquiries I have made, I learn that within the last ten years, no less than twenty-two paramount chiefs have been destooled, in addition to twenty-two others who have abdicated in that period—in most cases in order to forestall destoolment; that seven Stools of paramount chiefs are now vacant, and that in many States no paramount chief has succeeded in maintaining his place on the Stool for more than a very short time. In the case of subordinate chiefs, I understand the position is as bad or worse, and since my arrival in the Colony, rioting has occurred in small villages over Stool disputes.

Now I want to make it quite clear that such disorders will not be permitted and will be put down with a strong hand. It is intolerable that the peaceful life of the community should be disturbed by irresponsible minorities or by a few irreconcilables who will agree to no reasonable solution of any problem however trifling.[1]

Reduced power and prestige of the Chief

An important contributory factor in the disputes so strongly commented upon by the Governor was clearly put by the Chief Commissioner of Ashanti in the Annual Report on Ashanti for 1920:

Generally, Native Affairs in Ashanti have reached a stage of transition. A new generation which has grown up under the British Administration is coming to the fore. Prima facie also native institutions which suited the environment of the old order are hardly likely to be adapted as they stand to the radically changed and changing conditions of the present. A strong Central Government superimposed upon the tribal administration must affect adversely the power and prestige of the chiefs, and allegiance is apt to be transferred from the chiefs to Government. This accounts to some extent for the paramountcy cases, chiefs desiring to serve Government direct rather than through a paramount chief.[2]

The existence of the British Administration implies the reduced status and prestige of the chiefs. This is a most significant fact.

[1] Gold Coast Colony Legislative Council Debates 1942. The Governor's figures refer to the whole colony, but the picture is true of Ashanti.

[2] In 1920 the Chief Commissioner, Mr. Harper, heard three cases in which subordinate chiefs desired to withdraw their allegiance from their headchiefs and serve Government direct. These are the 'paramountcy' cases referred to.

In 1906 the Chief Commissioner reported of the Southern Province:

The Ashantis of the Southern District have given no trouble during the year. They have marked the year 1906 by their excellent behaviour, absolute obedience, and a desire to help and co-operate with Government. I think they have further begun to recognize that Government is the chief guardian of their interests, judging by the way they have sought advice on every matter, however small, that concerned them, and they have displayed a trusting and friendly spirit towards the Commissioner of their district that is most pleasing to record.[1]

This, the index of the success of the Administration, is the index of the decreasing authority of the chief over his subjects. When they regard the District Commissioner as the chief guardian of their interests, they take to him complaints which they would otherwise have taken to the chief. Under the British Administration the chief has become a subordinate authority. This is constantly in evidence in his relations with the District Commissioner, the police, the military, and other officials of the central government.

The military and police of the Government

After the Ashanti War of 1896 Government established in Kumasi an army consisting of Africans officered by Britishers. By 1905 military companies had been stationed at Kintampo and Sunyani as well. The relations between the army and the people of Ashanti were at first unfriendly. The Chief Commissioner admitted this in the Annual Report for 1905.[2]

The relations between the Army soldiery and the people leave much to be desired. In a country where power is synonymous with abuse, it is practically impossible to prevent petty roadside thieving and general imposition, and it is only by constant vigilance that these misdeeds can be kept within bounds.

No Ashantis were admitted in the army until 1917. The chiefs and people of Ashanti had by then become amenable to the new régime, and had demonstrated their loyalty to the British Government by generous contributions to the War Fund. The Chief of Adansi alone gave £1,000 towards the third aeroplane that Ashanti contributed as its gift to Britain for the prosecution of the war.

[1] *Colonial Reports: Ashanti*, 1906.   [2] Ibid., 1905.

After this demonstration of loyalty the Gold Coast Regiment was opened to Ashanti recruits in 1917. At the close of the year the Chief Commissioner reported:

By far the most important event of the year was the decision to throw the Gold Coast Regiment open to Ashanti recruits. Although the decision was not enthusiastically received, the chiefs vied with each other to supply men, and this occasioned much friendly rivalry. Altogether, about 1,000 Ashantis joined the Regiment. The Acting Governor accompanied by Colonel Heywood paid Ashanti a visit in March and held recruiting meetings at Obuasi, Mampong, and Juaso besides Coommassie. Thus encouraged and stimulated, the Ashantis overcame their ingrained dislike of the Regiment, and actually joined the Force that they had been taught to look upon as their natural foe.[1]

The hostility between the regiment and the people does not survive. Most of the men who fought against the British have died. Many Ashantis again joined the regiment during the Second World War. But the people know, and the regiment is a reminder to them, that Britain has abolished their military sovereignty.

This is relevant in considering the position of the chief in Ashanti to-day. As has been shown, the Ashanti military organization has been preserved in the political organization. The military exploits of their ancestors are still the basis for determining rank and prestige among the chiefs.

In October 1946 the Ashanti Confederacy Council divided the chiefs into three grades. This was primarily for the purpose of fixing the rate that each chief should pay as *aseda* (token of thanks) when he took the oath of allegiance to the Asantehene on his enstoolment. But it also indicated precedence. The Kuntanasihene, who was placed in Grade II, asked that he should be placed in the first grade, because Kuntanasi formerly occupied an important place in the Ashanti military organization. The Asantehene asked him to give an historical instance of any war in which Kuntanasi had played a prominent part. As the Kuntanasihene could not give any instance his request was considered a presumption, and the Nsutanahene had to intercede for him before the matter was dropped.

Before the British Administration the chief was the military leader of his people. This enhanced his prestige and importance. He is no longer the military leader, and the people do not look to

[1] Ibid., 1917.

him for defence, but to the Government. This means for the chief the loss of some prestige and authority.

The maintenance of law and order is also very largely the function of the police and administrative officers of the Government.

With the improvement in trade and communications that followed the *Pax Britannica,* many towns and villages in Ashanti increased in population as a result of the influx of immigrants from other tribes. Trade with the Northern Territories increased, and immigrants from there made such places as Kintampo, Wenchi, Ejura, Juaso, Ejisu, Bekwai, and Obuasi busy centres of activity. The chiefs found it more and more difficult to keep order, especially amongst residents who did not belong to their own tribe. Mining centres like Obuasi, or new trade centres like Ejura, became centres of frequent disturbances. The Moshi and Wangara people from the Northern Territories in particular caused a great deal of trouble. They were responsible for many cases of highway robbery or 'robbery with violence', and there were frequent fights between them and the local people.

One such fight occurred at Bekwai in 1919 between the people of Bekwai and the Moshi residents. The Moshis were fired upon, and ten of them were killed and seventeen injured. The Bekwaihene was tried by Government for this, and was not only fined £500 but was also sentenced to three years' imprisonment. The chief died in prison while serving his sentence.

Conflicts of this nature between the traditional native authorities and the immigrants were kept in check by the more powerful British Administration. Government police were employed to maintain law and order. By 1923 police detachments had been established in all the principal towns in Ashanti: Kumasi, Obuasi, Bekwai, Juaso, Kintampo, Ejura, Sunyani; many other towns have received detachments since, so that Government police are now found nearly everywhere in Ashanti. They derive their authority from Government and are under the control of police officers, the most senior of whom are British. The result is still further to decrease the prestige and authority of the chief over the area under his rule.

Although the functions of the police in the maintenance of law and order and the protection of property were generally appreciated, it was evident during the period of my field-work in Ashanti (1941-2) that the relations between Government police and the people were marked by mutual hostility, suspicion, and fear rather than trustfulness and co-operation. The public generally complained that the police, African and European alike, were brusque, curt, and domineering; the police on the other hand said the people were not co-operative, and that there were many serious offences committed each year, including homicide, which the police were unable to prosecute because the people would not report them or help the police to obtain the necessary evidence. This attitude was common throughout Ashanti.

The chiefs frequently complained that the Government police did not show them due respect. It is not necessary to labour this point, and a recent occurrence will suffice to illustrate the lowered prestige of the chief *vis-à-vis* the Government police. In July 1946 the Chief Commissioner of Ashanti left Kumasi to travel to England on sick-leave. The Asantehene decided to go to the railway station on the morning of his departure to say good-bye to him. When the Asantehene's car arrived at the railway station he found the gate leading to the platform shut. An African Government policeman stood behind it. The Asantehene's private secretary went to speak to him, but he refused to open the gate to let them through, because he had received instructions not to let any Africans in at the gate. He opened the gate for some white officers who came later. In the end the Asantehene himself got out of his car, and walked to the policeman to remonstrate with him. There are many situations like this in which the latent tensions inherent in the fact of British rule come to the fore. There are two authorities, the superior and the subordinate, with parallel, and in some cases duplicated, hierarchies of officials. The whole cadre of administrative officers, police, and soldiery of the central government is evidence that ultimate authority rests not with the chief and his people but with Government. This obvious fact, that Ashanti lost its political sovereignty in 1896, is the predominant factor to be taken into account in considering the present position of the chief.[1]

Loss of political sovereignty illustrated

No incident has brought home to the Ashanti more poignantly than did the unique incident of the desecration of the Golden Stool the fact that the nation had lost its political sovereignty.

[1] See Chap. VII, 'Local Government'.

As has been explained, the Golden Stool is the symbol of the national unity of the Ashanti. It is the most sacred national shrine. In 1895 the Ashantis accepted the deportation of the Asantehene rather than risk the loss of the Golden Stool in a war which they feared they might lose,[1] and it was Governor Hodgson's demand for it that led to the rising in 1900.[2]

The Gyasehene, who had the custody of the Golden Stool, caused it to be hidden at the village of Wawase, near Abuabugya. In 1920 Asubonten, the Gyasehene, requested a road to be made between Abuabugya and a neighbouring village. In August 1920 the construction of this road began under the supervision of the Government road-overseer. At a certain point in the road the road-overseer suggested a diversion almost at right angles to the road on which they had been working in order to avoid a difficult patch. The headman of Abuabugya, who was with the men working on the road, seemed very uneasy about this decision, and watched the men anxiously as they were at work along the diversion. One of the men, Kwadwo Buo, struck a box with his axe, and the others gathered round to see what was in it. With great difficulty the headman of Abuabugya, Danso, persuaded them not to dig out the box, which he said was a fetish against smallpox.[3]

The following night Danso and five other men removed the box to Abuabugya and hid it in the room of one Yenkyira. The box contained the historic and sacred Golden Stool. The six men swore an oath never to reveal the secret. But the suspicions of some of the men who were working on the road had been aroused. One Seniagya, a professing Christian, and a stool-carrier to the Asantehene, heard where the Golden Stool had been kept. He persuaded Yenkyira and Danso to share with him the gold ornaments adorning the Golden Stool. The stool, he said, was what was sacred, not the ornaments. So the three men despoiled the Golden Stool of its ornaments. One Yoko found them while they were sharing the ornaments and demanded and received a share. Rumours of what had happened got about, and the matter was reported to the Kumasi chiefs.

Inquiries were made and the facts came to light. It was discovered that a certain goldsmith, Kwadwo Poku, had received

---

[1] Rattray, *Ashanti*, p. 291.   [2] Claridge, op. cit., vol. ii, p. 438.
[3] Ashanti had been ravaged by a smallpox epidemic in 1918.

one of the gold bells off the stool to melt down. The gold fetters that bound it had been pawned for 30*s*., and most of the gold ornaments and insignia had disappeared. On the evening of 12 September 1920 the Kumasi chiefs reported to the Chief Commissioner that the Golden Stool had been desecrated.

This to the Ashanti was the most serious and heinous crime that anyone could commit. It has already been explained that a crime in Ashanti was a religious offence, which threatened the relationships between the community and the royal ancestors and the gods that guarded it.[1] The desecration of the Golden Stool was a capital crime. It was sacrilege as well as a betrayal of the nation. No crime in Ashanti law could be more outrageous.

The following day the whole of Ashanti was thrown into consternation. The people put on their russet cloths of mourning (*kuntunkuni*). The chiefs held a meeting at Apremoso (the place of cannons) where Asubonten, the custodian of the Golden Stool, and Seniagya were brought before them, charged with the desecration of the Golden Stool. A detachment of Government police sent under a European Police Commissioner to watch the proceedings took the two men away to the police station and kept them under police custody, because it was feared they would be killed.

A series of interviews between the Chief Commissioner and the chiefs followed. In the end the chiefs were permitted to try the men subject to the following conditions:

1. The inquiry was to be held not at Apremoso but in the open space behind the police barracks where, if necessary, police reinforcements could appear at a few minutes' notice.
2. Government police were to be at the inquiry to maintain order and preserve peace.
3. The accused would attend under armed police escort.
4. Witnesses were to be summoned and any further arrests were to be made through the Commissioner of Police.
5. The accused and the witnesses were to be under police protection.
6. The inquiry was to be conducted according to the principles of British justice.
7. When any confession or admission of guilt was made, the Commissioner of Police was to be called to hear it.

---

[1] See Chap. IV, 'Administration and Justice'.

8. At the conclusion of the inquiry a report was to be made to the Chief Commissioner, who would consider the question of guilt and the nature of the punishment to be inflicted.

The Kumasi chiefs began the inquiry in the presence of several thousand people. A few days later they reported to the Chief Commissioner that the nature of the case was such that it could only be tried by a full council of the Ashanti Union, consisting of all the headchiefs of Ashanti. The Chief Commissioner gave permission for the chiefs to come to Kumasi, but the number of followers each headchief could bring was limited to fifty.

The hearing began again on 23 September under the presidency of the Mamponghene, as there was no Asantehene in those days, Prempeh having been deported to the Seychelles Islands in 1896.

After a trial lasting four days the national court found Seniagya, Kwadwo Danso, Yenkyira, Yoko, Kwadwo Poku, and Asubonten guilty because they, 'being natives of Ashanti and subjects of the Golden Stool of the Ashanti Nation, did expose, steal, destroy, sell, and otherwise unlawfully deal with and use the said Gold Stool, thereby betraying the said Ashanti Nation and laying it open to disgrace and ridicule, and debasing the name and fame of Ashanti, much to the annoyance and provocation of all people, young and old, thereby giving occasion for disturbance and bloodshed but for the intervention of Government.'

The court passed a sentence of death, pointing out that in the old days men had suffered death for crimes which were less serious. It was deemed necessary that the men should die, their guilt having been established, in order that, as one of the chiefs put it, the nation might be appeased; for their deed had affronted both the living and the dead.

It is noteworthy that although the report made by the chiefs to the Chief Commissioner was that the Golden Stool had been desecrated, the wording of the judgement was to the effect that the culprits had been guilty of stealing. This phraseology is indicative of the influence of Government, and of the stipulation that 'the inquiry was to be conducted according to the principles of British justice'. To the people the important thing was not the stealing but the desecration, which amounted to sacrilege. It was with this in mind that they passed the sentence of death.

The Chief Commissioner studied the report of the inquiry, and directed that Asubonten should be tried again, as he did not consider the evidence against him strong enough to warrant his conviction. More convincing evidence of his guilt was produced at the second trial.

There were eight other people who were tried and convicted of buying the gold ornaments; as five of these were found guilty on the uncorroborated evidence of Seniagya alone, the Chief Commissioner acquitted them. The three others were made to testify on oath that they had none of the gold ornaments in their possession. The Chief Commissioner agreed that the others had been justly found guilty, but firmly refused to confirm the death sentence. No constitutional body of Ashanti chiefs had the right to inflict capital punishment. That was the fact of the new political situation. What the chiefs regarded as a national Council was to Government only an *ad hoc* Committee of Inquiry; it had no legal authority to pass a death sentence. Government substituted banishment overseas for the death sentence.

At every stage of this incident the authority and control of Government was in evidence, from the arrest of the criminals throughout the inquiry to the final sentence. What to the Ashanti was a most heinous and sacrilegious crime had been committed against the whole nation. It was in Ashanti law more serious than murder or treason, but the guilty men could not be killed. When the chiefs talk about this incident even now, they show very deep feelings of sorrow. They shake their heads and say, '*Oburoni yɛ duru*' (The white man is heavy, i.e. powerful). Several chiefs said it was a great national humiliation.

This brought home not only to the chiefs but also to the people the fact that Ashanti was not a sovereign nation.

The support which Government gives to the chief is on the basis of the chief's subordinate status. The chief's powers are limited and defined by ordinances: both he and his subjects are under the control of the Government, which the people associate with limitless power, endless wealth, and a high prestige. By comparison, the chief has limited powers, scanty wealth, and a lowered prestige, daily in evidence in his relationships with the District Commissioner or Chief Commissioner or the Governor.

It is in these circumstances that the Ashanti chief to-day is called upon to perform many new functions of government,[1] and to

---

[1] See Chap. VII, 'British Rule and the Chief: II, Local Government'.

rule over subjects some of whom have acquired a new status in the community, having gained more power, greater wealth, and a higher prestige, because of the opportunities offered by the white man's presence, as Government official, trader, or missionary within the framework of British rule.

New functions of Government

By practice and precept the new régime has introduced a new concept of government.

It has provided medical services for the people. African hospitals were built at Kumasi (1905), Obuasi (1908), Sunyani and Kintampo (1909); and in addition Government medical officers worked in Mampong, Nkoranza, and Odumasi.[1]

Sanitary services were also provided in different parts of the country. By 1905 Kumasi already had a number of new wells, streets, latrines, and incinerators. The Government constructed wells at Obuasi in 1910, and in the same year an incinerator was built at Kintampo. The chiefs were taught by word as well as by deed. In 1910 the Chief Commissioner reported:[2] 'No opportunity has been lost of impressing on the chiefs and residents in the out-lying towns and villages the paramount importance of cleanliness, pure water, and sanitary dwellings.' The lesson was already being learnt, for he also added: 'I found a most gratifying desire on the part of the chiefs to have their villages better laid out. Every assistance that the limited staff could give was afforded them.'

Many of the towns and villages were rebuilt under the direction of administrative officers and Government road overseers. Amongst the places rebuilt were Kintampo and Ejura (1913), Wenchi (1914), Sunyani (1917), and Obuasi and Kumasi were regularly being added to and improved. The Report in 1918 gives an indication of the progress that was being made. 'The demand by natives for village overseers to lay out and improve their villages generally, still continues to a gratifying extent. A better type of house is springing up throughout the country, and an endeavour at ornamentation of exteriors and planting of flowering plants is to be noticed.'[3]

The Government opened up the country with roads. Towards

---

[1] There are at present (1947) only two Government hospitals in Ashanti, one in Sunyani and one in Kumasi.

[2] *Colonial Reports: Ashanti*, 1910.   [3] Ibid., 1918.

the end of 1908 a Government Road Department for Ashanti was formed. The construction of the Kumasi–Tamale Road, a distance of 240 miles, commenced in February 1909; at the end of that year the first 4½ miles of the road, from Kumasi to Pankrono, were opened to motor traffic. The 850 labourers who worked on the road were recruited from many tribes, particularly from the Northern Territories of the Gold Coast. Besides the main road, about 65 miles of district roads were built in that year under the supervision of African contractors with unpaid or partly paid labour supplied by the chiefs. About 800 men supplied by the Chief of Bechem worked every day for a period of three months on the Bechem–Berekum road begun in that year. The official report on the roads constructed in 1911 contained the information:

Eighty-five miles of district roads were built, and seventy-eight were guttered and stumped at a cost of £3,000, five hundred pounds of which was expended on tools. This works out at the rate of £30 a mile, without taking into consideration the 78 miles of remade roads. When the thickly wooded nature of the country is taken into consideration, more than full value is realized for the outlay; in fact, the Ashantis may be said to be building their roads free of charge, receiving in return presents to encourage the movement.[1]

Little encouragement was needed, for the chiefs and people were eager to have roads because it made it easier for them to sell their cocoa. Road construction went fastest in the Southern and Central Provinces, where there was plenty of cocoa.

By 1934, through the joint efforts of the chiefs and the Government, there were 1,655 miles of motorable roads in Ashanti, maintained as follows:

Class A: Main trunk roads, maintained by the Government Public Works Department: 401 miles.
Class B: Roads which are necessary for trade and communications, but are not trunk roads, and are maintained under the supervision of administrative officers: 524 miles.
Class C: Minor roads, under the supervision of chiefs: 730 miles.

By 1937 there were 489 miles of road in Class A and 706 in Class B.

A network of telephone and telegraph services and post offices built by Government linked distant places in Ashanti, and Ashanti

[1] *Colonial Reports: Ashanti,* 1911.

with the Northern Territories and the Colony. By 1922 Kumasi was linked with both Secondi and Accra by rail.

Agriculture also received the attention of Government. The people were encouraged in a number of different ways. Government organized agricultural shows to which many chiefs from Ashanti and the Colony were invited. The chiefs were supplied with cocoa and rubber seedlings, and Government agricultural overseers went round the towns and villages to give talks to the people about the planting of cocoa and rubber. Courses of instruction were arranged at different times at various centres. Numerous charts were issued on cocoa diseases and the care of cocoa. Experimental plantations of rubber were established at Kintampo and Sunyani in 1910, and chiefs' model farms at Juaben, Ejisu, and Mampong in 1918. The growing of rice was encouraged in the northern districts, and in 1920 Government even experimented with a motor-tractor at Ejura.[1]

To provide educational facilities a Government boys' school was built in Kumasi in 1909, and a girls' school in 1914. Two more boys' schools were built, one at Sunyani in 1914 and the other at Juaso in 1920. A junior trade school was opened at Mampong in 1921, and in 1924 a Government agricultural training centre was built in Kumasi.[2]

In providing health services, communications, and schools, in encouraging agriculture and trade, the Administration was introducing and teaching a new way of government. This development affects the present position of the chief. New functions are now expected of him. The community has been taught to look to the ruler for the provision of welfare services. This increases the activities and responsibilities of the chief, and alters his traditional role.[3]

Trade and commerce

The trade of Ashanti has expanded vastly under British rule. Like the rest of the Gold Coast, the economic life of Ashanti has centred round the cocoa industry[4] and gold mining.

[1] The experimental farms have been abandoned. The experiment with the motor-tractor was also abandoned. The consumption of kerosene was high, and stoppages were frequent owing to hidden roots and stumps. It was found necessary to keep two men employed to remove them. The tractor did not prove an economic possibility. Unfortunately figures of costs are not available.

[2] Later developments are discussed below under 'Education'.   [3] See Chap. IX.

[4] See Shephard, *Report on the Economics of Peasant Agriculture in the Gold Coast*.

During the year 1905 numerous new cocoa plantations were started in Ashanti, mainly in the southern and eastern parts. Between that year and 1914 the industry expanded rapidly. The amount of cocoa exported from Ashanti from the first farms cultivated between 1896 and 1900 was 179 tons; by 1911 the export had risen to 4,170 tons. The high prices of cocoa so stimulated production that more and more areas were brought under cultivation, even to the neglect of food farming. In 1912 'a note of alarm was raised by the chiefs, who complained that the people were neglecting their farms in favour of cocoa cultivation'.[1] The same alarm was raised by the chiefs in 1938:

Already there have been more than sufficient cocoa farms cultivated at the discount or neglect of food farms. Almost all the forests in Ashanti have been converted into cocoa farms. All attention has been diverted from the cultivation of foodstuffs farms on the pretext that there is not much money in food farms as compared with cocoa farms and therefore it is not worth while wasting one's time and energy over them. Unless farmers disabuse their minds of this wrong notion, it is feared that in less than five years from now the country may suffer very considerably from famine. To avoid this eventuality, it is absolutely necessary that the Council should pass a resolution making it an offence for any person to make cocoa farms in Ashanti.[2]

In 1938, when the chiefs raised the alarm, 90,000 tons of cocoa were exported from Ashanti.

The cocoa industry brought Ashanti into the orbit of world-trade. Its prosperity became dependent on conditions in overseas markets. When the price of cocoa rose, more land was brought under cultivation; when it fell, the farms were neglected. The following description of conditions in 1916 is quite typical of the people's reaction to a low price for their cocoa:

During the year, 14,772 tons of cocoa were exported, as against 17,939 tons in 1915, a decrease of 3,167 tons. This was in no way due to a decrease in the quantity produceable by the natives of the Dependency [i.e. Ashanti], but solely to the fall in prices which so militated against the industry that many farmers did not even trouble to pick their fruit, while others refused to sell at such low prices, openly stating that they would rather lose all on a gamble for a rise in price than

[1] *Colonial Reports: Ashanti*, 1912.
[2] Minutes of the Confederacy Council (1938).

dispose of the beans for such poor returns. This in spite of frequent warnings and explanations as to the cause of the fall in the market.[1]

But in 1919, 'with the high prices offered for cocoa, the natives had a tendency to neglect food crops, other than the quantity required for their own consumption'.[2] Cocoa became the 'financial barometer' of Ashanti as of the Colony.[3] The standards of living of the people are dependent on the amount of money put into circulation during the cocoa season.

The cocoa industry not only accelerated the movement from a subsistence economy in Ashanti, but it was also directly responsible for the provision of a network of roads which broke down isolation. In 1914 Government recognized that 'the question of transport had assumed serious proportions, the fact being that the cocoa industry has outstripped the existing transport facilities of the country.'[4] So did the merchants, for in that year the Kumasi Chamber of Commerce requested the construction of a branch road of about ten miles long to Effiduase, a rich cocoa centre, to enable lorries to go there.

Besides cocoa Ashanti exported rubber, kola, cattle, and hides, but cocoa soon outstripped all other exports in importance and value.

Like cocoa rubber depended on economic conditions overseas, and was subject to fluctuations in price. It had a fairly regular demand until 1913, and then for almost ten years no rubber was exported from Ashanti, owing to a falling off in the demand. In 1925 the price of plantation rubber rose so high that wild rubber was in demand again, and 300 tons were exported that year. The demand fell off again, and no rubber was exported till the Second World War, when the occupation of Malaya by Japan in 1941 made it necessary for Britain to turn to other sources for her supply of wild rubber.

Mining has been another source of gainful employment, and also a source of revenue to certain stools from concessions granted to mining companies. The mining industry has not had the same widespread effect on the economic life of the people that cocoa has had, but since 1905 the mines have kept between 3,000 and 5,000 Africans in Ashanti (mostly non-Ashanti) in regular

---

[1] *Colonial Reports: Ashanti*, 1916.   [2] Ibid., 1919.
[3] Shephard, op. cit., p. 1.   [4] *Colonial Reports: Ashanti*, 1914.

employment. Of the important trade centres in Ashanti to-day, Obuasi and Akrokerri sprang up in connexion with the mines opened there in 1905, and Konongo owes its expansion to the mine started there in 1924.

The cocoa industry, the construction of roads, the opening of the mines, all caused a great expansion in trade.

The effect of this trade on Ashanti was most apparent in Kumasi, which was symbolic of the change that was taking place in varying degrees in all parts of Ashanti. Kumasi quickly became the chief trading centre for Ashanti, and by 1907 there were already eleven European firms established there.

From the Northern Territories came traders bringing cattle, sheep, shea-butter, and hides, and taking back to the north salt, cloth, kerosene, and kola. Some of these traders from the north settled in Kumasi and traded in kola, which they exported to Nigeria. Until 1916 the kola trade brought more money to the people in Ashanti than any other export. In that year the amount of kola exported was valued at £150,000. After 1916, however, cocoa outstripped kola in quantity and value. There were others who came from the Northern Territories every year about November and stayed till April or for longer periods, to take on temporary work on the roads or on the cocoa-farms, not only in Kumasi but also in other towns in Ashanti, chiefly Obuasi, Bekwai, Ejisu, Juaso, Kintampo, and Wenchi. There were also immigrants who came to Kumasi from the coast to seek lucrative employment as labourers, skilled artisans, or petty traders.

Syrians, too, were attracted to Kumasi by the prospects of making money quickly. By 1923 a considerable amount of the transport service of Ashanti was already in their hands. To-day they own most of the commercial buildings in Kumasi.

With all this trade, and the influx of immigrants, Kumasi expanded rapidly. In 1906 its population was estimated at 6,250; when the census was taken in 1911, a population of 18,853 was recorded. This increased to 23,694 in 1921. By 1931 the population had risen to 35,829.[1]

As the town grew the trade expanded still further. The European firms increased in number and established branches in the interior. There was a good market in Kumasi not only for European goods but also for foodstuffs required for the growing

[1] In 1948 the population of Kumasi was 70,705 (census figures).

population. This gave economic opportunities even to the more distant towns. Snails from Ahafo and Wam were regarded as a delicacy, and between 1907 and 1913 the trade in snails from these areas was valued at £50,000 a year. Fish came from the Colony in increasing quantities. Five hundred and nineteen tons were imported in 1910; two years later the import of fish was 989 tons.

The women in the hinterland found in Kumasi a ready market for the produce of their farms, and by 1920 they already controlled the food and petty trade in the Kumasi market.

From all these various activities, from the sale of cocoa, kola, rubber, cattle, or hides, of foodstuffs or fish or snails, or European goods; from work on the road or farm or mine as skilled or unskilled labourers, from employment with trading firms as clerks or commercial middlemen, the people earned money, and bought more and more goods. The imports were an ever-expanding assortment of goods. The people spent their money on whatever new commodities the trading firms brought from Europe. It was the supply that created new desires and stimulated an acquisitive and insatiable demand.

The rise in the standards of living was reflected in the building of new and better houses. The thatch-covered houses were rapidly displaced by houses of swish, brick, or cement, with iron and shingle roofs. In 1905 sixty such houses were built in Kumasi, and the town has kept, and often exceeded, that pace to the present day. Kumasi has grown into a busy urban centre with large buildings and shops owned by Africans, Syrians, and Europeans. From Kumasi hundreds of lorries go out to all parts of Ashanti every day, taking goods and new ideas. Every part has been affected by the expansion of trade during the last forty years.

New types of social personalities have emerged, from the unskilled labourer or carrier, the lorry driver, the absentee landlord, the petty trader, to the lawyer or doctor. There are new social groups as well: combines like the United Africa Company, rings like the Northern Territory Carriers (*kaayakaaya*), and trade unions like the Ashanti Lorry Drivers' Union. They mark the changes taking place in the social structure.

All this trade and economic activity has brought prosperity, but also litigation and indebtedness resulting from slumps or lack of regulated short-term loans, and many other social and political problems, some of which may be briefly examined here to illustrate how increased trade and commerce are affecting the political structure of Ashanti.[1]

Some social and political consequences of trade and commerce

We have noted that in Ashanti the ownership of land is vested in the stool and the right of usufruct in the lineage.[2]

During the last forty years cocoa has been planted extensively. Most farms are cultivated and owned by individuals, or occasionally by a group of kinsmen. On the whole, the cocoa industry has grown as a result of individual toil and enterprise. All the work involved—clearing the land, obtaining and planting the seed, caring for the farm, picking and preparing the crop for sale—has been done by the farmer, assisted by his wives and children, or by hired labour paid for by himself. Cocoa remains in bearing longer than food farms of plantain or cocoyams. Its introduction is causing a transition from lineage to individual claims of ownership of land.

Moreover, when a man has been helped by his wife and children to cultivate a cocoa-farm, he wants to leave the farm, or a part of it, to them. But by the legal rules of inheritance amongst the Ashanti property should be passed on in the matrilineal line to one's brothers or sister's children. It is in this way that what begins as individual property becomes lineage property in the long run.

A man may leave his cocoa-farm to his children, or give it to them in his lifetime, but such a gift must be made in the presence of witnesses, and the consent of his matrilineal lineage is required to validate it. This consent has often been refused, and there has been frequent litigation between a man's wives and children on the one side, and his matrilineal kinsmen—nephews, brothers and sisters—on the other.

The question has been discussed by the chiefs at the Confederacy Council on several occasions. It was first discussed at its session in 1938, but the chiefs were unable to reach a decision. The Asantehene reopened the subject at the 1941 session:

I brought up this question at our last session but we did not come to a definite decision about it. One fact with us Ashantis is that we

[1] See Chap. IX, 'The Chief to-day', where some more political consequences are discussed.
[2] See Chap. I, ' The Constitutional Aspect of Chiefship'.

appear to be too conservative. We always like to stick to custom even though it may have outlived its day. I do not deprecate the idea of brothers and nephews succeeding their deceased brothers or uncles, neither do I propose that the custom should be abolished, but I want you to understand that our children are blood of our blood and bone of our bone for whom we are accountable to God for bringing them into this world. God and our country expect us to make provision for the children we bring into this world. They and their mothers help us in our farm and domestic work. Sometimes you find that all your nephews and nieces do not come near you at all. It is only your children who care for you. Is it not fair then that we should make provision for them and their mothers who look after our interests and welfare, so that they may not become useless and wretched after our death? I would advise you to consider this question very carefully and favourably.[1]

The following discussion ensued:

Mamponghene: This is a difficult problem to be solved. We have our established custom and therefore it is not proper to make a ruling that widows and children should have a share in their husband's and father's property. We should not disturb our established custom. But a father who is satisfied that his children and or his wife have faithfully served him, can make them a gift. I therefore beg to oppose this item.

Asantehene: I do not mean to change our established custom. I only want the Council to give consideration to wives and children who have faithfully served their husbands and fathers.

Mamponghene: This subject has been fully discussed by me and my people, and they are of the unanimous opinion that I should oppose it. I tried to explain the circumstances to them, but they were emphatic in their opposition.

Offinsuhene: While supporting the Mamponghene in every respect, I beg to explain that if this Item were allowed to be made an Order it will doubtless disturb our custom with the result that there will be incessant litigation between wives and children on the one part and nephews on the other.

Ejisuhene: Personally I would have liked the idea that provision be made for children and widows, but in view of our law of inheritance I do not see how I can accommodate this Item to it. A father when alive can make provision for his wife and children who have faithfully served him. I therefore oppose this measure.

Asantehene: It has been opposed by the Mamponghene and supported by the Offinsuhene and the Ejisuhene that there should be no ruling

---

[1] Minutes of the Ashanti Confederacy Council (1941).

or order made by the Council regarding this Item. Those who are in favour may please show in the usual manner.

NOTE. Unanimously carried, so no ruling was made.[1]

The matter came up again for discussion in 1942, when the Asantehene proposed a variation in the existing custom so that 'when a person makes a gift of his own personal or self-acquired property to his children or to any other person in the presence of accredited witnesses, whether the relatives of the donor approve of it or not, it becomes valid'.

After a lengthy discussion this was passed by the chiefs. Cocoa is compelling a change in the traditional laws of inheritance.

There is a tension in the social structure which is a counterpart to the economic tension about property and inheritance. In the matrilineal system of Ashanti one result of the laws of succession was to emphasize and maintain a closer bond between brother and sister than between husband and wife. The lineage derived considerable strength from the solidarity of siblings. The desire to pass on some of a man's property to his sons instead of siblings has resulted in a weakening of the bond between siblings, which shows itself in strained relationships and frequent quarrels, especially between a man's wives and his sisters who are the mothers or potential mothers of his sons and nephews respectively.

Within the lineage itself there are nowadays quarrels and dissensions between a man's brothers and his nephews or between matrilineal cousins over the inheritance of cocoa-farms and houses. A farmer at Daho near Mampong summed up the situation concisely in a sentence: '*Cocoa see abusua, paepae mogya mu*' (Cocoa destroys kinship, and divides blood (relations)).

Further, with the new opportunities of making a living, the bonds of kinship are no longer as advantageous as before, and are, indeed, a burden to the more enterprising members of a lineage. Many traders and literate young men prefer to work away from home in order to escape the importunate demands of their kinsfolk for financial assistance. A woman trader who had left her home to go and live at Obuasi said she had to leave home because her kinsfolk bought her things on credit, and never paid her. She could not very well sue them in court for the money because they were her relations. In consequence, her business was failing, and

---

[1] Minutes of the Confederacy Council (1941).

she finally decided to leave home. Many literate young men have similarly left home, or when in Government employment have begged not to be stationed in or near their homes because they are unable to save any money there, and in fact often run into debt when they are near home owing to the demands of their kinsfolk for money for subsistence or clothing or the expenses of a funeral or litigation. So the ties of kinship are weakening because certain types of economic pursuits do not succeed in the framework of the close kinship ties of the Ashanti matrilineal society.

This social tension has a corresponding political aspect. The weakening of kinship solidarity strikes at the root of the political structure, for the chief and also his council are elected on the basis of kinship and matrilineal succession. There is now as much squabbling amongst kinsmen for political office as for cocoa-farms and houses.[1]

Moreover, the traditional political system carried with it the corollary that allegiance was personal, not territorial. A man remained a subject of his chief wherever he lived and worked because the ties of kinship remained the same. Trade and commerce and improved communications have dealt a blow to this tribal conception of citizenship.

People have travelled from the Northern Territories or the Colony to Ashanti in search of employment. Some of them have settled there more or less permanently. There are many people from these areas who have lived in Ashanti most of their lives, but they are outside the Ashanti political structure. They are 'strangers', no matter how long they live there.

Even Ashantis are 'strangers' outside their own Divisions. There are many Ashantis living in Divisions other than those in which they are subjects by kinship. This is particularly so in Kumasi, where the opportunities of employment have attracted people from all parts of Ashanti. With reference to the kinship political organization, these Ashantis are strangers, just as are the settlers from the Northern Territories and the Colony.

These permanent but 'stranger' settlers, who have no political status in the traditional organization based on kinship, present the chiefs with a new problem, which has arisen most acutely in connexion with taxation.

The Ashanti Confederacy Council decided to impose an annual

[1] See Chap. IX, 'The Chief to-day'.

levy to establish a National Fund for the general development of the country. Two questions at once arose. The first was whether or not the residents in Ashanti who are not Ashantis should pay the levy. When the matter was discussed in 1943 the Mampong-hene expressed the opinion that non-Ashantis living in Ashanti should pay because the fund would be 'used to develop the country from which they also will benefit. For example, when with the fund schools and hospitals are established, they will be open to them as well.' So it was moved and carried unanimously that non-Ashantis should pay the levy. No schools and hospitals have yet been built. The first disbursements from the National Fund have been for the award of scholarships for which only Ashantis were eligible. The Fantis have declaimed against this discrimination.

The second question was whether Ashantis should pay the levy to the Divisions in which they were resident or the Divisions they 'served', that is, of which they were subjects by kinship. This proved to be a very controversial question. Finally, it was decided that 'in the collection of the National Fund, persons pay to the Divisions in which they have been resident for six months or more, and not to the Divisions they serve'. This accepted citizenship on a territorial basis.

But the very next day the Kokofuhene raised a new problem.

Kokofuhene: With regard to the decision taken yesterday on the National Fund that people should pay to the Divisions in which they are resident, I would like to know what happens in the case where a whole village owes allegiance to a stool other than that on whose land it is placed. Does it pay to the Division it serves or to the Division whose land it occupies?[1]

The decision arrived at was that the 'village should pay to the Division it serves'. In endorsing this decision, the Asantehene said:

'Although the village is built on some other Division's stool land, it is protected by the Division it serves, and so should pay the National Fund to it.'

This decision accepts the principle of citizenship based on

[1] Minutes of the Confederacy Council (1943). For example, the village of Badu owes allegiance to the Kyidomhene of Kumasi, but the village is on Wenchi land, and the people pay cocoa tribute to Wenchi. See Chap. V, 'The Ashanti Union', for a list of such places. It is another point against the conception of Ashanti land-tenure as being feudal. Here are people who pay tribute for the land to one chief, and owe military service to another.

kinship, and conflicts with the first decision. At the 1945 session the Nsutahene reopened the subject for discussion.

Nsutahene: I would like to suggest the following amendment to the committee's first recommendation: That every Ashanti should pay the levy to the Division he serves, irrespective of where he lives; but that strangers (i.e. non-Ashantis) be made to pay to the Divisions in which they reside.

Secretary to the Council: I must enlighten the council that a Divisional Chief cannot compel his subjects living outside his Division to pay the levy since he has no territorial jurisdiction over them.[1] This fact was pointed out in a recent case at the Divisional Court, and also by His Honour the Chief Commissioner recently, during his discussions with the Standing Committee on the Agenda for this session.[2]

After another lengthy discussion it was again agreed that 'each Division should collect only from residents who have been in the Division for six months or more'.

The position is still confused. For example, Kumasi subjects may obtain building plots at a nominal rent of 1s. a year; other Ashantis resident in Kumasi are strangers and have to pay rents varying between £2. 10s. and £10 a year or more for building plots. Another instance is in the award of scholarships. Many Divisions now award scholarships to primary and secondary schools, but only the children of 'subjects' are eligible, although residents (strangers) are liable for the annual levy, and for rents for buildings and cocoa-farms. These practices show that the chiefs still think of the political structure in terms of kinship.[3]

The foregoing has shown some of the results of the impact of trade and commerce on the Ashanti political structure. Economic activities are weakening kinship ties; opportunities for travel and employment have brought large numbers of permanent settlers into tribal areas; the provision of the amenities expected of a modern Native Authority necessitates taxation; this has been found to be more satisfactory on a territorial basis than on the basis of personal allegiance; but chiefship itself is on a tribal basis, and tribal loyalty discriminates against taxpayers who are not subjects of the Divisions in which they are resident.

[1] The Native Authority Ordinance confers jurisdiction on a territorial basis. See next chapter.   [2] Minutes of Confederacy Council (1945).

[3] e.g. one Division has refused a scholarship (1946) to the winner, a girl who was born in the Division and has lived there all her life, because she is a subject of a village one mile away. The village lies outside the Division in which the girl is resident.

The conflict involved in this situation is one of the problems of chiefship in Ashanti to-day. The community over which the chief and his council rule now includes permanent settlers who are outside the kinship political organization.[1]

Education

It was the Basel and Wesleyan Missionaries who led the way in carrying education to Ashanti, and educational work is still very largely in the hands of the Missions.

In 1905 the Basel Mission had ten schools in Ashanti with a roll of 207 pupils. The Wesleyans had seven schools with a total roll of 219 pupils. Education at first made slow progress. The reason, according to official reports, was that the Ashantis were unwilling to send their children to Mission Schools because they would be made Christians. In 1907, for example, the Chief Commissioner reported:

The instruction given in Mission Schools is of necessity of an elementary character, and, as stated in last year's report, education among the Ashantis will progress but slowly, if at all, until Government Undenominational Schools have been established. The chiefs regard the Mission Schools as a means to an end, i.e. the proselytism of the children, and fear the consequent repudiation of the chiefs' authority, and their obligation to the tribal Stools.[2]

A Government boys' school was opened in Kumasi in 1909. Two years later it was reported that a decided improvement in Ashanti in favour of education was noticeable, and that many applications for government schools had been made.[3]

Two more schools were opened by Government in 1914—a girls' school in Kumasi and a boys' school in Sunyani; but the Missions had made a much bigger advance.

The schools in Ashanti in that year were:

Basel Mission	. .	23 schools with a total roll of 724 pupils.		
Wesleyan Mission.	.	13	,, ,, ,,	617 ,,
Roman Catholic Mission	4	,, ,, ,,	340 ,,	
Zion Mission	. .	3	,, ,, ,,	86 ,,
Government	. .	3	,, ,, ,,	555 ,,
Total .	. .	46		2,322

[1] The way this problem has been tackled is discussed in the next chapter, on 'Local Government'.

[2] *Colonial Reports: Ashanti*, 1907.   [3] Ibid., 1911.

The reason for the interest in education was economic. Primary school education led to lucrative clerical jobs. This fact, which was noted early, still provides the motive for the support of schools by the chiefs. In 1914 it was reported:

Education in Ashanti is so far only popular in the Central and Southern Provinces where natives can best realize the value of knowledge owing to constant contact with Europeans and educated natives. Chiefs appear anxious for their sons to learn all they can at the schools available so that their progeny may be in a position to compete with literate coast people and no longer remain at the mercy of alien clerks.[1]

Many more schools were opened by the Missions in the ten years between 1914 and 1924. In the latter year there were 186 primary schools in Ashanti with a total roll of 3,824 pupils. In the same year the Wesleyans opened a Training College for teachers, catechists, and ministers, and the English Church Mission a Theological Training College (St. Augustine's) for priests in Kumasi.

The Government has opened no schools in Ashanti, since the addition of the Mampong Trade School (1921) brought the number of Government schools to a total of five. But Mission schools have steadily increased.[2]

It is the political consequences of the spread of education that concern us here.

Education has raised a class of educated commoner *vis-à-vis* the illiterate chief and council. In the few but increasing cases where the chief is educated the majority of his council are illiterate. These educated commoners are employed as clerks, teachers, cocoa-brokers, shopkeepers. They have a high prestige in the community due to their wealth, occupation, or literacy, and they seek to exercise an effective influence in the political and social life of the community corresponding to their enhanced status. But they find that the traditional political organization places authority in the hands of the chief and his illiterate council, whom they consider unprogressive or reactionary.

In nearly every Division in Ashanti the educated youngmen have formed literary societies and 'Progress Unions', which are active political groups. In recent local political disputes (1942–6) considerable influence was exercised by such literary societies at

[1] *Colonial Reports: Ashanti*, 1914.
[2] There were 866 primary schools in Ashanti in 1948, classified as: Government 4, Assisted 84, Approved 58, Designated 240, non-Designated 480.

Juaben, Bekwai, Kumawu, and Offinsu. In each case the candidate elected as chief was the one who had the backing of the educated youngmen. In Kumasi, the six unofficial members of the Confederacy Council were selected from the Kotoko Society, a literary and political society of educated men, mostly middle-aged. The younger Ashantis in Kumasi have formed the Ashanti Youth Association, also an active political group. In the 1946 election of a candidate to represent the municipality of Kumasi at the Legislative Council, of the two candidates who had any chance one was backed by the Ashanti Youth Association, the other by the Kotoko Society. The candidate of the Ashanti Youth Association won the election.

The electors have realized that education is now indispensable for the functions of a chief, and there has been a marked tendency to elect literate chiefs. Of twelve elections to head stools since 1942 six of the candidates elected were literate. This can be the better appreciated when consideration is given to the fact that the percentage of illiteracy in Ashanti is over 90. The six candidates were elected to the stools of Juaben, Berekum, Offinsu, Ejisu, Essumeja, and Bekwai. All these stools rank high in the Ashanti Constitution.

The existence of these groups of educated men has given an added virulence to the contest between youth and authority. Both the chiefs and the Government have been concerned about this political problem raised by the spread of education. They are faced with small but influential groups of literate men who seek more political power than is allowed them in the traditional political organization. The conflict contributes to the insecurity of the chief's position.[1]

Christianity

Christianity came into immediate conflict with the chiefs in Ashanti. In 1905 the Chief Commissioner reported: 'Native converts cut themselves so completely adrift from the rest of the community that the chiefs are afraid to encourage a movement that experience tells them will, in course of time, undermine their power.'[2]

The official policy regarding the conflict was put by the Governor:

The tendency of Christian converts to alienate themselves from the

[1] See Chap. IX.   [2] *Colonial Reports: Ashanti*, 1905.

communities to which they belong is very marked, and is naturally resented by the chiefs, who claim their hereditary right, in which they are supported by Government, to make the converts in common with their fellow tribesmen obey such laws and orders as are in accordance with native custom, not being repugnant to natural justice, equity and good conscience.[1]

Five years later the Chief Commissioner again reported: 'Christians in the villages have had a tendency to refuse the ordinary services to their chiefs on the ground that they cannot take part in fetish observances.'[2]

The Government took the view that while Christians were naturally freed from fetish observances, they were to perform the ordinary obligations and services imposed on them by native custom in which fetish ceremonies were not involved. The Missions on the whole accepted this in principle.

In several cases the new Christian converts formed communities apart from the heathen. This was encouraged by Government, because it lessened daily bickering.[2]

In 1911 the number of Christian converts in Ashanti was 7,168 among a total population of 287,814. This was a small proportion, but the friction between the chiefs and the converts had got much worse. In March 1912 the Governor of the Colony visited Kumasi to help to deal with the situation. He met a committee consisting of the Chief Commissioner, three other government officials, and representatives of the Missions—one Wesleyan, three Basel, and two Roman Catholic missionaries. They were all Europeans.

This committee drew up rules for the chiefs and the Churches. The two rules regulating political relations were, first: 'No Christian shall be called upon to perform any fetish rites or service, but shall be bound to render customary service to his chief on ceremonial occasions when no element of fetish practice is involved'; and secondly, that 'an effort should be made to draw a distinction between fetish and purely ceremonial service'.

When a convert refused to perform any hereditary service required of him on the ground that it was 'fetish', the District Commissioner decided whether or not the service demanded was fetish.

The Christian Church in Ashanti expanded but slowly until 1921 when there was a phenomenal increase in the membership of the

---

[1] *Colonial Reports: Ashanti*, 1905.   [2] Ibid., 1910.

Church. Over 15,000 converts were baptized in that year, mainly into the Wesleyan community. The man responsible for this movement towards Christianity was Sampson Opon, an illiterate African from Wam, in Western Ashanti.

The people became more favourably disposed towards Christianity. In 1923–4 the Chief Commissioner paid tribute to the work of the Missions:

The writer desires to record the excellent work which is being performed by the various Missionary bodies in Ashanti. The relations between the Christian and the non-Christian African generally have been very friendly.... There is and always has been a tendency for the Christian, especially the newly converted, to ignore his allegiance to his chief, but during the present year this particular phase caused no trouble. How far Christianity has penetrated the life of the people it is difficult to discover, but there is no doubt that its influence is for good law and order.[1]

The chiefs must have been similarly convinced. Since 1923 they have co-operated with the Churches in building schools. There are many chiefs who are adherents or members of one or other of the various denominations of the Church. Meetings of the Confederacy Council and Divisional Councils begin with prayers, and the number of Christian converts has increased considerably.

But the conflict between Christianity and the chiefs is real, and has not been solved. It was revived when, at its session in September 1941, the Confederacy Council decreed that farming on Thursdays was to be an offence.[2] As a result of this order, representatives of the Churches—Protestant and Roman Catholic—sent a joint memorandum to the Asantehene.[3] Subsequently, the representatives met the whole council, and later met a committee appointed by the council to discuss the matter, but no satisfactory agreement was reached.

The essential points raised in the memorandum were as follows:

Paragraph 1. In the first place we wish to take this opportunity of placing on record our regret that so often in the past there has been a cleavage between Christians and non-Christians in this country, and our resolve to do all in our power to bring these two sections within the community together.

[1] Ibid., 1923–4.
[2] Thursday is the 'natal day' of Mother Earth. See Chap. II.
[3] The full text of this memorandum is given in Appendix III.

Paragraph 2. We must, however, state our conviction that in so far as some elements of the cleavage are due to difference of belief, the purpose of reconciliation cannot be furthered by any discussion which unduly minimizes these differences. We are forced to recognize that in some of its aspects Ancient Ashanti Religion asks an allegiance to certain spiritual powers which the worshippers of the God and Father of our Lord Jesus Christ cannot give.

Paragraph 6. On the part of the chiefs we would ask that they accept as a fact the existence of Christians as members of their State and lay down ways by which they can show their allegiance to their chiefs without at the same time offending their Christian conscience.

Paragraph 7. . . . If no recognized place exists in Native Customary Law for those who do not believe in 'fetish', has not the time come in view of many changing circumstances for the adaptation of Native Customary Law in order that it may include in its provisions all loyal citizens?

Paragraph 9. As regards the observance of Thursday: We feel that we cannot ask this of our members, in that to refrain from work on Thursday would be to them a confession of faith in Asase Yaa and her relation to harvest and famine and therefore a denial of the Fatherhood and providential care of God.

The cleavage centres round two questions. Belief, and the liberty of the Christian. They are both political as well as religious questions.

This can best be understood in relation to ancestor-worship. The whole legal and political system of Ashanti is bound up with ancestor-worship, which provides an organic unity between political and religious authority. The ceremonial rites connected with it have already been described.[1] The main features may be briefly recalled. Ancestor-worship is based on the social organization. The rites have reference to the chief's royal ancestors, to whom offerings of food and drink are made. The symbols used and the things prayed for are objects of common interest to the community—food, health, fecundity. By the rites the community expresses its sense of dependence on the ancestors for its welfare, and its belief that the ancestors watch over the conduct of its members, ceasing to send them blessings and punishing them with sickness and misfortune if they fail in their duties. The rituals reaffirm and strengthen the sentiments of solidarity and continuity of the people. Ancestor-worship is the basis of the chief's authority

[1] See Chap. II, 'The Religious Aspect of Chiefship'.

as well as the sanction of morality in the community. The chief is the one 'who sits on the stool of the ancestors'. This is the position which Christianity assails.

The things which Christians have refused to do on religious grounds cover a wide range, from swearing an oath in the traditional way, providing a sheep for sacrifice at the hearing of a case, carrying a stool or sword on ceremonial occasions, to doing communal labour on the road.

When Christians in the villages are asked why they refuse these services they usually reply: 'I now go to church, I am not under the chief,' or 'The priest (Father or *Sofo*) says we must not do them', or 'It is against the law of the Church'. They see the question in terms of regulations issued by the priest or minister. By becoming Christians they have put themselves under a new authority. Their disputes are settled by the catechist, the leaders of the congregation, or the priest or minister. Their conduct is regulated by Church law and discipline. They regard themselves as a separate community under the authority of the European missionary who is the head of the church. This is how most Ashanti Christians think of their new status. That is how the chiefs see it too. In a society in which political and religious office are combined, the chiefs regard the request for the recognition of the existence of the Christians and for the adaptation of native law as a request for the surrender of authority. As they see it, the Christian Church requests that they should not have power to legislate on certain things for certain members of the community, because the Church claims the right to legislate on these things for those of the chief's subjects who have embraced the Christian Faith. Christianity challenges the traditional position of the chief as the religious as well as the political head of his tribe.

The controversy about the observance of Thursday is therefore also a political question concerned with the exercise of authority. The Ashanti Confederacy Council of Chiefs ruled that there should be a ritual relation between every Ashanti and the fifth day of the week—Thursday. As those 'who sit upon the stools of the ancestors', the chiefs had the right to make such a rule. The representatives of the Church contended that the rule should not apply to Christians, because only the Church should legislate for them on religious matters, and in fact that the Church had already established a ritual relation between Christians and the first day of the week.[1] The traditional authority is confronted by another authority.

The deadlock in this particular case was resolved by the Chief Commissioner refusing to sanction the order of the Confederacy Council. This sanction was required before the rule could become law.

This leaves the conflict itself unsolved. To recognize the existence of Christians in the community, the chief must surrender to the Church his traditional authority as a religious head. This is the problem which Christianity presents.

Social change

In this chapter we have briefly surveyed the major forces that have produced radical changes in Ashanti society. During the last forty years, through British rule, the expansion in trade and commerce, the introduction of education and Christianity, there has been a social revolution in Ashanti. New ways of life and new beliefs threaten the framework of Ashanti institutions and values. A vastly greater number of individuals have been brought into effective social relations. The society has become more complex. As in other African communities brought into contact with European civilization, the processes of disintegration have been faster than the processes of reintegration on a new level.[2] We have not attempted in this chapter even to list the whole series of interconnected social problems that arise from the resultant disequilibrium in the society; but concentrating our attention on the chief, we have indicated how each of the major forces of social change has produced some disintegration in the political structure. It is against this background that the present position of the chief in Ashanti can be understood. In the next chapter we discuss further changes effected by British rule by considering the powers of the chief as defined by government legislation.

[1] 'There exists a ritual relation whenever a society imposes on its members a certain attitude towards an object, which attitude involves some measure of respect expressed in a traditional mode of behaviour with reference to that object.' Radcliffe-Brown, 'The Sociological Theory of Totemism'. *Proceedings of the Fourth Pacific Science Congress*, 1930, vol. iii, pp. 295–309.

[2] For general observations on this see: Godfrey and Monica Wilson, *The Analysis of Social Change*; M. Fortes, 'An Anthropologist's Point of View' in *Fabian Colonial Essays*; R. Firth, *Human Types*, chap. vii; Malinowski, *The Dynamics of Culture Change*.

CHAPTER VII

BRITISH RULE AND THE CHIEF
II. LOCAL GOVERNMENT

The Native Authority Ordinance

IN 1924 Government passed the Native Jurisdiction Ordinance, which defined the powers and duties of the chiefs in Ashanti. When the Ashanti Confederacy was restored in 1935, the Native Authority (Ashanti) Ordinance (Cap. 79 of the Laws of the Gold Coast) was passed. It is under this ordinance that the chiefs at present exercise their powers and duties.

For administrative purposes Government divided Ashanti into seven administrative districts, as follows:

District	Area (square miles)	Population (1931 Census)
Kumasi . . .	3,169	172,198
Bekwai . . .	2,205	73,025
Obuasi . . .	2,208	40,797
Mampong . . .	3,349	50,295
Ashanti-Akim . .	4,580	53,690
Sunyani . . .	3,850	82,742
Wenchi . . .	7,218	105,331
TOTAL . . .	26,579	578,078

The administrative staff of the central government in charge of this area consists of the Chief Commissioner, representing the Governor, an Assistant Chief Commissioner, and fourteen District and Assistant District Commissioners. The central government has also its police establishment and its technical departments—education, medical, agricultural, forestry, public works, treasury, lands, judicial, &c.

Each District of which an Administrative Officer is in charge usually consists of several Native Authorities. The ordinance defines a Native Authority as 'any chief or other native or any native Council or group of natives or native Councils declared to be a Native Authority under this ordinance for the area concerned'.

The Divisions of Kumasi, Mampong, Juaben, Nsuta, Bekwai,

Kokofu, Adansi, Kumawu, Essumeja, Offinsu, Ejisu, Agona, Banda, Wenchi, Mo, Nkoranza, Jaman, Berekum, Dormaa, Techiman, and Abeasi within the Ashanti Confederacy have all been declared Native Authorities, and the head chief of each Division has been appointed President of the Native Authority for his Division.

A chief, according to the ordinance, is 'a person whose election and installation as such in accordance with native Law and Custom is recognized and confirmed by the Governor by notification in the *Gazette*, and includes the Asantehene, but does not include any person from whom the Governor for any reason which appears sufficient, withdraws such recognition by notification in the *Gazette*'. This leaves no doubt as to which is the supreme authority.

The chief is elected and installed in accordance with native law and custom, but he must be recognized by the Governor before he can exercise the functions of his office. This recognition is usually given, provided the candidate has a valid hereditary right, and has been duly elected in accordance with the customary constitutional practice. But the recognition may be withheld, as has been done in the case of Bekwai, where at the moment of writing there is no chief because Government has refused to recognize the candidate the people have chosen—an ex-chief who has been twice destooled. The principle is clear that the choice of a chief is not entirely dependent on the will of the people.

Powers and duties of Native Authorities

Government not only appoints a Native Authority, but also prescribes its powers and duties. These may be divided into two broad categories: administrative and judicial.

The duty of a Native Authority is to maintain order and good government in the area over which its authority extends. For this purpose the ordinance gives it certain defined powers: it may interpose to prevent the commission of any crime within the area of its authority; it has power to direct any native to attend before itself or any Government officer; it may issue orders to be obeyed by such natives within its area as may be subject to its jurisdiction for certain purposes set out in the ordinance,[1] and generally for the improvement of sanitation and for the better preservation of health. Subject to the approval of the Governor it may make

[1] See App. V for the full text, giving the list of such purposes.

rules 'providing for the peace, good order, and welfare of the natives within the area of its authority'.

It may, with the approval of the Governor, and shall if so required by the Governor, establish a native treasury in the area under its control. It may, again with the approval of the Governor, 'levy upon the natives living within the local limits of its jurisdiction, rates, dues, tributes, and fees for such purposes as the Governor may from time to time by order direct'. Where a treasury is established, the ordinance lays down that moneys received from the following sources shall be paid into it:

1. Moneys paid in respect of stool lands by way of rent, tribute, or profit from the produce of the land.
2. Court fines and fees.
3. Market rents, slaughter-house fees, cattle-kraal rents, and other similar dues.
4. Interest on money invested or lent by the Native Authority.
5. Money derived from rates, dues, tributes, fees, levies, or other taxation imposed by the Native Authority.

Judicial functions: The Native Courts (Ashanti) Ordinance

Native courts have been established under the Native Courts (Ashanti) Ordinance, 1935 (Cap. 80 of the Laws of the Gold Coast) within the areas of the Native Authorities.

The ordinance defines the jurisdiction of the courts and the law to be administered.

A native court is to administer the native law and custom prevailing in the area of its jurisdiction 'so far as is not repugnant to natural justice or morality or inconsistent with any provisions of any other ordinance; provided always that in regard to criminal offences by virtue of native law and custom such court shall take cognizance only of such offences as from time to time may be prescribed by order of the Governor'.

There are four grades of native courts, A, B, C, and D, and the jurisdiction of each court is normally as follows:

Grade A

A Grade A court has jurisdiction in all disputes relating to the ownership, possession, or occupation of land in the Confederacy:

(*a*) Arising between two or more head chiefs or chiefs belonging to two different Divisions, or between a head chief and a person subject to the jurisdiction of such head chief by virtue of the Native Authority (Ashanti) Ordinance.

(b) In which for any reason no other native court has the requisite jurisdiction.

(c) Which are transferred to the court by the Chief Commissioner.

Only one Grade A court has been established. This is the Asantehene's Court A, which exercises jurisdiction within the Confederacy over the area covered by the twenty-one Divisions specified above.

The head chiefs of the Divisions and the senior chief of each of the seven Kumasi 'clans' are members of the court. The Asantehene is president of this court, and the maximum and minimum number of persons competent to transact its business are respectively five and three.

The court is, in addition to its original jurisdiction, a court of appeal:

(a) In cases relating to the ownership, possession, or occupation of land from all Grade B and C native courts within the Confederacy.

(b) In appeals from native courts of appeal situate within the Confederacy transferred from a magistrate's court under Section 24 (4) of the ordinance.

Grade B

The jurisdiction of a Grade B court is:

(a) Civil action in which the debt, demand, or damages do not exceed £100.

(b) Suits relating to the ownership, possession, or occupation of land within the area of its jurisdiction.

(c) Suits for divorces and other matrimonial causes between natives married under native law and custom.

(d) Suits to establish paternity of children other than suits in which some question affecting rights arising out of any Christian marriage is or may be involved.

(e) Suits and matters relating to the succession to property of any deceased native who had at the time of his death a fixed place of abode within the area of jurisdiction of the native court.

(*f*) Criminal cases in respect of any offence which in the opinion of the native court can be adequately punished by a fine of £50 or six months' imprisonment or by both punishments.

Grade C

The original jurisdiction of a Grade C court is similar to that of a Grade B court except that in civil actions it is limited to cases where the debt, demand, or damages do not exceed £50; in succession suits to cases where the whole value of the property of the deceased does not exceed £200, and in criminal cases to offences which can be adequately punished by a fine of £25 or three months' imprisonment or both.

Grade D

A Grade D court has jurisdiction similar to that of a Grade C court save that in civil actions it is limited to £25, has no jurisdiction in succession suits, and it may only hear criminal cases which can be adequately punished by a fine of £5 or one month's imprisonment or both such punishments.

In addition, the Native Courts (Criminal Code Enforcement) Order has conferred power upon all native courts in Ashanti, to the extent of their jurisdiction, to enforce the provision of Book II other than Title 12 of the Criminal Code (Laws of the Gold Coast Cap. 9) and to impose penalties on natives subject to their jurisdiction who offend such provisions. This gives the courts jurisdiction in offences against the person, such as assaults; offences against rights of property, such as stealing, misappropriation and fraud, receiving, unlawful possession, damage to property; and offences against public order, health, and morality such as drunken, riotous, and disorderly conduct, or nuisances in streets.

Appeals

The ordinance makes provision for appeals.

In land cases within the Confederacy an appeal lies from a native court of first instance to the Asantehene's court A, thence to the Chief Commissioner's court, and a further appeal lies from the Chief Commissioner's court to the West African Court of Appeal. Leave may be granted for a further appeal to the Privy Council.

In civil cases other than land cases an appeal lies to a native Court of Appeal, if there is one so constituted for the area; if one has not been constituted the appeal goes to the magistrate's court constituted by a District Commissioner. A further appeal lies to the Chief Commissioner's court, and thence to the West African Court of Appeal. The magistrate's court constituted by the District Commissioner may transfer the case to the Asantehene's court A, from which again an appeal lies to the Chief Commissioner's court.

In criminal cases an appeal lies from the native court to the magistrate's court and thence to the Divisional court presided over by a judge.

Constitutional matters

A native court may not hear matters of a constitutional nature dealing with the election, installation, and deposition of chiefs. The Chief Commissioner may transfer such matters to a Committee of Inquiry or to the Confederacy Council. But, normally, constitutional matters lie within the jurisdiction of the Divisional Council, which is 'the Native Authority appointed for a Division when composed of the head chiefs, chiefs, and councillors'. An appeal lies from the decision of a Divisional Council to the Chief Commissioner.

The persons over whom a Native Authority may exercise its powers are the 'natives'. A native is defined as 'a person of African descent: provided always that the expression shall not include any person who does not belong to a class of persons who have ordinarily been subject to the jurisdiction of native tribunals'.

To sum up, a Native Authority is responsible for the maintenance of order and good government within its territory. It has power to make rules and issue orders on certain subjects; it has judicial functions defined in the order establishing the native court or courts in the area of its authority; it is expected to establish a treasury to meet the costs of the administration of its area and the provision of health and social services.

A Native Authority is protected by Government in the exercise of these powers. It may inflict penalties (fines and imprisonment) on those who disobey or do not carry out its orders and rules. Also, Section 12 (1) of the Native Authority (Ashanti) Ordinance provides that

any person who conspires against or in any manner attempts to undermine the lawful power and authority of the Asantehene, any Native

Authority, or any member of a Native Authority shall be guilty of an offence, and shall be liable on conviction thereof to a fine of one hundred pounds or to imprisonment with or without hard labour for one year, or to both such fine and imprisonment, and shall be liable to be removed from Ashanti or into any part of Ashanti outside the area of such Native Authority's jurisdiction.

Proceedings under this section require the consent of the Governor, and no removal order can be enforced until it has been confirmed by him. But it provides a strong sanction for the power of a Native Authority.

Native Authority under Government control and supervision

A Native Authority is under the careful control of Government in the exercise of the powers given it.

As has been in evidence in the above account, certain measures of control are vested in the Governor. It is he who appoints Native Authorities. The rules which they are permitted to make are subject to his approval, and may be revoked by him at any time. The establishment of a native treasury and the imposition of any rates, fees, or other taxation also require his approval, as do the annual estimates of revenue and expenditure which a Native Authority must submit to him.

Other measures of control are exercised by the Chief Commissioner. When a Native Authority applies for the Governor's permission to impose a tax, it must submit for the Chief Commissioner's approval the amount payable by every individual, the persons to whom the levy or tax shall apply, the purposes to which the proceeds of the tax shall be put, and the period within which the tax or levy shall be collected. The Native Authority requires the approval of the Chief Commissioner before it can contract any debt of more than £100. The appointment of employees for carrying out the provisions of the Native Authority Ordinance requires the approval of the Chief Commissioner. The Governor's powers to establish native courts have been delegated to the Chief Commissioner, who also has the power to review the proceedings of such courts. He may at any time terminate the appointment of any officer of a native court.

But the most supervision is done by the District Commissioner, as may be judged from the following outline of some of the powers given him under the Native Authority (Ashanti) and the Native Courts (Ashanti) Ordinances.

Whenever in the opinion of a District Commissioner it is expedient that any order should be issued which a Native Authority is empowered to issue, he may call upon the Native Authority to issue and enforce any such order, and should the Native Authority neglect or refuse to issue the order the District Commissioner may himself issue it.

In respect of any rule or tax approved by the Governor, the Native Authority must submit to the District Commissioner for his approval rules regulating the method of collection, the persons to be employed in collecting, and the safe custody of the money.

No payments other than as approved in the estimates should be made by a Native Authority without the authority in writing of the District Commissioner. The Native Authority is to appoint treasurers and other officers as in the opinion of the District Commissioner may be necessary. The treasurers shall produce on demand all documents and books of accounts for inspection and audit by the District Commissioner or any officer deputed by him for the purpose. Where a Native Authority keeps a bank account, disbursements other than current expenses must be paid by cheque signed by the senior member of the Native Authority and the treasurer, and must be countersigned by the District Commissioner, who shall first satisfy himself that the disbursements are lawfully due.

A public audit of all accounts of a Native Authority shall be held half-yearly at such time as may be notified by the District Commissioner, and for the purpose of such audit a balance sheet shall be prepared in such form as the District Commissioner may direct.

No debt shall be contracted on behalf of a Native Authority without the approval in writing of the District Commissioner. A Native Authority shall, if so required by the District Commissioner, make a declaration of all its outstanding debts; these shall be inquired into by the District Commissioner at a meeting of the Divisional Council. All debts so declared and approved shall be entered in a register of stool debts.

Where there is a market within the area of a Native Authority, it shall provide stalls roofed with iron sheets or some other material approved by the District Commissioner and the Senior Health Officer, Ashanti. For keeping the market clean it shall be the duty of the Native Authority to provide such number of sanitary labourers and to pay them at such rates as the District Commissioner may direct.

With regard to native courts, at such times and in such form as the Governor shall direct a report of all cases tried in such courts shall be submitted to the District Commissioner. The latter shall at all times have access to all native courts in his District and to the records of native courts, and on the application of any person concerned or of his own motion may:

(*a*) Review any of the proceedings of a native court whether civil or criminal, and may make such order or pass such sentence therein as the native court could itself have made or passed.

(*b*) Order the case to be retried by the same native court or any other native court of competent jurisdiction.

(*c*) Order the native court to review its judgement.

(*d*) Order the native court to take further evidence either generally or on some particular point.

(*e*) Order the transfer of any case or matter to a magistrate's court, the Chief Commissioner's court, or to any native court of competent jurisdiction.

This review of the Native Authority (Ashanti) and Native Courts (Ashanti) Ordinances summarizes the statutory powers of a Native Authority, and the supervision and control to which it is subject in the exercise of its powers.

The Native Authority at work

To see how a Native Authority functions within this statutory framework we may give a brief account of two Divisions— Wenchi and Kumasi.

The Native Authority of the Wenchi Division consists of the Wenchihene and his councillors: the Gyasehene, the Adonten-hene, the Kontihene, the Akwamuhene, and their subordinate councillors.

The population of the largest town in the Division, Wenchi, was given as 5,310 in the 1931 Census. It is both the capital of the Wenchi Division and the headquarters of the Wenchi District.

The greater part of the population consists of settlers from the neighbouring Division of Banda and from the Northern Territories. The largest groups are the Wangaras, Jiminis, and Dagombas. There are also Hausas from Nigeria and immigrants from other parts of Ashanti and the Colony. Most of the people from the Colony are Kwahus from the Eastern Province. They are mainly engaged as traders, running small shops of their own.

There is a Government police station in Wenchi and also a post office. The District Commissioner's offices, bungalow, and clerks' quarters are about a mile from the town. These institutions are outside the sphere of the Native Authority.

There is a Methodist church, and also a Methodist school opened in 1917. The school now has all classes from kindergarten to standard seven, the primary school leaving class. The manager, an English missionary, lives about a quarter of a mile from the school. There are also a Roman Catholic church and junior school, opened three years ago.

Besides the town of Wenchi there are twenty villages in the area of the Wenchi Native Authority. The principal of these are Droboso, Jensoso, Koase, Nkonsia, Akrobi, and Yoyoano.

The Wenchihene is the President of the Native Authority. The present Wenchihene and his councillors are all illiterate. A considerable amount of administrative responsibility therefore falls on the registrar, the finance clerk, and the police staff, none of whom has had more than a primary school education.

The Native Authority often meets to discuss matters referred to it by the District Commissioner or the Ashanti Confederacy Council. The registrar, who is also the State Secretary, is responsible for the secretarial work. Much of this consists of correspondence with the District Commissioner. All the letters are read and interpreted to the chief and his councillors by the registrar, and their replies are written, read back to them, and signed on their behalf by him. The registrar also drafts any rules or orders which the Native Authority makes. This draft is usually corrected by the District Commissioner.

The drawing up of estimates of revenue and expenditure is done by the finance clerk in consultation with the chief and his councillors, but they find it complicated, and a great deal of help is given by the District Commissioner, who advises not only on the preparation of the estimates but also on the purposes on which the

Division should spend its revenue. The latter is raised from cocoa tribute, ground rents, market and slaughter-house fees, and from a direct annual levy, two-thirds of which is retained in Wenchi and one-third paid into the Ashanti Confederacy National Fund. Most of the revenue is spent on paying the staff of the Native Authority, but Wenchi has a State Dispensary, provides its own sanitary services, and makes generous contributions towards education. In 1945 it voted £600 for a new classroom block for the Methodist senior school.

Wenchi has a Grade C native court of which the Wenchihene is the president, and the Kontihene, Adɔntenhene, Gyasehene, Nifahene, Twafohene, Akwamuhene, and the queen-mother are members. The maximum and minimum number of persons competent to transact the business of the court are respectively five and three.

The court deals with three classes of cases.

1. Offences under native law and custom.
2. Offences under the Criminal Code, Book II.
3. Civil cases.

It has been explained that the offences of which the chief took cognizance in Ashanti law were religious offences.[1] This is borne out by a list drawn up by the Confederacy Council at its 1946 Session, setting out the offences for which native courts demand the slaughter of sheep. This is because these offences are religious, and a piacular sacrifice is deemed necessary. The list is as follows:

A. *Offences against stool and traditional office-holders*

  (*a*) Insulting and assaulting of State dignitaries (i.e. traditional office-holders).
  (*b*) Assault or fighting in the house of a State dignitary.
  (*c*) Cursing any individual, or a State dignitary.
  (*d*) Exchange of blows between two State dignitaries.
  (*e*) Having sexual connexion with the wife of a State dignitary.
  (*f*) A State dignitary putting himself or being put into fetish.
  (*g*) A woman in her menstrual period entering the house of a State dignitary.
  (*h*) Disrespecting an oath which had been sworn.

[1] See Chap. IV, 'Administration and Justice'.

B. *Sexual offences*

(*a*) Incest (*mogyadie*).

(*b*) Having sexual connexion with a woman in the bush.

(*c*) Having sexual connexion with a woman during her menstrual period.

(*d*) Having sexual connexion with a pregnant woman who is not one's wife.

(*e*) A woman swearing an oath during her menstrual period.

(*f*) Swearing the oath to deny a sexual act which had in fact taken place.

C. *Offences against the gods*

Entering or polluting a sacred grove or shrine or stream.

The nature of these offences has already been discussed.[1] The chief and his councillors are familiar with the procedure in such offences, and the registrar's work is merely that of recording the proceedings of the court.

Most private wrongs or injuries were expected to be settled by arbitration. The method by which such wrongs were brought before the chief by swearing his oath has been explained.[1] The procedure in such cases is again well known to the chief and his councillors, although in this as in the other cases listed above there have been some modifications in procedure. An example will make this clear.

K. Y., a Kyidɔmhene, swears the chief's oath (Thursday) asserting that K. F., a commoner, has insulted him and called him an extortioner. K. F. responds (*de ntam boso*) by swearing that he has not insulted K. Y. M. B. hears the two men swear the oath, arrests them and takes them to the chief's Ɔkyeame (spokesman), who puts them before the chief and reports the incident, M. B. confirming the report. A date is then fixed for the hearing, and the two men may be released on their finding sureties. Each party has to find his supporter (*kyigyinafo*: one who stands behind one). Such a supporter is required by native customary law to stand surety for a litigant and to accept responsibility for any debts or obligations that may be incurred at the trial.

In former times, if anyone failed to find a supporter he was

---

[1] See Chap. IV, 'Administration and Justice'.

put in log (*wɔbɔ no pam*) till the trial was over. This was to make certain that he did not escape. The head of one's house or lineage usually stands as one's supporter: this emphasizes lineage solidarity. A man who in such a situation fails to find a supporter amongst his kinsmen regards himself as having been disowned by them.

At the date fixed for the hearing the parties appear with their supporters. Each of them would have paid 7*s.* to M. B., who arrested them. They will also be required, as they have sworn a chief's oath, to deposit £3 each (*dwomtadi*) towards the expenses of the suit. As this is a case in which the issue is one of insult to a stool elder, a sheep has to be sacrificed. Each party is therefore required to deposit a further £1. 3*s.* 6*d.* (*dwan sika*: sheep money).[1] The innocent party will receive back his deposit, and the guilty party will pay the expenses of the case from his.

The hearing then begins. K. Y., who first swore the oath, becomes the plaintiff and tells his story first. K. F. and the councillors cross-examine him. K. F. similarly tells his story. Neither statement is given on oath.

In the old days, both K. Y. and K. F. then agreed on one witness who gave evidence on behalf of both parties. The messenger whom the court sent to call this witness was sworn, first on an *ɔbosom* (god) and then on the chief's oath, not to discuss the case before the court with the witness.

Before the witness arrived the Ɔkyeame turned to the two parties and said: 'You, plaintiff, this is what you assert, and you, defendant, this is what you assert; if the witness comes and says this or that, you, plaintiff, are right; but if he says thus and thus, you are guilty.' This procedure was called *sigyinae* (setting the support). What the Ɔkyeame did was to single out the essential points which would prove the truth or falsehood of the statement of the plaintiff or defendant.

When the witness arrived he was sworn and asked to say what he knew of the dispute. After he had given his sworn evidence the Ɔkyeame would pronounce one or other of the parties guilty according to his evidence. The sentence was pronounced in a set formula:[2] '*Wate dee dansefo aka; sɛ wamfa amma ha ma yɛamfa aso pa*

---

[1] These are the rates as standardized in the Native Courts (Ashanti) Ordinance.

[2] On this procedure see Rattray, *Ashanti Law and Constitution*, pp. 281–3; I have observed the same procedure in many native courts.

antie, na womaa abaa bi so bɔɔ Ɔkyeame, woku no, wodi no aboa—wodi fɔ.'
(You have heard what the witness has said; had you not come here
for us to listen (to your case) with good ears, but had lifted some
stick and hit the Ɔkyeame, you would have killed him as if he
were a beast; you are guilty.) The meaning of this formula is
obscure, but the import is that if the guilty party had not submitted the issue for adjudication, but had taken the law into his
own hands and punished his opponent he would have treated him
like a beast.

When the judgement had been pronounced, the court heralds
sprinkled white clay on the one acquitted. He was then asked to
pay a customary fee (*aseda*: token of thanks), because he was being
let off after he had sworn the oath which was a tribal taboo.

The guilty party and his supporter then begged the elders to
apologize to the chief, for he had been found to have used the
oath without good cause. (*Me dwane toa mo mema Nana dibem*: I flee
to you; I give *nana* (the chief) the justice of his cause.) He would
then be made to pay a fine.

This procedure has now been modified. Both plaintiff and
defendant may call separate and any number of witnesses, who are
cross-examined by the court and the parties. Plaintiff, defendant,
and witnesses now give their evidence on oath.

Thus, in our example K. Y.'s witnesses are first called; when
they have given their statements they are cross-examined by both
parties and the court; K. F.'s witnesses speak next. The councillors
deliberate together at the close of the evidence, and the Ɔkyeame
pronounces the judgement in the set formula. The bill of costs is
then worked out by the Registrar, who informs the guilty party.
If there is an appeal to the District Commissioner's court, native
law is applied by him.

Of the offences that the court may hear under Book II of the
Criminal Code there are some, like stealing or assault, which are
familiar as offences in native law; others, like receiving or unlawful possession, present technical difficulties. The procedure is more
formal, and the councillors need the help of the registrar regarding
such points as admissible and inadmissible evidence, what statement requires corroboration, and so on, because on appeal to the
magistrate's court English law becomes applicable, and there are
cases in which the judgements of native courts are reversed on
technical grounds. The tendency, therefore, is for the native courts

to copy the procedure in the magistrate's court, with the Native Authority police conducting the prosecutions.

It is, however, with the procedure in civil suits that the native court is most unfamiliar. There are many cases for the recovery of debt, or for damages for insult or personal abuse. The former class of case was rare in the subsistence economy of fifty years ago, but has become more numerous since the new economy involves many commercial transactions. Cases of insult or abuse were formerly mostly settled by arbitration as far as commoners were concerned; but these can now come before the court by summons, and a large number of actions for defamation are brought before native courts. The councillors are unfamiliar with contractual relations, or with the assessment of damages, or with the whole process of executions against property or persons (writs of *Fi: Fa* or *Ca: Sa*), and both councillors and litigants have to rely on the Registrars for much help in such cases.

The table on p. 154 is an analysis of the returns of cases heard by native tribunals in the Wenchi District for the second half-year of 1941. It shows that the largest number of criminal cases dealt with were assaults and sanitary offences; and the largest number of civil cases were suits for the recovery of debts, or damages. All these are types of cases which are comparatively new to the tribunals.

It is notorious that there is much bribery in connexion with trials in native courts. A Commission of Inquiry into expenses of litigants in the courts of the Gold Coast appointed in 1944 confirmed this: 'I am', the Commissioner wrote, 'driven to the conclusion that in a regrettable number of cases certain members of the Tribunal, their officers and clerical staff have accepted gifts in money or kind, sometimes solicited, and sometimes unsolicited, from litigants or intending litigants.'[1] My own investigations support this statement.

Native courts have shown a tendency to impose heavy fines, and litigants frequently go to the District Commissioner to beg him to exercise his powers of revision and reduce fines and fees imposed by the native courts; others appeal to the magistrate's court.

[1] Havers, *Report of Commission of Inquiry into Expenses incurred by Litigants of the Gold Coast and Indebtedness caused thereby*, 1945, p. 10. Corruption and bribery are general throughout the Gold Coast, and are not confined to the courts. It is one of the community's responses to the new economy, which has made people very acquisitive.

	Wenchi	Techiman	Nkoranza	Drobo	Banda	Mo	Suma	Seikwa	Nsawkaw	Seketia	Totals
CRIMINAL CASES											
Assault	12	8	7	7	2	1	12	6	2	6	63
Putting into fetish	1	1	..	1	..	..	..	3	..	..	6
Insult to chiefs	1	1	..	4	..	..	..	..	..	..	6
Stealing	..	..	4	5	..	1	1	6	3	5	25
Using insulting and de-famatory words	..	..	..	..	..	..	..	1	2	1	4
Sexual offences	3	3	4	5	4	4	..	..	..	..	23
Criminal oath cases	2	..	..	4	..	..	..	2	1	4	13
Disobeying lawful order	..	..	..	1	..	..	..	3	..	..	4
Breach of peace	..	..	..	3	1	..	3	2	1	..	10
Sanitary cases	385	109	..	..	..	..	..	20	..	..	514
Causing injury or wound	..	..	..	..	..	..	..	3	2	..	5
Threatening	..	2	1	1	..	..	1	..	..	..	5
Fraud and receiving	..	1	3	1	..	..	1	..	1	..	7
Illegal cutting of wood in forest reserves	..	1	3	1	..	..	1	..	1	..	7
CIVIL CASES											
Debts	15	4	51	..	..	3	..	1	..	5	79
Damages	8	6	12	..	..	1	..	3	..	3	33
Oath cases (civil)	4	2	6	..	..	..	..	2	..	5	19
Marriage suits	2	2	2	..	..	1	..	..	..	..	7
Judicial relief	1	1	..	..	..	1	..	..	..	..	3
Labour contracts	1	..	2	..	..	1	..	..	..	..	4
Interpleader suits	..	..	2	..	..	..	..	..	..	..	2
Land	..	..	1	..	..	..	..	..	..	..	1
Cocoa tribute	5	..	..	..	..	..	..	..	..	..	5

Participation in local administration

We have said that many of the people who live in Wenchi are settlers from the Northern Territories and the Colony. The various communities have appointed their own headmen. The Kwahu traders, the Ashanti traders, and the various groups—Wangaras, Jiminis, Moshis, Hausas, and Dagombas—have each appointed a headman. The Banda headman is the chief of the Zongo, where all the 'strangers' live, but he has no effective control over the heterogeneous population of the Zongo. These settlers pay house rent, farm rent, or the annual tax, but they are not members of the Native Authority. They are regularly consulted on all matters that concern them, and when necessary are invited to meetings of the Native Authority or to sittings of the court, but they do not share the responsibility for any decisions that are taken. They all tend to look upon the District Commissioner as their 'Master and Protector', and they take most of their complaints and questions to him.

The headmen who live in the villages have also very little share in the administrative work of the Division. The Divisional Council of which they are members meets when there is a constitutional case to be settled, or when some rule or regulation to be made is regarded as important enough to warrant a full meeting of the Divisional Council; or the Council may meet to discuss matters referred to it by the Confederacy Council. The headmen may also come to the public audit of the native treasury held twice a year. Otherwise their participation in the new administration is small.

The schools are managed by the missions, though the Native Authority may vote money to assist education; the treasury and court work devolve mostly upon the literate staff; administrative instructions from the District Commissioner are dealt with by the Wenchihene and the councillors on the spot, and even they depend largely on the staff and on the District Commissioner. Many complaints which would formerly have been settled by the elders and village headmen now go to the court by summons; and there are some people who, when they do not resort to a lawsuit, take their complaints to the District Commissioner; so although the elders and headmen still settle cases by arbitration, their traditional role as peacemakers within the community is of decreasing importance, as they are not called upon as frequently as in former times.

When the religious festivals come round, then the Wenchihene goes to each village in turn and joins the headmen and elders in sacrifice to the gods. All the headmen also meet in Wenchi for the periodic religious ceremonies already described.[1] It is then that they feel they have a definite place in the community, and share a sense of oneness and of belonging together.

But the actual exercise of the powers of a Native Authority—making rules and regulations, working out estimates of revenue and expenditure, making provision for schools, health and welfare services, dispensing justice under the twofold criteria of African and European principles of law—are matters in which their role is a subordinate and not very significant one.

[1] See Chap. II, 'The Religious Aspect of Chiefship'.

The Kumasi Division

The Native Authority for the Kumasi Division consists of the Asantehene and his Kumasi councillors: Adɔntenhene, Akwamuhene, Ankɔbeahene, Gyasehene, Kontihene, Kyidɔmhene, Oyokohene, the Tafohene, and their councillors. In addition, there are forty-nine subordinate Native Authority areas in the Kumasi Division, and the chiefs of these areas and their councillors are subordinate Native Authorities within the Division. The more important of these areas are Banko, Bompata, Agogo, Obogu, Bechem, Nkwanta, Nsoatre, Odumase, Sekitia, Sekwa, Suma, Nsawkaw, Kuntanasi, and Akropong. Ten of the chiefs in the Division are literate. The courts established within the area of the Kumasi Native Authority were the Asantehene's Native Court B, eight 'clan' courts of the C Grade for the Adɔnten, Akwamu, Ankɔbea, Gyasi, Konti, Kyidɔm, Oyoko, and Benkum clans, and seventeen courts of the D Grade in each of the areas specified above.

There was a disproportionate centralization of courts in Kumasi. This caused much inconvenience and expense to the people in the neighbouring areas who had to travel to the courts. It also gave opportunities for the kind of bribery and corruption already referred to. For these reasons Government closed the Kumasi clan courts in 1945. They have been replaced by a Kumasi Division court of the C Grade, and a Kumasi Division Appeal Court, and area courts are being opened (1946) throughout the Division. A discussion of the courts in Kumasi is not attempted here, as these changes have taken place since my field-work was done.[1] But the remarks made about the Wenchi Court regarding procedure are of general application throughout Ashanti.

The Divisional Treasury was also centralized in Kumasi, and the people of the subordinate areas had little to do with it beyond paying their taxes and tribute. In 1945 the Chief Commissioner reported of the Kumasi Treasury:

One regrettable exception to the general development of Native Authority Treasuries is that of the Kumasi Divisional Council. Administration is inefficient, and the amount devoted to the development

---

[1] The establishment of the area courts for the outlying places, and the appointment of more representative panels to the courts have cured many of the ills listed above.

services has been meagre, although a belated contribution of £4,000 was made for education. The cause for this unsatisfactory state of affairs appears to be the lack of interest shown by the people of Kumasi in their local administration.[1]

It must be added that the belated contribution was made on the insistence of Government that more of the revenue should be spent on development.

So a new policy was adopted in 1946. Of this, the Chief Commissioner writes:

A policy of financial devolution has also been adopted, and it is proposed that each area shall have a sub-treasury subordinate to the Kumasi Divisional Treasury. Already, there are signs that the resultant increased control over revenue and expenditure by the peoples of these areas is arousing enthusiasm for the Treasury System, and they have in many cases applied for the imposition of levies for development purposes.[2]

These extracts are of further interest as showing the standards that Government sets before the Native Authorities, and by which it judges their success in administration. The leading part that Government plays is also in evidence from the second extract: the policy of financial devolution is one which has been initiated by Government.

In Kumasi town there are the Cantonments, the headquarters of the Gold Coast Regiment, and also a residential area where the Chief Commissioner, the judge, magistrates, police officers, and other civil servants of the central government live. There is a government police establishment maintaining order, protecting property, controlling traffic, checking crime, effecting arrests, and conducting prosecutions in Government courts. There are many technical departments of Government: the post office, education, agriculture, public works, &c. There are numerous churches and schools. All these are institutions outside the sphere of the Native Authority.

Kumasi also contains large groups of Syrians, Indians, and other strangers who do not come within the definition of 'native', and are therefore outside the jurisdiction of the Native Authority.

There are large communities from the Northern Territories:

[1] *Gold Coast Legislative Council Debates, 1945 Session*, Appendix.
[2] Ibid., *1946 Session*, Appendix.

Dagombas, Moshis, Wangaras, &c., and Fantis, Ewes, and Gas from the Colony. Each community has appointed a headman, but the headmen have little real authority over their respective groups, each of which consists of persons from widely separated areas even when they come from the same region, all attracted to Kumasi by the economic opportunities the town offers. There is often little sense of unity amongst them.

The Kumasi Native Authority usually refers matters which concern these non-Ashanti residents to the respective headmen and sometimes invites them to its meetings. Otherwise these residents, though they pay taxes, have no part in the affairs of the Native Authority. They, as well as the Syrians and the Indians, mostly take their complaints and questions to the District Commissioner.

The Kumasi Native Authority has both administrative and judicial functions; constitutional cases within the Division are dealt with by the Divisional Council.

As regards administrative functions, the Kumasi Native Authority discusses matters referred to it by the Chief Commissioner, the District Commissioner, the Confederacy Council, or the Kumasi Town Council. It also considers and takes decisions on reports or recommendations submitted by its Education or Finance Committee.

New Government policy—Advisory Committees

Both these bodies are examples of a new Government policy. The Native Authority (Colony) Ordinances 1944 passed for the Gold Coast Colony made provision for the appointment of a Finance Board for each Native Authority Treasury. The members of the Board may be persons other than hereditary rulers. The Ordinance also provided that 'it shall be the duty of every State Council as soon as may be after the commencement of this Ordinance to make a declaration in writing specifying by office or name the persons who are members thereof, and the State Council may thereafter from time to time as the necessity arises vary such declaration'.[1] The aim of this was to enable Native Authorities to introduce new blood into their councils and many of the Native Authorities in the Colony have taken advantage of this and given the younger men representation on their councils.

[1] *Native Authority (Colony) Ordinance*, 1944, Sec. 24 (1).

At the 1946 Session of the Gold Coast Legislative Council the Governor said in his opening address :

On the subject of Native Authorities, there is one point to which I would like to refer. I am a great believer in the value of Native Administrations, and I feel that these administrations are strengthening themselves very greatly by introducing into their Councils and Finance and other Committees a number of the younger and progressive elements of the population as they have done in a large number of cases in the Colony. Such a step strengthens—not weakens—a State Council. It gives those better educated persons apart from the traditional rulers, an opportunity for more direct participation in the administration of their country, and it provides a useful outlet for the constructive energies of responsible men who might otherwise take up an attitude of irresponsible opposition to the traditions of native administration.[1]

The policy has not been given statutory effect in Ashanti, but it has been adopted in practice, and the Native Authorities have been encouraged to set up various Advisory Committees: town boards, education and finance committees, to which some of the younger men have been appointed. This is an attempt to solve the problem of an educated class *vis-à-vis* the traditional rulers referred to in the previous chapter.[2] It is a very recent policy, which it has not been possible to study on the field, and one which is really too early to yield any reliable social results. But two indications of the effect of the new policy are given in the Chief Commissioner's report on Ashanti for 1946 :

Owing largely to the activities of the Kumasi Finance Advisory Committee, the administration of the Kumasi Divisional Treasury was considerably improved, and the costs of administration of the Kumasi Division were reduced from 97% in 1943–4 to 77%.

That is, whereas in the 1943–4 financial year 97 per cent. of the total expenditure had been on administrative costs, mainly salaries; in the following year administrative costs had been reduced to 77 per cent., and more money made available for development.

Of the Mampong Division he also reported :

General progress has been most marked in the Mampong Division where a Divisional Treasury was established in addition to existing sub-Division Treasuries and a considerable increase in revenue and

[1] *Gold Coast Legislative Council Debates, 1946 Session.*
[2] Chap. VI, 'British Rule and the Chief: I. Social Change'.

development occurred. A new layout was evolved for Mampong Town, and the Mampong Town Committee has already carried out important anti-erosion works and street construction.[1]

That this marks a change of policy may be judged from the fact that when in 1942 the Mampong Literary Club (Kontonkyi Club) asked that an Advisory Finance Board to the Native Authority might be formed, the chief objected. Many of the Divisions now have town boards, and education and finance committees.

Many of the other functions of the Kumasi Native Authority are carried out by its paid clerical staff. It is seldom that the administrative functions of a Native Authority bring all the members together. In particular, the members of the many subordinate Native Authorities of the Kumasi Division have had little part in direct administration. It is the religious ceremonies that bring them together; and occasionally, when there is a major political dispute, the full council of the Division meets. Normally, it is in the offices of the secretaries and clerks that most of the administrative work is done. The Asantehene visits the Chief Secretary's office every morning to deal with complaints, sign letters, or discuss matters arising out of official correspondence. The Asantehene has a separate office of his own in the palace where he deals personally with correspondence, answers telephone calls, and issues instructions. He is also kept busy settling complaints out of court. Some of these he deals with in his office at the palace, in the presence of a few of his elders and Akyeame, and sometimes one or other of the secretaries. Other complaints are settled in the Chief Registrar's office where the complainants await the Asantehene's daily visits. Others are settled at *Adwarease*, that is, 'at the bath'. It is a traditional custom that chiefs and councillors as well as commoners who have questions or complaints to put before the Asantehene do so at the palace immediately after his bath when he sits to deal with such matters. Complaints are also settled at *Kwakwiram*, one of the inner halls of the palace. There are always small crowds at these places waiting to lay their complaints personally before the Asantehene. The matters dealt with are various: marriage disputes, matters affecting chiefs and their kinsmen, assaults and insults, breaches of custom, stool disputes, and so on. Some of these are referred to the courts, but many of them are settled cheaply in this traditional way by which any one may

---

[1] *Gold Coast Legislative Council Debates, 1946 Session*, Appendix.

claim the personal aid of the Asantehene. The chiefs of the various Divisions similarly settle complaints out of court among their subjects, though they are not called upon to exercise this function as often as in the past when there were no District Commissioners, or civil summonses by which private injuries were brought before the courts. The oath was used but sparingly, for it was expensive. Whether one was found innocent or guilty, one incurred a debt, for the use of the oath was the transgression of a tribal taboo. As the Ashanti proverb has it : 'The chief's oath is like the hole in which yam is planted; no one falls into it and comes out scot-free.'[1]

There are separate Treasury offices where the financial clerk and his staff deal with the finances of the Division. As in other Divisions the sources of revenue are land rents, court fines and fees, various licences, royalties from mines or timber concessions, cocoa tribute, and the direct annual tax. The expenditure is mostly on the costs of administration, but, as is now general throughout Ashanti, the Kumasi Division votes generous grants for educational work.

The Kumasi Native Authority has a number of road-overseers who are in charge not only of the roads and bridges which come under the supervision of the Native Authority, but also of the sanitation and cleanliness of the neighbouring villages. It has also a Native Authority prison and police station in Kumasi.

It is relevant to point out that Kumasi has a town council which is a body independent of the Native Authority. The Kumasi Town Council was constituted by ordinance in 1943, and it replaced the Kumasi Public Health Board which, inaugurated in 1924, was constituted under ordinance in 1937. The town council consists of three official, three nominated, and six elected members. The official members are government representatives, and the Assistant Chief Commissioner is the President of the town council. The Asantehene and the Kumasi Divisional Council nominate two members, and the Kumasi Chamber of Commerce one member. The town has been divided into six wards for electoral purposes, and each ward elects a member.

The town council exercises powers provided under certain Government ordinances, principally the auction sales, diseases of animals, liquor licences, mosquitoes, motor traffic, and the petroleum ordinances. Amongst its duties the town council regulates the sale of fish, vegetables, and other foodstuffs within

[1] Ɔhene ntam te sɛ bayerɛ amena; obi ntɔ mu mfa ne ho mfiri tɔtr otɔo mfi adi da.

the town of Kumasi; it provides, maintains, and supervises the public markets, slaughter-houses, public latrines, &c.; it supplies electric lighting, regulates any trade or business which may be injurious to public health, and makes rules for the use and conduct of public vehicles plying for hire. It has generally power to 'undertake all other works, matters and services necessary for or conducive to the public safety, health or convenience as it shall think fit'.[1]

The provision of services for the urban area of Kumasi is thus the responsibility not of the Native Authority but of a new rival body the members of which are partly nominated and partly elected by ballot.

This review has made it clear that a chief no longer rules in his own right. Native Authorities have their powers and duties prescribed and closely supervised by Government. It is Government policy that determines what purposes a Native Authority pursues. At present, from the Government point of view, a Native Authority best discharges its functions when it has an effectively run Treasury and is able to provide health and welfare services and development works. This again may be illustrated from the Chief Commissioner's report on Ashanti for 1945:

During the last two years steady progress has been made in the development of Ashanti Native Treasuries. The revenue has risen from £51,500 in 1942–3 to an estimated figure of £109,000. The increase is partially due to the National Fund which in its first year produced approximately £22,400, and to numerous levies imposed by the Divisional Council for development works and for the liquidation of debts. Of the national levy, two-thirds are spent in the Division in which it is collected and one-third is paid to the Confederacy Council, and all is to be spent on development or welfare services. A notable feature has been the increased interest in education. In 1941–2, the Native Treasuries contributed some £461 while the expenditure for 1944–5 is estimated at £13,778.[2]

The response which the Native Authorities have given to Government lead and policy is best told in figures. On p. 163 is a summary of the revenue and expenditure of Native Authorities in Ashanti for the last six years. It may be stated that Government policy has been to make grants to Native Authorities based on the

[1] *Kumasi Town Council Ordinance* (1943).
[2] *Gold Coast Legislative Council Debates, 1945*, Appendix.

amounts that each Native Authority spends on education and development works. A Native Authority gets from Government a grant equivalent to its own expenditure on these items.

Native Authorities Finance—Ashanti

	1941–2 Actual	1942–3 Actual	1943–4 Actual	1944–5 Actual	1945–6 Actual	1946–7 Estimated
REVENUE	£	£	£	£	£	£
1. Taxation	1,956	3,880	6,220	37,267	38,231	67,890
2. Court fees				12,422	19,011	25,443
3. Licences and other fees	24,797	30,480	19,607			
				42,736	56,042	65,277
4. Land: Rent, tolls, &c.	12,595	13,304	42,636	13,393	14,441	21,284
5. Government grant (grant in aid)	294	123	313	713	34,057*	29,079†
6. Interest and recovery of loans	5,091	2,054	3,553	1,054	964	880
7. Miscellaneous				2,341	4,289	3,049
TOTALS	44,733	49,841	72,329	109,926	167,035	212,902
EXPENDITURE						
A. *Administration*						
1. Administration	30,499	33,330	46,567	26,961	32,868	36,766
2. Divisional				15,117	19,198	31,064
3. Judicial				1,787	2,540	6,987
4. Police				3,144	3,875	8,833
5. Prisons				781	843	1,174
6. Miscellaneous (including litigation and debts)	3,183	2,590	2,189	11,900	10,797*	16,769†
B. *Developments*						
7. Development recurrent	729	648	1,306	2,075	6,277	8,805
8. Education	365	869	1,711	5,596	25,971*	51,958†
9. Medical and health	963	2,194	2,877	5,031	6,656	15,935
10. Agric. and forestry				149	237	1,299
11. Miscellaneous services	689	684	86			
				6,875	6,596	7,306
12. Extraordinary works (capital works)	3,335	4,428	3,761	7,791	21,718*	43,030†
TOTALS	39,763	44,743	58,497	87,207	137,576	229,926

* Including some £4,000 grants by one Native Authority to another paid out under heads 6, 8, and 12.

† Including some £3,000 grants by one Native Authority to another paid out under heads 6, 8, and 12.

For these new functions of a Native Authority competent staff and Advisory Committees have been found to be more effective and to play a more important part than the traditional councillors whose direct participation in administration is now small.

The District Commissioner, representing the central government, plays a more important role than the chief. He has wider powers, and is more familiar with the Government policy which directs and inspires the actions of the Native Authority. The chief's subjects and the strangers living in his Division, whether within or outside his jurisdiction, seek the help of the District Commissioner in some cases more than they do the chief's. The Native Authority has not full control over the area within its authority, but shares it with the more powerful Government.

The result of all this has been to weaken the personal ties between chief and subject. This is partly responsible for the all too ready disposition of the subject to destool the chief that has been manifest in the frequent constitutional disputes.[1]

But within the limits prescribed for them, the Native Authorities are learning their new functions. A big step was taken when in 1942, inspired by the Government, the Confederacy Council decided to impose an annual tax throughout all the Divisions within the Confederacy, and to establish a National Fund for the development of the whole nation. We now proceed to the examination of the work of this new Native Authority, the Ashanti Confederacy Council.

[1] See Chap. IX, 'The Chief to-day' below. Also compare Nadel, *A Black Byzantium*, 1942, p. 168: 'Two competing authorities of different range of power existing side by side and concerned with the same or closely similar domains of social life must be in danger of frustrating each other, as individuals dissatisfied with the decisions of one may be tempted to obtain help from the other. The elimination or surrender of the weaker authority is the result.'

CHAPTER VIII
THE ASHANTI CONFEDERACY COUNCIL

T HE Ashanti Confederacy Council as restored by Government in 1935 is governed by legislation defining the area of its authority, and setting out its powers and constitution.[1] It is still undergoing rapid changes in its constitution and powers. New laws are passed every year as experience dictates to enable the council to extend its activities. This chapter covers the work of the council during the first ten years of its existence.

The Ashanti Confederacy Council is a Native Authority for a specified area which includes the Divisions of Kumasi, Mampong, Juaben, Bekwai, Essumeja, Kokofu, Nsuta, Adansi, Kumawu, Offinsu, Ejisu, Agona, Banda, Wenchi, Mo, Abeasi, Nkoranza, Jaman, Berekum, Techiman, and Dormaa. These cover an area of 24,560 square miles, and have a total population of 818,944 (1948 Census).

The members of the council are the Asantehene, the head chiefs of the Divisions specified above, the chiefs of each of the nine Kumasi clans,[2] and seven Extraordinary Members from the Kumasi Division. The present members of the council (1946) are the following:

Ex-officio members

1. *Asantehene*
2. *Mamponghene*
3. *Juabenhene*
4. *Nsutahene*
5. *Bekwaihene*
6. *Kokofuhene*
7. *Essumejahene*
8. *Dormaahene*
9. *Adansihene*
10. *Nkoranzahene*
11. *Offinsuhene*
12. *Ejisuhene*
13. *Kumawuhene*
14. *Agonahene*
15. *Techimanhene*
16. *Jamanhene* (Drobo)
17. *Wenchihene*
18. *Berekumhene*
19. *Bandahene*
20. *Abeasehene*
21. *Mohene*

---

[1] The main ordinances are set out in Apps. IV and V.

[2] 'Clan' here is used in the sense in which it is used by Government to indicate the military groups of mixed lineages formed for the defence of Kumasi. These groups are the basis of the civil administration of Kumasi. See Chap. V, 'The Ashanti Union'. This use of the word is applicable to Kumasi only, not to the rest of Ashanti.

Clan chiefs

22. *Kontihene*	Kumasi	27. *Gyasehene*	Kumasi
23. *Akwamuhene*	,,	28. *Kyidɔmhene*	,,
24. *Adɔntenhene*	,,	29. *Ankɔbeahene*	,,
25. *Tafohene*	,,	30. *Manwerehene*	,,
26. *Oyokohene*	,,		

31–7: Seven Extraordinary Members, appointed by the *ex-officio* members of the council

Mr. J. B. Edusei

Dr. I. B. Asafu-Adjaye

Mr. E. O. Asafu-Adjaye (Barrister-at-Law)

Mr. H. A. Hayfron Benjamin (Barrister-at-Law)

Mr. I. K. Agyeman

Mr. J. S. Kankam

Mr. C. E. Osei

Co-opted members

38. *Asantehemaa* (queen-mother of Ashanti)

39. *Kuntanasihene*

40. *Sumahene*

41. *Danyasehene*

42. *Asokorehene*

43. *Nkwantahene*

44. *Beposohene*

The Confederacy Council has recognized 38–44 as members, but their names have not yet been published in the Government *Gazette*.

Powers of the Ashanti Confederacy Council

The council is authorized to exercise the powers conferred upon Native Authorities by sections 6, 7, 8, 15, and 16 of the Native Authority (Ashanti) Ordinance.[1]

By section 6 the council may 'interpose for the purpose of preventing, and to the best of its ability to prevent, the commission of any offence within the area of its authority by any native subject to its jurisdiction'.

Section 7 enjoins every native to attend before Government officers when so directed by the Ashanti Confederacy Council. Section 8 empowers the council to issue orders to be obeyed by

---

[1] See App. V for full text.

such natives within its area as may be subject to its jurisdiction for all or any of the following purposes:

(a) Prohibiting, restricting, or regulating the manufacture, distillation, consumption, &c., of intoxicating liquors.

(b) Prohibiting, restricting, or regulating gambling.

(c) Prohibiting, restricting, or regulating the carrying and possession of weapons.

(d) Prohibiting, restricting, or regulating hunting and fishing.

(e) Prohibiting any act or conduct which might cause riot or a disturbance or breach of the peace.

(f) Preventing the pollution of water.

(g) Prohibiting, restricting, or regulating the cutting or destruction of trees.

(h) Requiring natives to report cases of infectious or contagious disease.

(i) Requiring natives to report offenders.

(j) Requiring the birth, death, marriage, or divorce of any native subject to its jurisdiction to be reported.

(k) Prohibiting, restricting, or regulating the movement of livestock through the area of its authority.

(l) Prohibiting, restricting, or regulating the burning of grass or bush.

(m) For the purpose of exterminating or preventing the spread of tsetse fly and locusts.

(n) Prohibiting, restricting, regulating, or requiring to be done any matter or thing which by virtue of any native law or custom for the time being in force, and not repugnant to morality or justice, it has power to prohibit, restrict, regulate, or require to be done.

(o) Prohibiting, restricting, or regulating the construction of buildings.

(p) Requiring the removal of dangerous or ruinous buildings and of buildings constructed in contravention of any order issued under the Native Authority (Ashanti) Ordinance.

(q) Generally for the improvement of sanitation and for the better preservation of health within the area of its authority.

(r) For any other purpose whether similar to those hereinbefore enumerated or not which may, by notice published in the *Gazette*, be sanctioned by the Governor either generally or for any particular area.

Section 15 empowers the Confederacy Council to make rules providing for the peace, good order, and welfare of natives within the area of its authority, and to impose as penalties for the breach of any rule a fine of £50 or imprisonment with or without hard labour for two years, or both such fine and imprisonment.

Section 16 authorizes the Confederacy Council to establish a native treasury, with the approval of the Governor.

Native Law and Custom

The scope of the Council's activities was widened by the Native Law and Custom (Ashanti Confederacy) Ordinance 1940.[1] The important provisions of the ordinance are in clauses 3 (1) and 4 (1). Clause 3 (1) reads:

> The Confederacy Council may at any time record in writing a declaration of what in its opinion is the native law and custom within the Confederacy relating to any subject, and submit such declaration to the Chief Commissioner for the consideration of the Governor in Council.

Clause 4 (1) reads:

> The Confederacy Council may submit to the Chief Commissioner for the consideration of the Governor in Council any recommendation for the modification of native law and custom which it may consider expedient for the good government and welfare of the Confederacy.

Constitutional Cases

Constitutional cases are specially provided for. An amendment to the Native Authority (Ashanti) Ordinance (No. 2 of 1940) empowers the Chief Commissioner to transfer constitutional disputes to a Committee of Inquiry or the Confederacy Council. The relevant sections of this amendment are the following:

> 11 B. Provided that if the cause, matter, question or dispute arises within the Confederacy, the Chief Commissioner may either appoint a Committee of Inquiry or refer the same to the Confederacy Council for decision.
>
> 11 C. The Chief Commissioner may in his discretion transfer to the Confederacy Council for decision any cause, matter, question, or dispute of a constitutional nature which is pending before a Divisional Council within the Confederacy.
>
> 11 G. (1) For the purposes of 11 B and 11 C the Confederacy Council shall be constituted by the Asantehene (who shall be president) and

[1] See App. VI.

four other members, of whom at least two shall be Head Chiefs of the Divisions specified as being within the Ashanti Confederacy.

(2) In case of the temporary illness or absence of the Asantehene, the Asantehene may appoint a Head Chief to act as President of the Confederacy Council for the purpose of this section until he shall resume the duties thereof.

This summarizes the main ordinances governing the Ashanti Confederacy Council. By them the council is constituted a Native Authority over the Divisions which are within the Confederacy. It may make rules for certain specified purposes, and, generally, for the 'peace, good order and welfare of the natives within the area of its authority'; it may declare or modify native law and custom, and it may adjudicate in matters of a constitutional nature referred to it by the Chief Commissioner.

The Union and the Confederacy

An examination of these ordinances shows that in certain important respects the Confederacy Council is different from the old Ashanti Union.

The membership of the Confederacy Council follows the traditional lines of the old, except that a departure has been made by the appointment of seven educated members to represent the views of the educated commoners of Kumasi. But the functions of the Confederacy as defined in the ordinances are different from those of the Union. The former is to be an administrative body with legislative and judicial powers. The latter was primarily a military council, which also met periodically on ceremonial occasions, and was occasionally summoned to meet as a judicial council.

The Ashanti Confederacy Council is made a Native Authority for the Divisions within the Confederacy. This involves the necessary consequence that the Ashanti Confederacy Council and the Divisions, or regional Native Authorities, both operate directly upon the people. Every native is in effect subject to two Native Authorities, the general and the regional, both of which now make laws and regulations which affect him directly.

Another important change is this. With regard to the powers conferred by sections 6, 7, 8, 15, and 16 of the Native Authority (Ashanti) Ordinance, the same matters lie within the spheres of both the general and regional Native Authorities. They may both legislate on the matters within the scope of these sections con-currently for the same area. The ordinances do not say which law is to prevail over the other in the event of both the general and regional governments legislating upon the same subject; but no conflict came to my notice in the course of my field-work. The ordinances do, however, set aside the principle which governed the old Ashanti Union, namely, that each of the Divisions was solely responsible for matters which affected itself alone. Each Division had a greater degree of autonomy. The Confederacy Council may now not only legislate directly for the subjects of the Divisions, but may legislate concurrently with the Divisions upon certain subjects.

The Confederacy Council has legislative powers but no execu-tive agents of its own. In practice, the chiefs of the Divisions are the executive agents of the council. When it makes laws affecting the Divisions, it is left to the chiefs to enforce them. An example of this practice may be given. In 1938 the council made an order prohibiting the planting of new cocoa-trees. The penalty for con-travening the order was a fine of £5 or two months imprisonment, in addition to the destruction of the cocoa-trees planted.

It was left to the chiefs to enforce this order in their Divisions. In 1945 the Chief Commissioner wrote to the Asantehene inform-ing him that Government Departmental officers had reported that new cocoa had been extensively planted in North-western Ashanti, particularly in the Dormaa and Nkwanta areas, contrary to the order made by the Confederacy Council. The Chief Commissioner pointed out that it was unfair for individuals in certain areas to be prosecuted if chiefs in other areas did not take steps to enforce the orders of the council.

When this matter came up for discussion at the council, the representative of the Dormaa Division informed the council that he was not aware that some people in the Dormaa Division had been planting new cocoa. 'I can assure the council', he added, 'that the Native Authorities in the Dormaa Division are very particular about this order of the Council and would not spare anyone they discover disobeying it.'[1]

The Nkwantahene said: 'I have never condoned the infringe-ment of this order of the council in my sub-division. Rather, to my disappointment, the summonses I prepared for execution against

---

[1] Minutes of the Confederacy Council (1945).

those I found disobeying the order were not allowed by Government.'

The Mamponghene, who was presiding in the absence of the Asantehene, observed, 'You have heard the explanations of the Dormaa Representative, and the Nkwantahene. In the circumstances, I advise that we do not press the matter any further, but ask the Native Authorities of Dormaa and Nkwanta Divisions to see to it that this order of the council is strictly enforced.'[1]

The Chief Commissioner's letter, and the subsequent discussion at the council make clear what the constitutional practice is. The Confederacy Council legislates for the Divisions, and leaves it to the Native Authorities of these Divisions to enforce the orders. It may be added that there is no legislation prescribing what action the Confederacy Council can take against a Native Authority which does not enforce its orders, or refuses to do so.

This raises the question of the sanctions for the powers which the Confederacy Council is authorized to exercise. As regards the Ashanti Union, the sanctions for duties or levies which it could exact were the religious sanctions of sentiments of attachment to the Golden Stool, and reverence for the ancestors, and the secular sanction of force. The Asantehene could declare war on a recalcitrant member.

A recent occurrence showed how the powers of the Confederacy Council may be enforced. In 1945 the Bekwai Native Authority declared that it had ceased to be a member of the Confederacy Council, and the Bekwaihene refused to attend the meetings of the council. As there was no way of dealing with the matter, the council decided to refer it to the Chief Commissioner for the information of Government. The Asantehene remarked that in the old days there would have been only one way of dealing with the matter, namely, by waging war against Bekwai. Government dealt with the matter by empowering the District Commissioner of Bekwai to exercise the powers of a Native Authority within the Bekwai Division.[2] The Native Authority was divested of all its powers by order of the Governor. The chief and all the elders of Bekwai were subsequently destooled by the people of Bekwai and their successors agreed to rejoin the Confederacy Council. The

---

[1] Minutes of the Confederacy Council (1945).

[2] Order No. 19 of 1945, made under section 3, sub-section 9, of the Native Authority (Ashanti) Ordinance.

authority of Government is thus the ultimate sanction for the powers which the Ashanti Confederacy Council now exercises.

The range of interest of the Confederacy Council

A survey of the topics that the Confederacy Council has discussed at the seven sessions it has held since 1938 will indicate how it has used its powers, its development, and the range of its interests.

First Session held in 1935

The council appointed five Extraordinary Members to represent the educated section of the community. These were all residents of Kumasi.

Under section 15 of the Native Authority Ordinance it made two sets of rules, one for the control of company hunting, and another prohibiting the sale of cocoa that had not been thoroughly dried.

A lengthy discussion was held regarding the large sums of money expended on funeral customs, and a committee was appointed to consider the question and draft rules for modifying the customs so as to cut down the expenditure of time and money.

A second committee was appointed to consider the question of stool debts, and to suggest ways and means whereby any debts or liabilities of stools might be paid off.

The council decided that each chief attending a session of the council should bring with him only four of his elders, a spokesman (*Ɔkyeame*) and a clerk. This was to cut down expenditure.

A long time was spent discussing whether or not an apology rendered by anyone through the Golden Stool should be refused. That is, if anyone approached the Asantehene to intercede on his behalf in any cause or matter, should such apology be refused by the one to whom it is rendered when the Asantehene acts as mediator?

Another question discussed concerned bribery and corruption in connexion with the election of chiefs. The council agreed that measures should be taken to check the practice whereby electors accepted bribes from candidates for election to stools.

The council considered a proposal to impose an annual levy and decided that it could not recommend the levy because, if it were imposed, the people would cease to render their customary services to the chiefs.

Second Session, 1936

The council passed rules governing the behaviour of stool royals. It also agreed to send a petition to Government for the restoration of Kumasi lands to the Golden Stool.

Third Session, 1938

The council agreed to institute a National Fund by a levy of sixpence on every load (60 lb.) of cocoa sold in Ashanti. The Asantehene explained, 'What we want is a National Fund to enable us to carry on a progressive programme of public and social services for the benefit of the whole Ashanti people.'[1] Although a resolution was passed, the fund was not instituted, because the council had not been given powers by Government to enable it to impose such a levy.

A resolution was passed prohibiting the planting of new cocoa-trees, in order to direct attention to the growing of food crops.

The expenses connected with the destoolment and installation of chiefs were considered, and a committee was appointed to discuss 'the offering and accepting of bribes in connexion with the destoolment and election of chiefs, and to make recommendations'.

Another committee was appointed to discuss the custom dealing with the recovery of marriage expenses from the wife on the dissolution of a marriage, and to suggest modifications.

This committee was also asked to fix new rates of rent payable to the respective stools by cocoa-farmers. A rent of one penny per tree had been found excessive.

The council resolved that cinematograph films shown in Ashanti should be censored. The Asantehene explained that: 'The object of introducing this by-law was to stop the screening of certain films which have had a detrimental effect on the morals of the majority of our children in this country.'[1]

Fourth Session, 1941

The council discussed the custom whereby a deceased husband's or father's property was inherited by his maternal kinsmen to the exclusion of widows and children. It was pointed out that

[1] Minutes of the Confederacy Council (1938).

the custom led to frequent litigation between widows and children on the one side, and nephews on the other. The council was unable to make any ruling on the matter.

A considerable part of the session was spent in considering Captain Warrington's *Notes on Ashanti Custom*. It was decided in the end to appoint a committee to review the notes and submit its recommendations for the approval of the council.

Cocoa tribute was again discussed, and the council decided that farmers should pay a tribute of one farthing per tree instead of the previous scale of payments drawn up by the committee appointed by the council at its third session in 1938.

The council drew up a list of acts which were considered to be offences according to native law and custom. The offences included farm-work on Thursdays.

Fifth Session, 1942

In order to encourage the tapping of rubber, which had become important for the war, rules were passed to regulate its sale. Similar rules were passed regarding palm-trees.

Rules were passed modifying the custom of renewing one's allegiance to one's chief by the 'drinking of fetish',[1] to enable Christians and Mohammedans to swear according to their religious belief.

A deputation representing the Christian churches in Ashanti met the Confederacy Council and protested against compelling Christians to observe Thursday as a sacred day. The council appointed a committee to meet the representatives of the churches to discuss the matter further, as no agreement was reached about it.

To encourage Ashanti youths to enlist for service in the army, a resolution was passed permitting a man serving in the forces to claim an adultery fee of £9. 6s.

The council again varied the rents payable in respect of cocoa. It decided that cocoa tribute should be on the basis of 1d. for eight trees, and that no tribute should be paid in respect of trees which were not in bearing.

The committee appointed to consider Captain Warrington's *Notes on Ashanti Custom* submitted its report.

It was unanimously decided that a National Fund should be

---

[1] This consisted of drinking a mixture of rum and medicine washed from the top of a shrine (*obosom*).

established, and that an annual levy of 2*s*. per man and 1*s*. per woman be collected for this purpose. Of the total sum collected in each Division, the Division was to retain two-thirds, and pay one-third into the central fund.

A rule was made to the effect that all marriages under native law and custom should be reported to the chief, and that a registration fee of 5*s*. should be paid in respect of every such marriage.

A committee was appointed 'to consider the Native Authority and Native Courts (Ashanti) Ordinance and make necessary amendments or recommendations regarding same for submission to Government for consideration'.

The Committee appointed to discuss Captain Warrington's *Notes on Ashanti Custom* was asked to consider and submit Estimates for the buildings and staff of a special secretariat for the Confederacy Council.

Sixth Session, 1943

The Confederacy Council discussed a Government Ordinance to establish an Advisory Council for Ashanti and decided to ask Government to repeal the Ordinance, and give Ashanti representation in the Legislative Council.

The council decided to accept the oath of a Christian as an alternative to the swearing of the Great Oath as a method of bringing causes before native courts for judicial settlement.

Two chiefs, the Denyasehene and the Sumahene were made members of the council.

The next question discussed was whether or not the property acquired by a chief out of his personal allowance should remain his on his deposition or abdication. It was agreed that on vacating a stool a chief might retain any property so acquired by him, but that he might leave any regalia he had made as his contribution to stool property.

A committee was appointed to consider the custom of mortgaging farm-lands, and to submit recommendations for checking the practice.

The Asantehene informed the council that, acting on its recommendation, Government had approved that charges brought against Divisional chiefs should be heard by the Confederacy Council instead of the Divisional Councils concerned. The scales of fees payable at the hearing of such constitutional cases were fixed.

The Asantehene undertook to appoint 'guardians' to act as intermediaries between himself and any destooled chiefs who stayed in Kumasi.

It was decided that chiefs and other State officials should contribute to the National Fund, and a scale of annual payments was drawn up for them.

The amounts that chiefs should pay when they took the oath of allegiance to the Asantehene on their enstoolment were standardized. For this purpose, chiefs were divided into four categories: Grades I, II, III, IV, the amounts payable being respectively: £37. 4s., £27. 18s., £18. 12s., for Grades I to III, and £9. 6s., £4. 13s., or £2. 7s., for chiefs of Grade IV who are all Kumasi chiefs.

A Confederacy Council Finance Board consisting of twenty-seven members representing all the Divisions was constituted.

The council decided that chiefs should be permitted to undergo surgical operations when a medical officer certified this to be necessary.

It was decided that non-Ashanti residents in Ashanti should pay the annual levy, and that Ashantis should pay to the Divisions in which they were resident and not to the Divisions of which they were subjects by birth.

The committee appointed to discuss with the representatives of the Churches the observance of Thursday as a sacred day reported that no agreement had been reached on the matter.

Seventh Session, 1945

Before this session the Standing Committee of the council discussed each item of the agenda. The full council met to consider the recommendations of the committee.

The council accepted the committee's suggestions for collecting the National Fund.

By-laws and regulations for game preservation were passed.

The council adopted the committee's recommendation that Government should be asked to amend its proposed Cocoa Marketing Scheme in order to give the producers a majority representation on the Board.

It was agreed that adultery fines should be standardized and that a uniform scale should be fixed for all the Divisions at the next session of the council.

It was also agreed that the offences for which, according to native custom, sheep should be slaughtered at the trial, should be specified and legalized by a special provision in the ordinance. The Standing Committee was asked to draw up a list for the next session.

The council supported the Standing Committee's recommendations to reject the Chief Commissioner's suggestion for a reorganization of the Confederacy Council, and decided to retain its present membership.[1]

The council approved a Five-Year Scholarship Scheme envisaging a total expenditure of £39,950 for the award of scholarships tenable at secondary schools and colleges in West Africa and at universities in Great Britain.

The range of the Council's interests

This synopsis covers the main topics discussed by the council at the seven sessions it has held during the first ten years of its existence. The disconnected list of topics can only be understood in their proper context and against the background of social change indicated in previous chapters. Here, it shows the total range of the interests of the Confederacy Council. It will be observed that the matters it has discussed cover every aspect of the national life: economic, political, social, and religious.

The topics which have received the most attention are cocoa and the chief. This correctly reflects the dominant interests of the community. The economic activities which are causing structural changes in Ashanti centre round the cocoa industry. The structural changes in turn have necessitated certain modifications in custom to accord with new social facts.

The position of the chief is a crucial problem in the whole process of social change. His personal insecurity has its counterpart in a general social insecurity.

The committee system

The summary also brings out the fact that most of the work of the council has been done by committees. This has been the most outstanding development of the Confederacy Council.

---

[1] The council at its meeting in October 1946 accepted the recommendations for a reorganization of the council.

The following *ad hoc* committees have been appointed:

First Session, 1935

  1. A committee of six members was appointed to consider the question of stool debts.

  2. A second committee of twenty-four members was appointed to consider funeral rites and to draft rules to govern their celebration.

Third Session, 1938

  3. A committee of twenty-six members was appointed to make recommendations on annual payments to be made by cocoa-farmers to stools, and also on the recovery of marriage expenses after divorce or dissolution of marriages under native law and custom.

  4. Another committee was appointed to discuss the offering and accepting of bribes in connexion with the destoolment and election of chiefs.

Fourth Session, 1941

  5. A committee of thirty-two members was appointed to review Captain Warrington's *Notes on Ashanti Custom*.

Fifth Session, 1942

  6. A committee of ten members was appointed 'to consider the Native Authority and Native Courts (Ashanti) Ordinance and make the necessary amendments and recommendations regarding same for submission to Government for its consideration'.

Sixth Session, 1943

  7. A committee of eight members was appointed to discuss the mortgaging of farm-lands and building-plots.

  8. A committee of eight members was appointed to consider 'the marriage policy regarding Ashanti royals as proposed by the Mamponghene'.

  9. A third committee was appointed to meet representatives of the Churches to discuss the observance of Thursday as a sacred day.

Permanent committees

In addition to these *ad hoc* committees, three permanent committees have been appointed: the Ashanti Confederacy Education Committee, the Confederacy Standing Committee, and the Confederacy Finance Board.

The Education Committee consists of twelve members, and was responsible with the Standing Committee for drawing up the Ashanti Confederacy Scholarship Scheme.

The Finance Board consists of twenty-seven members, representing the Constituent Divisions of the Confederacy. Its function is to control the expenditure of the central Confederacy Fund raised from the annual levy. It has also been entrusted with the task of revising the salaries paid to employees of the Native Authorities.

At the fifth session of the Confederacy Council held in 1942 the Asantehene suggested to the council that in view of its increasing duties, and of the difficulties of travel due to war-time restrictions, a Standing Committee should be appointed to act for the council. The suggestion was accepted, and the committee which had been appointed to review the *Notes on Ashanti Custom* was appointed a Standing Committee of the Confederacy Council.

At the next session, in 1943, the Asantehene again suggested that it would help to expedite the work of the council, and ensure that matters which came before it were thoroughly discussed if a Standing Committee considered every item of the agenda for each session beforehand, and submitted recommendations for the consideration of the full council. A committee of fifteen members was accordingly appointed. This committee replaced the previous one of thirty-two members which had originally been appointed to consider Captain Warrington's *Notes on Ashanti Custom*.

The Secretary of the Confederacy Council is an *ex-officio* member of the Standing Committee. The rest are selected by the council. The committee (1946) consists of fourteen members, seven of whom are chiefs. It has no legislative powers, and acts only in an advisory capacity. Its main function is to make recommendations for consideration by the plenary session of the council. The Asantehene expects to be consulted before the recommendations of the committee are submitted to the full council. In practice, no recommendations have been submitted without his previous consent.

The literate members of the Council

A noteworthy feature of the Confederacy Council is the part that the literate members have been enabled to play. They have served on many of the committees. The following table makes clear the extent to which they have been used.

In 1942 the full council consisted of 39 members of whom 11 were literate. In 1946 the membership was 44, of whom 17 were literate.

The composition of the various committees was as follows:

Year	Committee	Total number	Number of literates
1935	Committee on stool debts	6	2
	Committee on funeral custom	24	1
1938	Committee on annual rent and marriage . .	26	3
1941	Committee on Ashanti custom . . .	32	2
1942	Committee on Native Authority and Native Courts Ordinance	10	8
1943	Committee on mortgaging of lands and building plots	8	6
	Committee on marriage policy of Ashanti royals .	8	3
PERMANENT BOARDS MEMBERSHIP			
1946	Finance Board	27*	27
	Education Committee	12*	12
	Standing Committee	14	12

* Includes co-opted representatives who are not members of the council.

The table shows that on matters of native law and custom the committees have consisted of a majority of the illiterate chiefs who are the better informed on such matters. On those dealing with modern changes such as education, the mortgaging of lands, finance, or ordinances, the literates have been in the majority on the committees. The numbers of literates on the permanent committees indicate the increasing influence that the literate members of the council are exercising on its deliberations.

The evolution of the committee system, and the blend of literates and illiterates on the various committees, are evidences of the way the Confederacy Council is adapting itself for its new functions. We see at work the process by which it is changing from a cumbersome deliberative body into an administrative machinery.

The Asantehene as President of the Council

The President of the Confederacy Council is the Asantehene. His constitutional position is defined in sections 4 and 5 of the Ashanti Confederacy Council order.[1]

> Section 4. The Asantehene when present shall preside at the meetings of the said Council, and when he is from any cause whatsoever unable to attend a Head Chief or Chief nominated by the Asantehene, or in default of such nomination the next senior Chief present, shall preside.
>
> Section 5. The said Council shall be deemed to be properly constituted for the transaction of any business, if in the opinion of the Asantehene or of the person presiding in his absence the attendance of members is sufficient for the business to be transacted: Provided that in exercising his discretion the Asantehene or person presiding in his absence shall so far as practicable be guided by Native Customary Law.

This is all that is said. The Asantehene shall preside over the meetings of the council. He may in his absence appoint someone to preside, and he may at his discretion determine a quorum for the transaction of the council's business. His position has therefore to be studied from what he has actually done in the council.

The evolution of the council has depended very largely on the personality of the present Asantehene. His has been the predominant influence. This may best be shown from a study of the work and discussions of the council.

When the Confederacy Council was restored, it was made a condition that the Asantehene should not interfere in the domestic affairs of the various Divisions. This proviso was based on information given to Government by the chiefs who declared that to be the principle and practice of the Ashanti Union.

At the first session in 1935 the Confederacy Council unanimously passed a resolution worded by the Secretary to the Council as follows:

The Ashanti Confederacy Council in Session do hereby resolve and it is hereby resolved that the Asantehene being the Supreme Ruler or the highest Native Authority in Ashanti should be the Supreme Arbiter of all matters relating to enstoolments and destoolments of chiefs within the Confederacy and forming part of this assembly, his decision to be final and conclusive in such matters.[2]

---

[1] See App. IV.   [2] Minutes of the Confederacy Council (1935).

This indicates the way in which the position of the Asantehene was regarded by the assembled chiefs in 1935. The resolution was not enforced, but in 1943 Government agreed that constitutional matters concerning the election and deposition of Divisional chiefs could be heard by the Confederacy Council presided over by the Asantehene.

At the same session the Confederacy Council unanimously accepted the following proposals made by the committee appointed to consider the question of stool debts.

It was unanimously agreed that every chief whose Stool is at present in debt should submit to his principal Elders an account of the said debt explaining the circumstances which necessitated the incurring of the debt. The Elders should agree to all items of expenditure which were reasonable and fair.

In the event of there being a deadlock as to the reasonableness of a particular debt, the chief should refer the matter to the Asantehene for determination, and his decision thereon shall be final and binding both on the said chief and on the said Elders of the Stool. The subjects of the Stool should then be called upon to pay the necessary debts agreed upon by levy in the customary manner.[1]

At the same session the Asantehene proposed that he might be permitted to visit the various Divisions so that he could have first-hand knowledge of what was happening in each Division. The chiefs by a majority rejected this proposal. This shows that the chiefs did not intend that the 'Supreme Ruler or highest Native Authority' should interfere in the affairs of their respective Divisions. The inconsistency between this and the previous Resolution is obvious, but it indicates that there was no clear conception of the powers of the Asantehene.

The discussions of the third session of the council in 1938 throw some light on the way the position of the Asantehene has been developing in the Confederacy Council. During a discussion on the Ashanti custom of inheritance he said:[2]

I would like you all to understand that the items on the agenda were prepared by myself and submitted to you for your views. In doing so, I must explain to you that it is not my intention to change the native Customary Law of inheritance by substituting sons for nephews, but

[1] Minutes of the Confederacy Council (1935).
[2] Ibid. (1938).

I think that the time has now arrived that something must be done for wives and children who have faithfully served their husbands and fathers.

This is typical of what happens at each session. The Asantehene prepares the agenda, and generally opens the session with a speech outlining the business before the council. He also opens the discussion on each item, explaining the reasons for introducing it for discussion, and as a rule, he sums up the discussion of the council.

At the 1938 session he opened a discussion on cocoa-farms as follows:

Before we discuss this important item I wish to explain to you what prompted me to add it to the agenda. Judging from the recent famine, one can realize that if we still go on cultivating cocoa-farms, without paying attention to foodstuffs farming, in the course of a few years we may suffer from famine.[1]

He summed up the discussion thus:

As we are all unanimous now, it is hereby prohibited that any person who cultivates any more cocoa-farms shall be guilty of an offence and on conviction thereof shall be liable to a fine of £5 or two months imprisonment with or without hard labour, and in addition the Court trying him should order that the trees thus planted should be uprooted. This law is to come into force from the first day of January 1939.[1]

At the same session in 1938 during a discussion about the election and deposition of chiefs the Asantehene made a statement which shows the growth of his authority as president of the Confederacy Council:

At the first Session of the Confederacy Council, it was ruled that a chief must be warned thrice before he could be destooled, and this meeting reaffirms that ruling. Therefore any chief who has not been thrice warned, if he is destooled by his Elders and reported to me, I will not sanction and report it to Government for confirmation, and Government always wants my recommendation in either destoolment or enstoolment affairs before it can take any action thereon; and before I do so I must satisfy myself that the procedure adopted was in accord with this decision.[1]

The Asantehene has, nevertheless, been most insistent that everyone should freely express his opinion during the discussions of

[1] Ibid.

the council. The following statement made at the 1941 session is typical of what he has repeatedly said at every session:

> Before we tackle the business for this morning, I would like to explain what is meant by 'Council'. I should make it plain to all that each chief is a representative of his Division, and is to voice out the views and wishes of his people. No chief is bound to take any opinion expressed by me if he finds that he cannot accommodate it to his. Every member has the right to express his opinion freely on any subject that may be brought forward for discussion. This is why the Council has been established.[1]

This repeated instruction has been necessary because many of the chiefs are reluctant to express their views especially if they do not accord with the Asantehene's. By custom and tradition no one may oppose the occupant of the Golden Stool who is believed to speak with the wisdom and authority of the ancestors whose place he fills. The tradition grew up at a time when the Asantehene was not the president of a council which discussed matters affecting every aspect of life and every Division within the Confederacy. The chiefs express their views more freely than before, but this ancient belief, bound up as it is with reverence for the ancestors, still inhibits free discussion. A number of chiefs have in conversation confessed to having kept silent on various occasions rather than oppose the views of the Asantehene. The Asantehene himself is aware of this, and that is why at every session he has asked that everyone should freely express his opinion.

There are occasions, however, on which the Asantehene acts on his own prerogative and informs rather than consults the council. In 1941 he increased the membership of the council by creating a new chief whom he introduced to the council in these terms:

> As the agenda have been gone through, I have the pleasure to inform the Council that the Asantehene Nana Agyeman created a 'Fekuo' (Company) which he never named. I have augmented it and named it Manwere. I therefore introduce it to the Asanteman. The Head of the Fekuo is the Manwerehene and it is of equal political status as any of the other Kumasi clans, that is, the Manwerehene is promoted to the status of a Palanquin Chief. I ask the Secretary of the Council to bring this to the notice of the Government for the Manwerehene to be recognized as a member of the Confederacy Council as any of the Kumasi Senior Clan Chiefs.[1]

[1] Minutes of the Confederacy Council (1941).

The chiefs recognized this as an ancient prerogative of the Asantehene, and thanked him on behalf of the new Manwerehene.

Another instance may be cited. At the session of the council in 1943 the Asantehene informed the council: 'I have recommended to the Government to approve of the Denyasehene being made a member of the council. I would like to know what members have to say about this.'[1]

The Juabenhene replied: 'We have nothing to say but to thank the Otumfuo on behalf of the Denyasehene for his recommendation.'[1] The Kokofuhene supported this, and the council approved of the action taken by the Asantehene and thanked him.

The chiefs realize that the success of the council is due to the leadership that the Asantehene has given. Among the many speeches paying tribute to his work, we may quote the Kyidɔmhene's as typical of what all the other chiefs said at the close of the session in 1945:

We have to thank the Otumfuo for his devotion to the Country, and especially to the Council. We must pray for his health and continue to be loyal to him.

In the early days of the restoration of the Confederacy, some of us did not appear to appreciate its full significance; but now we have seen and are seeing the fruits of that act. Posterity will bless the Otumfuo and all who worked to make the restoration possible.[2]

In reply to this and the other tributes the Asantehene said, *inter alia*:[2]

I must thank you all for the co-operation you have shown which has made this Session such a success. I cannot repress the expression of my gratification at realizing that you do now express your frank opinions on matters which are brought before the Council for discussion. This shows that you have now realized that this Council exists for all of us and not for any one man and that we are responsible, collectively, for any decisions taken by the Council.

Almost every member who has spoken has been thanking me as though by my own efforts alone we have had such a successful Session. If any people need special thanks for the expeditious way in which this Session has been conducted, it is the members of our Standing Committee. We cannot be too grateful to the Standing Committee for their work.

[1] Minutes of the Confederacy Council (1943).
[2] Ibid. (1945).

The Confederacy Council as defined by ordinance

We have looked at the Confederacy Council as defined by ordinances. It is a council with authority over a specified area over which it has been given certain powers. It may interpose to prevent crime, it may issue orders or make rules on certain subjects, and generally for the peace, good order, and welfare of the natives within its area; it may declare or modify native custom, it may establish a treasury, and it may adjudicate in constitutional cases.

In membership it has followed the traditional lines of the old Union, but has appointed commoners who are not chiefs.

We have analysed the subjects it has discussed, and have seen that they cover a wide range and bear on every aspect of the life of the community. In its discussions it has given most attention to economic and political changes, centring round the cocoa industry and the position of the chief, and has made rules to modify custom in an effort to deal with some of the problems of social change.

In accordance with the new concepts of the function of a Native Authority as set before it by Government, the Confederacy Council has established a National Fund, and has begun to assist in administration. It has given priority to education, and the first disbursements of the Confederacy Fund have been for the award of scholarships tenable at educational institutions in West Africa and Great Britain.

The council has legislative powers, but relies on the constituent Native Authorities to execute and enforce its orders. The ultimate sanction it can bring to bear on these Native Authorities is the authority of Government.

It is limited in its authority and is subject to the overriding powers of the Chief Commissioner and the Governor.

The Asantehene is the President, but his powers and duties are not defined. The old Union not being an administrative or legislative body does not provide precedents for the new functions. But the chiefs accord the Asantehene the respect they are accustomed to give to the occupant of the Golden Stool. Within the council he has played the leading role, and has exercised the biggest influence on its development. The agenda have been prepared by him or under his direction; he has taken a leading part in the discussions, and has guided both the council and the Standing Committee in their work.

The Confederacy Council and the people

We may now look at the Confederacy Council as a social institution.

The chiefs who are members of the council have taken the opportunity of their being in Kumasi to discuss their common problems. Groups of three or four, or sometimes more, arrange meetings of their own to consider points arising out of the discussions of the council or other matters of common interest. The groups for these private discussions consisted of members bound by different sets of ties. There were three forms of alinement.

A group might consist of chiefs who are members of the same clan. Thus the chiefs of Offinsu and other chiefs of the Asona clan used to meet together.

A second type of group consisted of chiefs of the same wing, following the old military organization of the Ashanti Union. The chiefs of Essumeja, Kumawu, Hemang, and others of the left wing held their own meetings.

These two types of alinement follow traditional lines, and show how the ties of clanship or comradeship in arms which strengthened the old Union persist to strengthen the Confederacy Council.

A third type of grouping consisted of chiefs bound by personal friendships. The Mamponghene, the Berekumhene, and the Essumejahene often met to discuss problems that were to come before the general meeting of the council.

Many such spontaneous meetings are held between the sessions of the council, and are evidence of the growing co-operation among the chiefs.

Also, the Confederacy Council has given the chiefs a new sense of security. It was at the request of the chiefs themselves that Government conceded that constitutional cases should be tried by the Confederacy Council. At such trials the court consists of other chiefs, and there is no doubt that they give their fellow chiefs the most sympathetic hearing.

During the hearing of a constitutional case which involved a Divisional chief, it was found that the complainants were all commoners backed by only one elder, the Kontihene. The council dismissed the case without inquiring into the charges on the ground that the charges had been preferred by commoners and one chief only. Later, I asked one of the members of the council why the charges had not been investigated. His reply was: 'We shall not dig our own graves (*yentwa yɛ'amana*). If we start inquiring into charges preferred by mere commoners, no chief will remain on his stool for more than three months.'

On the other hand, the commoners complain that the chiefs now can do just as they like, because, 'We have no money to go to Kumasi'.

Moreover, since the restoration of the Confederacy, many cases have been settled in arbitration by the Asantehene personally without their coming before the council. In this way many chiefs have been saved from the expenses of litigation or even destoolment. This has won the support of the chiefs for the council.

On the other hand, there was evidence of a belief among the chiefs that the Confederacy Council has reduced their autonomy and is increasingly subordinating them to the Asantehene. The literate commoners were more blunt in their criticism. They called the Confederacy Council a 'one-man show'. This is due to the fact that the chiefs, the people, and the Asantehene himself all have different conceptions of what the powers of the Asantehene were in the old days, and there is no definite guide either from tradition or from the ordinances to clarify the present situation. The lack of certainty finds expression in mutual distrust and suspicion and fear.

For example, several chiefs talked to me about an order passed by the Confederacy Council prohibiting the cultivation of cocoa. These chiefs came from Divisions where its cultivation had started late, and at the time the order was passed their subjects were just beginning to cultivate it extensively. They pointed out that it was in the areas where cocoa had been planted for a long time that there was danger of famine through the neglect of food farming. As the order was made to apply to all the Divisions, their subjects were kept poor, because they could not cultivate cocoa, and, added one chief, 'Although I sympathize with them, I cannot help them. To-day no one has power save the Asantehene.'

Another instance cited by the chiefs to support their belief that their power was reduced was the fact that the Confederacy Council had not only decided that all chiefs should pay the annual levy, but had also fixed higher rates for them. In the past chiefs did not pay levies, as they had no personal property distinct from stool property. The rate now fixed for chiefs varies from £1 to 5s. a year. The annual rate for commoners is 2s. per man, and 1s. per woman.

Another source of grievance is the extra expense to which the chiefs are put in attending the sessions of the council. They usually stay a fortnight or more in Kumasi during each session. They have the responsibility of paying the travelling expenses of their retinues of elders and attendants and finding them board and lodging in Kumasi. They are able to recover some of the expenses from their stool treasuries, but never all. The figures given me by the chiefs as representing their out-of-pocket expenses, excluding what they recovered from their stool treasuries, varied between £10 and £80 a session. Some of them have very poor quarters to live in when they visit Kumasi. For these reasons the chiefs, especially those who live a long way from Kumasi, absent themselves from meetings on such pretexts as lack of transport, urgent matters requiring their presence in their States, funeral rites, or ill health.

The biggest source of distrust, suspicion, and fear, however, is the advantage that the residents in Kumasi have taken of the chiefs who live outside Kumasi. The most noticeable thing that struck me when I began my inquiries in Kumasi in 1942 was the considerable intrigue that went on regarding constitutional disputes that came before the Confederacy Council. Bribes were given and received in all such cases. It was so common that everybody knew about it, and everybody talked about it.

When there is a constitutional dispute, both the chief concerned and his opponents, 'malcontents' as they are called, give bribes to the chiefs, registrars, secretaries, Akyeame (spokesmen), and others connected with the council to enlist their support. These sums of money are called 'presents'.

Besides those who are officially connected with the courts, there are some residents in Kumasi who collect money from the parties to a constitutional dispute which they promise to take to one or other of the chiefs known to be sitting on the case, or to the Asantehene. These men make a living in this way, as besides the money they receive for others, they are paid for their services. Some of the money so collected does not reach the chiefs whose influence it is meant to buy, but some of it does. Some influential chiefs have 'agents' who are known to have access to them, and who collect 'presents' for them in this way.

I received and checked up information on a number of such cases.

In one instance a candidate for the stool of an important Division sent £100 to another chief whose backing would secure him the stool. This candidate was in fact elected. The candidate sent the money to the influential chief through another chief. Both the chief who took the money to the recipient and his attendant who carried it confirmed this story.

I followed closely one of the constitutional disputes pending before the council during my field-work in 1942. The chief against whom his subjects complained had to come to Kumasi several times, staying from two weeks to a month each time. For about three months the 'malcontents' were continuously resident in Kumasi. The case was called and adjourned several times. On the night previous to the day on which the case was due to be heard, the malcontents distributed £50 'in presents' to three of the Kumasi chiefs who were known to be sitting on the case. The chief sent £100 to one of the members nominated to sit on the case. Both parties sent tips to various officers of the court. This particular dispute dragged on for well over a year, when it was finally settled in favour of the chief. He boasted that he had won his case with money (*Yede sika na yedi asεm*: We contest cases with money) as he had spent over £800. The malcontents spent £250.

Because of such incidents, there is much distrust and suspicion especially directed against the chiefs and residents of Kumasi whom the others regard as the 'Kumasifo' (people of Kumasi) who 'rub pepper into the eyes' (*twi ani mako*). I was given names of a number of prominent citizens and royals in Kumasi who were believed to make their living in this way.

Such abuses cause both chiefs and people to be suspicious of the Confederacy Council and to want to secede from it. The significance of the decision of the Bekwaihene to secede from the council lies in the fact that it was generally believed that other chiefs had held secret meetings with him, and had agreed to secede too. This is one reason why all the chiefs swore the Great Oath to deny any knowledge or complicity in the action. The anxiety of the chiefs may be seen from their speeches at the close of the 1945 session. I quote a few extracts from the minutes:

Ejisuhene: I would humbly pray the Otumfuo not to give ear to any flying reports. Ejisu has never rebelled against the Golden Stool in our long history and it will never rebel against it.

Offinsuhene: The Bekwai rebellion should be an eye-opener for all of us. We should be ashamed of what the Bekwaihene and his elders have done rather than follow their footsteps.

Essumejahene: I would like to begin by supporting what the Ejisuhene asked the Otumfuo that he may not heed the false news that some people with malicious intentions, disseminate concerning us. My State being the neighbour of the Bekwai State, it is easy for any one to harbour suspicions against me that I am concerned with the Bekwaihene's rebellious act. But I want to assure the Otumfuo and this council that I would be the last man to associate myself with the Bekwaihene's infidelity.

Mamponghene: I would also like to support those who beseech Otumfuo not to give ear to any people who may come to gossip to him about his Divisional chiefs. The intention of those people is only to create bad blood between the head and his chiefs, and if Otumfuo gives in to them, they will spoil the fine co-operation which we have built up since the restoration of the council.

The Asantehene: As regards what almost every speaker has touched upon, that I should not listen to gossip, may I point out that it has never been my habit to attach any importance to gossips. I am a ruler and I know that there are some people, some of whom are our own personal attendants who make a living by carrying news from one chief to another, and thus create dissensions between them.[1]

The Bekwai incident, however, did have repercussions which increased the suspicion and fear of chiefs and people alike. Within six months of the incident trouble had broken out in the Divisions of four of the chiefs generally suspected to have attended secret meetings with the Bekwaihene, as a result of which two of them were subsequently destooled. One of them, the Kuntanasihene, a member of the Confederacy Council, was deposed after he had been found guilty by the Kumasi Divisional Council of complicity in the Bekwai secession.

These incidents show that the Confederacy Council has not yet gained the strong support of the chiefs or the people. The strength of the old Ashanti Union was largely dependent on the fact that

[1] Minutes of the Ashanti Confederacy Council (1945).

it was a group organized for wars. But one of the first acts of Government was to put an end to warfare. A strong factor of the social integration of the Ashanti Union was therefore removed.

The Asantehene was exiled, and for over thirty years the Divisions managed their own affairs, subject to the control of District Commissioners. In 1935, the Confederacy Council was 'restored'. Although the council followed the old Union in its membership, in its powers and legal position it is in effect a new creation.

Sentiments of loyalty to the Golden Stool still remain, but that alone has not been enough to overcome the tendency of the different segments of the Confederacy to break away in order to maintain a greater degree of autonomy. The chiefs feel that the Confederacy Council has increased the domination of Kumasi over them. The reason why Kumasi is considered to be more powerful is that regarded as one of the component units of the political structure, on a par with other units such as Mampong, Bekwai, or Juaben, it is over-represented on the council.[1] The tendency to break away is strengthened by uncertainty regarding the powers of the Asantehene, or of the Confederacy Council in relation to the Divisions, by the extra financial burdens the chiefs have had to carry, and above all, by fears and suspicions caused by abuses such as have been described.

On the other hand, the chiefs feel a greater sense of security, and a new solidarity is being built around the idea of co-operation to improve the welfare of the nation as a whole; but this concept is still in its beginnings, and has not evoked strong sentiments of attachment.

So far, we have considered only the chiefs who are themselves members of the council.

The belief that the Confederacy Council has reduced the power of chiefs *vis-à-vis* Kumasi is most strongly held by those chiefs in the Kumasi Division who are not members of the Confederacy Council. This is most keenly felt by places like Agogo, Ahafo, and Bompata where the chiefs are responsible for the administration of larger areas than the Kumasi chiefs who represent them on the

[1] The Kumasi Division is the most populated of the Divisions, and on the basis of population it is probably not adequately represented. But the basis of representation is in terms of corporate units (Divisions) of the political structure. On that basis, Kumasi is over-represented, as compared with the other units.

Confederacy Council. The Kumasi clan chiefs have little interest in these areas. They do not inform the chiefs of the deliberations of the council. As one chief said, 'We only hear of the resolutions passed by the Confederacy Council through our District Commissioner. It is only when they want to collect taxes that they send the collectors to us.'

The result is that the people of these areas are completely ignorant of the work of the council, and are either indifferent or even hostile to it. The hostility has another cause. A visitor to any of the Kumasi courts where litigants from the outlying districts are parties to a suit hears the court members making such remarks as 'Do not tell us Ahafo tales', 'Do not tell us Asante-Akim tales', or 'Only an Asante-Akim man will behave in this way'. The people of these areas feel very strongly about these taunts, and complain bitterly about them. They regard them as expressions of the contempt in which the Kumasi people hold them.[1] This affects the social relationships of the Kumasi people, and those from Bompata, or Agogo, or Ahafo. The disparaging remarks give the latter a sense of injury and cause an estrangement which often leads to hostility. This is projected on to the political and judicial institutions which bring them into contact, and which are believed to have given the Kumasi people their advantage and sense of superiority. To them the Confederacy Council is a Kumasi institution. In my inquiries I found that affronted feelings caused by taunts or the fear of them underlay much of the adverse criticisms of the Confederacy Council made by the people who live outside Kumasi.

The ignorance and suspicion of the work of the Confederacy Council is general. My inquiries were conducted in the Divisions of Kumasi, Mampong, and Wenchi, and in none of these Divisions had the common people any adequate knowledge of the work of the council. The commoners are not consulted by the chiefs and elders, and they are not given a chance of expressing their views on the matters discussed. The educated commoners feel that they should be represented on the council. One of them, a trader in Kumasi, put the popular view in this way: 'Every day we see the chiefs going to the council. We have no say in what they discuss. When they come out they give us laws to obey. Most of these are

[1] This cause has since been removed by the establishment of area courts for these places.

in their own interest.' In 1935, the Extraordinary Members were selected from a list submitted to the council by the Asante Kotoko Society. The younger educated Ashantis consider that the Kotoko Society does not represent their views, as it is composed of older men, mainly resident in Kumasi. Many of them are cocoa-brokers or independent traders. Since 1935, changes in the personnel of the Extraordinary Members have been made by the Confederacy Council without reference to any outside body.

It is not only the literate commoners who feel that the council is not sufficiently representative. An illiterate cocoa-farmer, sixty miles from Kumasi, put what is a general criticism most clearly when he said: 'All I know of the Confederacy Council is that whenever the chief comes back from Kumasi he brings a new law. We must not hold funeral celebrations. We must not plant cocoa. We must pay a levy. When you ask why, they say, "The Council says so", or, "The Asantehene ruled it". To-day we have too many masters, the District Commissioner, the chief, the Asantehene, and they all make laws for us. When you serve too many masters, your head tears off (*Wo ti te*).'

We have shown that the units of administration in Ashanti are the lineage, the village, the sub-division and the Division, and that within each unit the head is expected to consult the members of his unit. The chief or Odekuro or elder consults his council, and each member in turn consults the members of the unit he represents. The machinery is democratic only if these consultations are held, and the popular checks are effective.

The Ashanti Union, as we have shown, was not part of the normal administrative machinery. But the Confederacy Council which has taken the place of the Union has legislative and judicial powers. The people have felt its influence in the laws it has passed, and in the levy it has imposed. The orders have come from a body over which they have no control. The Confederacy Council has not been integrated into the political structure of the community. It legislates directly for the ordinary man, but its powers do not derive from him, nor does he have a share in its legislative or judicial work. This is because the elders do not consult the people, and in particular, the villages and towns which are outside the capitals of the Divisions are left out of the picture. There is therefore a general indifference to or suspicion of the Confederacy Council. But sentiments of nationhood still persist and find expression in reference to the Golden Stool. The Ashanti still think of themselves as a nation bound by their common loyalty to the Golden Stool.

The general criticism of the Confederacy Council as an administrative organization with judicial and legislative powers sanctioned by the authority of Government does not affect the sentiments of attachment to the Golden Stool. The concept of the nation is mystical and derives from antiquity. The Golden Stool is a symbol of its unity and continuity. The Confederacy Council on the other hand is a machinery of government designed to achieve certain secular ends, and the condition of its success is that it should fit into the system of social groups by which the Ashanti regulate their political life.

CHAPTER IX

THE CHIEF TO-DAY

IN the preceding chapters we have examined the various duties of the chief, and the institutions through which he functions. The Ashanti chief thinks of himself and is regarded by his people primarily as 'he who sits upon the stool of the ancestors'. He is accorded reverence as the successor of his royal ancestors, to whom he performs sacrifices on behalf of the tribe. He is custodian of the tribal land, because the people regard the land as belonging to the ancestors. His judicial functions are exercised in connexion with offences which are religious and threaten the relationship between the community and the ancestors of the chief and the gods.

Though an aura of sacredness surrounds the chief, and his prestige is supreme, there are constitutional checks on the exercise of his powers. He rules with the assistance of a council, whose advice and consent he must obtain regarding all his activities.

The council consists of the elected heads of the lineages composing the Division (ɔman). This gives every member direct representation in the conduct of the affairs of the community on the basis of kinship.

Before the period of British rule the primary duty expected of the chief and his council was the maintenance of peaceful relations within the community and its defence from external attack. The community was welded together into a political unit by its common allegiance to the chief. The councillors were jointly responsible with him for the welfare of this unit. They sacrificed together to the chief's ancestors and prayed for the things which they considered essential for their continuity—health, food, fecundity. They guarded the laws and customs of the tribe. Most important of all, they were the captains of the tribe in war, when they fought to preserve their common inheritance. The chief was the link between the tribe and the Golden Stool, and so in this way the tribe was brought into the circle of the States which composed the Ashanti Union.

We have traced in the preceding chapters some of the changes that this system has undergone under British rule.

The Government has not interfered with the religious cere-

monies of the chief. He performs the *Odwera* and the *Adae* ceremonies to-day as his predecessors have always done. But the
libations and sacrifices he offers have lost their full significance for
some of his Christian subjects, who no longer believe that the crops
will fail or that misfortune will befall the tribe if the sacrifices to
the ancestors are not performed. Nevertheless, many Christians
still believe that the ancestors send help and blessing, and, above
all, they share with non-Christians the sentiments of unity and
continuity which are given expression at the religious ceremonies
centring round the chief.

We have shown how the chief's religious position is challenged
by Christianity.[1] Those of his subjects who are Christians—a few
on the grounds of conscience, many on the grounds of Church
law or teaching—repudiate the spiritual headship of the chief.

In the political sphere the chief is now under the control of
Government. Native Authorities are established by the Governor,
their powers and duties defined in ordinances, and their functions
supervised by the District Commissioner.

The more important functions expected of a Native Authority
are the administration of a good treasury and the provision of
social and welfare services. The chiefs have adapted themselves
to the new situation and have led in the construction of roads,
the establishment of treasuries, the building of schools, the provision of wells, sanitary services, and the like. The administrative
units of the old régime—the lineage, the village or sub-division—
have been less directly connected with these new tasks.[2]

The positive contribution of Government

It has been stated that the presence of an alien government as
a superior authority is one of the causes of the maladjustment of the
Ashanti political structure.

At the same time Government has made an important and
constructive contribution towards the political development of
Ashanti.

In the first place, Government has given Ashanti a new political
education. Its own system of rule, based on larger territorial units
than the Native Authorities, and the social services it has provided,
have taught a new conception of the functions of a government.

[1] See Chap. VI. The total number of Christians in Ashanti is less than a fifth of
the population.   [2] See Chap. VII.

Government has encouraged the Native Authorities to learn these new functions through the direct instruction of the District Commissioner, the establishment of native treasuries, and the award of Government grants to Native Authorities towards development schemes. When Native Authorities make grants to education or agriculture or provide their own wells or sanitary services, as they now do, it is a tribute to the work that Government has done in this direction.

In the second place, Government has made possible a centralized Native Administration which is able to provide these services. It has been shown that the cardinal principle of the Ashanti Constitution was to leave each unit—the lineage, the village, or the sub-division—to manage its own affairs with a minimum of interference from the Central Authority.

This was adequate when what was needed was unity for defence, and when the prime function of the local government was the maintenance of peaceful relations. To-day the Government has put an end to tribal warfare, and different tasks are expected of a Native Authority.

The provision of roads, wells, schools, and the like requires a centralized administration rather than small more or less autonomous units. This centralized administration the Government has provided in the Native Authorities and the Ashanti Confederacy Council, which derive their powers and duties from Government ordinances. Without the control and direction of Government such centralization as has already been achieved would not have come so quickly or so easily.[1]

The trend towards centralization has created its own problems. These have already been indicated. First, there is the problem of the relationship or integration of the Confederacy Council and the regional Native Authorities;[2] secondly, the problem of giving the smaller units within a Native Authority adequate participation in administration;[3] thirdly, the political system of Ashanti is based on kinship, but the tasks of a modern government require some kind of administration on a territorial basis. This is what Government is building up, and some disintegration in the existing structure is inevitable in the process of the change.

[1] See Chaps. IV and V, where the tendency against a centralized administration was noted.   [2] See Chap. VIII, 'The Ashanti Confederacy Council'.
[3] See Chaps. IV and VII.

We have used the terms 'disintegration' or 'disequilibrium' of the political structure of Ashanti to-day. What is meant may be gathered from the present state of Ashanti political institutions as described in the preceding chapters. Clear symptoms of the disequilibrium are also found in the present economic position of the chiefs, the practices connected with elections, and the frequency with which chiefs are destooled. They are all illustrations of a system which is out of balance.

Change in the chief's economic position

The chief's economic position has been assailed by the new changes. Formerly the chief's social personality was completely merged in his office. He could not own private property, and everything he possessed belonged to the stool. He could not engage in trade to enrich himself, but his Gyase subjects traded for the stool. He received tribute from his subjects—food, palm wine, game, animal skins—and when necessary special levies were raised to meet specific purposes. He could command the services of his subjects for tilling his farm, building his house, or cleaning the paths. Many palace attendants directly attached to him did his domestic work. He was wealthy in goods and services, but it was not all for his own benefit. 'When a chief has plenty of breast milk', runs the Ashanti proverb, 'it is the people who drink it.'[1] He provided food and drink for those who visited him, rewarded the services of his subjects, and distributed presents at religious festivals. As we have noted, one of the injunctions recited to a chief on his enstoolment was that he should be generous. Munificence bound his subjects to him. It was one of the sanctions of his authority.[2]

With the changes that have taken place, and the new economic opportunities offered by cocoa-farming and other occupations, the men have less inclination to perform customary services for the chief.

No subjects trade for the stool any longer. Many of the tributes in kind are no longer paid, and there are restrictions on the imposition of levies. The approval of the Chief Commissioner is required for the purpose for which the levy is to be used, and the Governor's approval for its collection.

Nevertheless, the chiefs have felt it an obligation to continue to

[1] 'Ohene nufu dɔɔso a, amansin na ɛnom.'   [2] See Chap. III.

dispense hospitality, reward the services of their subjects, distribute presents generously at religious festivals, and make donations towards the building of schools and churches, in order to maintain their prestige. They have also to feed and clothe their wives, children, and domestic staff.

The chief acquires private property

To meet such a situation some of the chiefs entered business and took to acquiring private property. In 1906 it was officially reported: 'Building operations have been the rule throughout the year. All the principal Ashanti Chiefs now own large European houses which they lease to strangers at good rentals.'[1] In 1909 it was again noted: 'The European firms showed commendable enterprise and several of the native Chiefs now readily engage in trading ventures foreign to them a short time since.'[2]

In 1942 the writer came across a chief who was a cocoa-broker and rubber processor, owner of a tile and water-cooler factory, and employed also a number of artisans doing various jobs for him. This was an exceptional case, but there are many chiefs who own private property—cocoa-farms and houses—and have their own savings in the bank or Post Office. A number of chiefs have opened accounts or purchased houses in the name of their relations—sons, sisters or nephews—in order to avoid comment and suspicion. But there is suspicion, and the chief's subjects call all such practices 'corruption'.

I was present at a meeting held in Kumasi in 1942 when the representative committee appointed by the Confederacy Council discussed the question regarding the ownership of private property by the chief. The committee stated the custom in the following terms:

When a Chief is in occupation of the Stool he is according to ancient custom incapable of owning any property apart from the Stool; he and the Stool are one. Before he accepts the Stool he is entitled to dispossess himself of his private property, particularly farm lands, and any Family property in his possession will revert to the Family.

The only manner in which the Stool can be said to owe money to the occupant of the Stool is in a case where the Chief himself, at the request of the Elders, negotiates a loan on behalf of the Stool and becomes a principal debtor.

[1] *Colonial Reports: Ashanti*, 1906.   [2] Ibid., 1909.

If a Chief engages in any business undertaking, he must obtain the consent of the Elders before doing so; any profit he makes is then a gain to the Stool, and any loss a Stool debt.

A Chief has no right to become security (i.e. stand surety) for any person without the consent of his Elders, and if by so doing he involves the Stool in debt this would be sufficient ground for his destoolment.

Before the Electors decide upon a candidate they enquire as to his private property and his private debts, and at the public ceremony of election he is questioned as to his property and his debts. If the candidate then declares his debts and is nevertheless elected to the Stool, his private debts are thereby accepted by the Stool and become Stool debts. If however he fails to declare his debts prior to his election, the Stool cannot accept responsibility for them and such debts become the debts of his family.

A Chief is not entitled to incur any debt on behalf of the Stool without the consent and approval of his Elders, and if money is borrowed by the Stool at least two of the Elders must be actual parties to the loan. If this is not done, the Elders may deny any liability on behalf of the Stool.[1]

This was a correct statement of the custom to which all the members of the committee agreed. The committee's report was later discussed by the Confederacy Council at its session in October 1942:

Kokofuhene: It is not in consonance with the law of equity that a Chief's private debts incurred by him should be borne by the State. I would suggest that a Chief embarking upon a business enterprise, should first gain the consent of his Elders, and if he makes any profit he is to enjoy it; but if he involves himself in debt, he should be personally responsible for it; the Stool is in no way affected.

Oyokohene: I suggest that if a Stool occupant undertakes any enterprise with the knowledge and consent of his Elders any profits gained or debts incurred by him should go to the Stool. This should be so because a Stool occupant cannot undertake any private work without first obtaining the knowledge and consent of his Elders.

Asantehene: This is a delicate question and requires careful consideration.

NOTE: After a lengthy discussion the suggestion made by the Kokofuhene was adopted.[2]

This is an example of the indefinite state Ashanti custom is in.

[1] From the Report of the Committee on *Notes on Ashanti Custom* (unpublished).
[2] Minutes of the Confederacy Council (1942).

The decision implies that the chiefs have abandoned the old custom and have accepted the principle that a distinction should be made between the chief's property and the stool's.

Another decision in line with this was taken with regard to the National Fund. It was decided that every chief was to contribute to it; we may quote parts of the Confederacy Council's discussion on the subject:

Adɔntenhene: The raising of a national fund is a necessity for our progress. Although in the ancient days Chiefs did not pay taxes, in this case it is necessary that we do so. I suggest that members of the Confederacy Council contribute £1 a head, sub-divisional Chiefs 10/-, and Adikrofo 5/-. Chiefs' wives should be exempted as suggested.

Kyidɔmhene: If a man knows for what purpose he is called upon to give his money, he does so without grudge. The purpose of this national fund is to raise money to implement schemes for the educational and social development of the country; and this in my opinion deserves the ungrudging support of the Chiefs. I agree with the amounts suggested by the Adɔntenhene.

Kokofuhene, Nsutahene, Oyokohene and the rest support the Adɔntenhene.

Mamponghene's Representative: I would respectfully beg to ask whether the £1 to be paid by each Divisional Chief should come from the Divisional Stool Treasury or from the Chief's own pocket?

Asantehene: The Chief has to pay it himself. Now the Council has decided to keep the Stool's money quite apart from the Chief's personal money; and so the Chief will be contributing nothing at all if his share should come from the Stool Treasury. Any Chief who is discovered to be using his Stool's money for this purpose is to be prosecuted.

Dormaa, Wenchi, Banda, Mo, Offinsu and Jaman Chiefs support the Adɔntenhene.

Asantehene: I thank you all for your kind consideration of this matter. I am sure that if you, the Chiefs, had refused to pay the levy, the Government would have hesitated to give its approval to it, and this would have rendered our fine scheme uncertain.[1]

At the same session the council discussed 'whether or not the property acquired by a Chief out of his personal allowance during his tenure of office remains his on his demise, deposition or

---

[1] Minutes of the Confederacy Council (1943).

abdication'. The custom had been that everything the chief acquired belonged to the stool.[1] Again, we may let the chiefs speak for themselves:

Mamponghene: As the State finances are now to be controlled by Boards to be appointed by every Division and a Chief will have no right to take any money from the State Treasury without the knowledge and consent of the supervising body, I am of the opinion that whatever property a Chief acquires out of his personal emolument should remain his exclusive property even if he vacates his office.

Juabenhene: I agree with the Mamponghene.

Nsutahene: I agree with the Mamponghene.

Bekwaihene: I agree with the Mamponghene.

Kokofuhene: My opinion is that whatever property a Chief acquires while on the Stool should remain the Stool's property even when he leaves the Stool. Every Chief is supposed to make something for his Stool and so add to the property of his ancestors' Stool.

Essumejahene: I agree with the Mamponghene.

Kumawuhene's Representative: I agree with the Kokofuhene's views.

Kuntanasihene: My opinion is that whatever Stool paraphernalia a Chief makes while in office with his personal money should go to the Stool even if he vacates it. Other properties he could take away with him.

Mamponghene: A Chief while in office might make Stool paraphernalia and offer them to the Stool as a present. This remains the Stool's property when the Chief leaves; but any other property which the Chief acquires for himself is his and he retains it even when he leaves the Stool.

Berekumhene: I agree with the Mamponghene.

Offinsuhene: I agree with the Mamponghene. A Chief might himself present certain things to the Stool, but he cannot be compelled to do so.

Nkoranzahene: I agree with the Mamponghene.

Adansihene: I support the Mamponghene.

Agonahene: I agree with the Mamponghene. If a Chief can own property exclusively then Chieftaincy becomes a trading affair or a profession.

Wenchihene: I support the Mamponghene.

Jamanhene: I support the Mamponghene.

Denyasehene: I support the Mamponghene.

Asokorihene: My opinion is that when a Chief leaves the Stool, half of the property he acquires for himself while on the Stool should go to the Stool and the other half should go to him or to his family.

Sumahene's Representative: I agree with the Mamponghene.

---

[1] See Chap. III, 'Chiefship and Land-tenure'

Tafohene (Kumasi Benkum): I agree with the Mamponghene.

Adɔntenhene, Kontihene, Akwamuhene, &c., all support the Mamponghene.

Asantehene: I would like to point out that our system of administration is changing and so we cannot accept old practices to be binding on us in these days. According to the new system under which Stool treasuries work, it will not be right to compel a Chief to surrender what he has acquired with his personal allowance, except, as the Kuntanasihene has pointed out, Stool paraphernalia such as State umbrellas, sandals, cloths, &c.

Mamponghene: I want to turn my suggestion into a motion: A Chief vacating his Stool retains the property acquired by him with his personal allowance, except paraphernalia which he may offer to his Stool as his contribution to the Stool property.

Juabenhene: I second the motion.

NOTE: Motion put to vote and passed by a majority.[1]

The different opinions expressed in this discussion are evidence of the uncertainty about Ashanti custom to-day. In this particular instance we find that the decision of the council amounted to making a change in the prevailing custom. But until changes have been made over the whole field, inconsistencies will remain to cause conflict. For example, offences against the person of the chief, such as insult or assault or adultery with his wife, are still treated as sacrilegious crimes. The chief's identity with the stool is then accepted, and in every such instance sheep must be sacrificed to the stool to expiate the crime.[2] The Confederacy Council in 1946 drew up a scale of the amounts payable (including the cost of the sheep to be sacrificed to the stool) by offenders who commit adultery with chiefs' wives. These are £148. 16s. for a chief in Grade I, £74. 8s. for one in Grade II, and £37. 4s. for one in Grade III.[3] The compensation that a commoner may claim from anyone committing adultery with his wife is £2. 7s.

Though the Confederacy Council has agreed on making a distinction between the private property of a chief and stool property, the people generally do not make such a distinction. So when a chief engages in trade, owns houses and farms, or keeps a private bank account, he incurs the suspicion and reprobation of his sub-

[1] Minutes of the Confederacy Council (1943).

[2] See Chap. IV, 'Administration and Justice', where the social identification of the chief and the stool was noted.

[3] The gradation of the chiefs is given below in this chapter, under 'Elections'.

jects. These things do not seem to them to accord with the chief's position, and they use them as a cause for destooling him. In one Division which I visited in 1942, during a political dispute, the ringleaders gave it as one of their reasons for destooling the head-chief: 'He minds his cocoa-farms more than the State. Let him give us our stool and take his farm.'

Stool debts

The difficulty of the chief is increased by the fact that many stools have been encumbered with debts. These usually arise from loans raised to erect stool-houses, celebrate the funeral of a deceased chief, make stool regalia, pay the debts of candidates elected to a stool, or for litigation, especially about stool lands. This last item has been the biggest single cause of stool debts.

Land has become enhanced in value owing to the mining, rubber, cocoa, and timber industries, and since these were intro-duced into Ashanti land disputes have been a perennial source of strife and litigation. There is hardly a Division in Ashanti which has not at some time or other during the last forty years litigated about its lands or boundary with another tribe or Division.

It would require much labour even to chronicle all such boundary and land disputes.

The earlier land disputes settled by Government clearly show the relation between litigation about land and the new industries which enhanced its economic value. Earlier settlements of boundary disputes are tabulated below. The list indicates that most litigation took place in the mining and cocoa areas in South Ashanti, but there were also boundary disputes in North Ashanti where, at the beginning of the century, the rubber industry was of some importance.

Boundary disputes settled in 1905
Central District: Effiduasi–Asokori (cocoa area).
   Petriansu–Konongo (mining and cocoa).
   Obogu–Bompata (cocoa).
Southern District: Mansu Nkwanta–Kumasi (cocoa).
North-western District: Wam–Ahafo (rubber).
   Wenchi–Techiman (rubber).
North-eastern District: Dormaa–Fakosi (rubber).

1907

Central Province: Kumawu–Mampong (cocoa).
Southern Province: Bekwai–Adansi (mining and cocoa).

The latter dispute was about land on which concessions had been taken.

1909

Southern Province: Bekwai–Adansi (mining).
  Bekwai–Denyase (mining).
  Akrokerri–Dompase (mining).

All these disputes were in connexion with concessions.
The Akrokerri–Dompase dispute caused a civil war.

1911

Southern Province: Abodom–Assechere (cocoa area).
  Bompata–Asankare (cocoa area).
  Denyina–Jachi (cocoa area).

1915

Central Province: Mampong–Agona (cocoa area).

1916

Southern Province: Pekyi–Trede (cocoa area).
  Nkawie–Mansu Nkwanta (cocoa area).
  Essumeja–Ofuasi (cocoa area).

The Essumeja–Ofuasi dispute gave rise to protracted litigation which ended in the Privy Council. It cost Essumeja over £2,800.

1918

Southern Province: Amoafu–Bekwai (cocoa area).

Litigation about land has persisted to the present day. A commission appointed by the Governor of the Gold Coast in 1944 to investigate 'the expenses incurred in the courts of the Gold Coast and indebtedness caused thereby'[1] reported on stool debts as follows:

It is abundantly clear from the evidence that the majority of States in the Colony and in Ashanti have been, and many still are, in debt. Though there are other contributing factors, litigation is undoubtedly the main cause of indebtedness. Stool debts caused by litigation generally arise out of litigation over land and particularly out of boundary

---

[1] The Havers Commission (1944).

disputes. The most expensive cases are boundary disputes between two Paramount Chiefs of adjoining States or disputes in which one or more Paramount Chiefs become involved. Land cases are always protracted and almost invariably go through a chain of Appellate Courts to the West African Court of Appeal and sometimes to the Privy Council. The African places a great store upon the land, for which he has a religious affection, apart from its commercial value. To the African mind his spiritual ancestors live on in the land, which he considers himself under a sacred obligation to preserve. Moreover, a Chief would run the risk of destoolment if he did not take every step, which his subjects thought could be taken to defend the Stool land. He is therefore compelled, even in cases where he does not consider the chance of success favourable, to carry the litigation to the utmost limit. Further, a large proportion of the population derives its livelihood from the soil. Therefore States, families and individuals are bound to protect their titles or perish. On the other hand, there have been many cases, where the area of the land in dispute and its value have been extremely small and quite out of proportion to the large sums expended in litigation. Vast sums are incurred by litigants in such cases. Fees to Counsel are bigger in land cases than in other civil cases, and the evidence showed that very large fees have been paid, more particularly in past years, to legal practitioners in the course of such cases. Some States are able to borrow money from rich Elders or friends. Others, who are less fortunate, are compelled to resort to moneylenders, who have seldom lent money at a rate of interest lower than 50 per cent. and sometimes at the rate of 100 per cent. Usually, they are compelled to mortgage part of the Stool lands as security for the loan. Not infrequently, States obtain the necessary sanction to raise a levy upon their subjects, and even if such sanction is not forthcoming the subjects of the State can usually be relied upon to make a voluntary contribution. Moreover, the cost of maintaining and transporting numerous witnesses is heavy. Similar disputes have given rise to widespread indebtedness of Divisional Chiefs, Chiefs, villages, communities, families and individuals.[1]

Of the cases cited in illustration the table on p. 208 gives the Ashanti ones.

The list is by no means complete, but it helps to show the extent and cost of stool litigation about land. It will give some idea of the lengths people are willing to go when it is pointed out that £1,885 was spent by the village of Ewisa, with a population of less than 1,000 souls.

As a result of stool debts many Divisions have been unable to

[1] *Report of Havers Commission of Enquiry*, p. 31.

Stool Debts arising from Litigation

Name of stool	Title of case (where debt arose in respect of one case only)	Approximate amount expended	Approximate amount outstanding, where known
		£	£
Assechere	Assechere v. Dadiase	1,940	1,940
Dadiase	,, ,,	1,972	1,972
Berekum	Nsoatre v. Berekum	1,500	..
Nsoatre	,, ,,	1,500	..
Nkwanta	Nkwantahene v. Bechemhene	770	695
Bechem	..	3,950	..
Nsuta	..	600	Nil
Beposo	..	100	30
Jamasi	..	150	80
Effiduasi	..	250	120
Asokore	..	180	70
Ejura	..	40	Nil
Mampong	..	300	Nil
Adansi	Kobinafori v. Obeng Akese (Decided by Privy Council)	8,000	..
Essumeja	Essumeja v. Ofuasihene	over 2,800	..
Adokwai	Adokwaihene v. Anofohene	375	295
Menji	Menji–Namasa–Nsawkaw	2,000	2,000
Nsawkaw	,, ,,	Large	800
Namasa	,, ,,	2,000	2,000
Nchiraa	Nchiraahene v. Buoyemhene	1,105	..
Offuman I	(a) Offuman I v. Offuman II (Concluded in Chief Commissioner's court)	1,325	800
	(b) Offuman I v. Offuman II (Techiman interpleading before Privy Council)	650	650
Offuman II	,, ,, ,,	1,664	664
Techiman	..	1,755	905
Wenchi	Wenchi v. Ewisa	165	20
Ewisa	,, ,,	1,885	447
Drobo	..	943	827

pay their staffs adequately, and the latter have in consequence resorted to imposing excessive fines and fees and to receiving presents from litigants.

The chiefs have not had adequate funds to maintain their prestige, and they have been tempted to exact levies, sell stool lands, or lease them to concessionaires at low rents in order to obtain money to meet their needs. The people have then charged them with extortion, corruption, or with being ignorant dupes, and have attempted, often successfully, to destool them.

Stool debts have also affected the smooth working of the Constitution. In certain instances stools have been offered by the
elders to candidates, who would otherwise not have been elected,
because they have undertaken to defray the stool debt.[1] It is
generally said that, as soon as the chief so elected had exhausted
what money he had, the people found reasons to destool him.

An ex-head chief of a Division, enstooled in 1940 and destooled
in 1944, corroborated this by saying that he had spent £1,000 in
paying the stool debt. He had sold his house and cocoa-farms to
raise the money, but as soon as the elders saw that he had no more
money left they found an excuse to destool him. Another ex-chief
of a Kumasi sub-division said he was offered the stool on his
promising to pay the stool debt, which amounted to £600. Three
months after he had been made a chief a section of the people rose
against him on the ground that he had no legitimate hereditary
title to the stool, and he was eventually destooled.

There is a recorded instance which happened in 1920. A candidate was offered the Kumawu stool on his undertaking to pay the
stool debt. He accepted the offer, but succeeded in persuading the
elders to sign a document making themselves responsible for
reimbursing him in case he was destooled. When this man became
a chief he proceeded to levy fines and fees in order to recoup himself. The people consequently refused to serve him, and brought
him before the Chief Commissioner.[2]

The loss of economic resources and the fact of stool debts
arising principally from litigation about land have not only deprived the chief of his traditional role as a repository of wealth and
bestower of largesse, and so of an important sanction of his
authority, but have also created a state of mutual suspicion and
fear between chief and subject. Owing to such a situation a chief's
activities are always suspect, and the community readily believes
stories of misappropriation or dishonesty, and succumbs to any
move to destool him.

Elections

We have explained that the Ashanti system of electing chiefs
combines kin-right with popular selection. The elders select a

[1] See Nkoranzahene's speech in discussion quoted under 'Elections', pp. 211–12
below, where this is corroborated. Also rules (3) and (4) made by Confederacy
Council regarding elections. [2] *Colonial Reports: Ashanti*, 1920.

candidate from the royal lineage of the particular tribe. As each matrilineal lineage consists of several subordinate branches, there are always a number of candidates available.

In the account of the election of the Chief of Wenchi, we noted that after a candidate had been nominated and accepted, the royal lineage held a special meeting at which differences between the chief-elect and any members of his lineage were settled, after which they swore allegiance to him.[1] The people realized that the smooth working of the system depended on harmony amongst the members of the royal lineage.

One of the characteristics of the Ashanti system to-day is that lineage solidarity is weakened, and royals compete jealously for the stool.[2] Whenever a stool falls vacant, the eligible candidates canvass for it by distributing presents and bribes to the electors. Moreover, the successful candidate always has rivals who are working against him openly or secretly. This not only adds to stool debts, but also contributes to the insecurity of the chief.

The chiefs have been very concerned about this matter, which they have discussed at several of the sessions of the Confederacy Council. The discussion they held in 1938 provides good evidence of the facts stated above. The men who have themselves been elected as chiefs are the best qualified to speak on the subject, and we may let them speak for themselves:

1938. Item 5. The offering and accepting of bribes in connexion with election and destoolment of Chiefs.

Asantehene: This subject was discussed at the last session of the Council, but at that time the Council had no power to make by-laws, therefore our decision in the matter could not have legal effect. As the Council has now been granted powers to do so, the subject is introduced again so that the necessary by-laws may be made.

Mampong Representative: The practice of offering and accepting bribes in connexion with election and destoolment of Chiefs is as bad as it is detrimental to the welfare of the country. It should, therefore, be prohibited and made a punishable offence. I suggest that by-laws be passed by the Council providing that any Chief found guilty of such offence shall be destooled and any youngman found guilty of the same offence shall be imprisoned for six months with hard labour.

Juabenhene: I support the view of the Mampong representative. A trader always wants to gain on his investments; in the same way if a person

---

[1] See Chap. I.   [2] See Chap. VI.

is compelled to spend all his money and to borrow in order to bribe the Elders of a Stool before he is elected to that Stool, he would naturally try to pay off his debt with Stool money and to have some profit whilst he is on the Stool. Moreover, as he is conscious of the fact that he might be destooled on the least pretence, he thinks more of his personal interest than the welfare of the Stool. Such a state of affairs is deplorable, and therefore its cause which forms the subject of our discussion should be removed. In the olden days affairs were not in such a deplorable state as they are to-day, and destoolments were of very rare occurrence.

Nsutahene: Bribery in connexion with destoolments and enstoolments is bad and should be stopped. I therefore support the previous speakers.

Agonahene: I support the views expressed by the previous speakers and would further suggest that royals should not be allowed to contest for a Stool. If and when a Stool becomes vacant the Elders should approach the Queen-Mother for a candidate and in consultation with the Gyase and Ankobea Chiefs and the members of the Stool family, she should nominate a candidate and the Elders may accept or reject her nominee without allowing any of the royals to influence them in any way in their decision.

Nkoranzahene: In certain cases if a Stool becomes vacant, wealthy sub-jects of the Stool try to bribe the Elders concerned in order to gain election. Under these circumstances, the royals too start to give bribes in order to ensure election to the Stool. Whilst, therefore, agreeing with the previous speakers, I should like to suggest further that any subject of a Stool who tries to contest for that Stool should be banished from the Division concerned.

Oyoko Clan: We agree with the previous speakers and would add that certain Chiefs instigate the subjects of another Chief to destool their Chief. By-laws should therefore be passed to the effect that any Chief who is found guilty of such an offence will be destooled.

Asantehene: The matter under discussion is so important that I should like all present to listen attentively. It is a disgrace for any Chief to neglect to train his nephews who will succeed him in future. The practice of offering and accepting bribes in connexion with the enstoolment or destoolment of Chiefs is also very bad and should be stopped. . . . I request the Committee which was appointed yesterday to deal with the question of the payment of annual 'sheep' in respect of cocoa-farms to deal with this subject also.[1]

The committee appointed later submitted its suggestions, which the Confederacy Council adopted. 'After a lengthy discussion the

[1] Minutes of the Confederacy Council (1938).

Committee was of the opinion that the practice of people offering and accepting bribes to destool or enstool a chief has become very common and has been the source of political unrest in this country.' It made the following recommendations:

1. It shall not be lawful for any member of a Royal Family to contest for a Stool whenever a Stool becomes vacant, and he shall not canvass for votes from any Elder of the Stool.

2. Any member of a Royal Family who contests, offers, or accepts any bribe in any form in any enstoolment case shall be guilty of an offence and shall be struck off the roll of the Royal Family and shall forfeit his right of succession to the Stool.

3. It shall not be lawful for any Elder or Elders to nominate, elect, or install any candidate on any Stool other than a member of the Royal Family of such Stool.

4. Any Elder or sub-chief who offers or accepts a bribe in an enstoolment case, or nominates, elects, or installs any candidate other than a member of the Royal Family of any such Stool, or breaks away from the Elders' meeting with the intent to prolong or delay the enstoolment of a Chief shall be guilty of an offence and shall on summary conviction thereof be removed from his office and destooled.

5. Any subject of a Stool who offers or accepts a bribe in an enstoolment case or interferes with or canvasses votes for any candidate shall be guilty of an offence, and shall on summary conviction thereof be liable to imprisonment for a term not exceeding six months with hard labour.

These regulations reveal the abuses which have been practised in connexion with stool elections, and give evidence of the tension already alluded to regarding the weakening of lineage solidarity and the competition amongst matrilineal kinsmen for the inheritance of offices and property. The rivalry is heightened as regards chiefship owing to the prestige attached to the office.

Quite apart from these abuses, the permitted customary donations in connexion with stool elections make it expensive for anyone to become a chief.

The chief-elect makes a donation (*aseda*: token of thanks) to the elders when he is offered the stool. The customary amounts donated range from £4. 13s. in the case of a village headman or an elder, to £93 in respect of the Golden Stool. The amounts paid vary between these two limits, according to the rank of the stool.

Then there is *abradie*, the customary sums or drinks a new chief distributes to his principal elders and other chiefs of his clan or wing to 'inform them that he has come to sit in the place of his ancestors' (*wabɛtena ne nananom anam mu*). The amounts that different chiefs spend on this vary from £25 to £100.

Thirdly, there is the *nsuaaka* (allegiance oath debt), the amount a chief pays when he takes the oath of allegiance to the Asantehene. The sum depends on the chief's place in the following gradations:[1]

Grade I: Chiefs pay £37. 4s. These are: Mamponghene, Juabenhene, Nsutahene, Bekwaihene, Kokofuhene, Adansihene, Kumawuhene, Essumejahene, Adɔntenhene Kumasi, Nkoranzahene, Dormaahene, Techimanhene.

Grade II: paying £27. 18s. Offinsuhene, Ejisuhene, Agonahene, Kontihene Kumasi, Akwamuhene Kumasi, Denyasehene, Wenchihene, Berekumhene, Asokorihene, Kuntanasihene, Sumahene, Drobohene, Nkwantahene.

It is of interest to note that the chiefs of Mo, Abeasi, and Banda, who belong by prestige to this grade, asked the Confederacy Council to place them in Grade III, because the donation for Grade II is too high.

Grade III: paying £18. 12s. Kyidɔmhene, Gyasehene, Oyokohene, Ankɔbeahene, Manwerehene of Kumasi, Abeasihene, Mohene, Amakomhene, Tafohene, Antoahene, Assamanghene, Bandahene.

Grade IV: All other chiefs not included in the above grades. The amounts they pay vary from Division to Division and range from £2. 7s. to £9. 6s.

The fourth item of expenditure at elections is *nsanom* (drinking of wine), the amount spent on drinks and entertainment during the rites of election and installation. Again the actual amounts spent vary from chief to chief. The range is from £20 to £100.

The total cost of an election to a chief of Grade I or II is usually more than £150. Some chiefs are known to have spent more than £800, and one informant estimated that he had spent over £1,000. Many of them borrow the money to meet these expenses and thus add to the financial burden of their office. It also affects their

---

[1] See Chap. VIII, 'The Ashanti Confederacy Council'. The fees were standardized at its session in 1943.

tenure of the office, for a chief known to be in debt is always in danger of destoolment.

Insecurity of the chief's office

All these show the predominantly characteristic feature of chiefship in Ashanti to-day—its insecurity.

Before 1900 chiefs were mostly destooled for failure to consult the elders or the breaking of custom, though there were other causes.[1]

Nowadays the most common cause is that of 'misappropriating stool funds'. This has become a prominent charge against chiefs since the 1920s. We have referred to the series of constitutional disputes that occurred in 1920 at Offinsu, Kumawu, Bekwai, Agogo, and Agona.[2] A common feature of all those destoolment cases was the charge of the maladministration of stool revenues. The charge now regularly appears in every destoolment case. Of recent cases that have been heard by the Confederacy Council one may cite the cases of Wenchi, Nkoranza, Agona (1942), Kumawu, and Techiman (1944), in all of which the chiefs were accused of misappropriating stool funds.

Some subsidiary charges also recur: that the chief has violated native custom; that he has broken the laws to which he assented on his enstoolment; that he does not add to stool property; and that he does not keep up appearances as befitting his rank. With native custom in its present confused state it is always possible to find a custom that the chief has violated. For example, a chief who owned private property (houses and cocoa-farms) was said to have violated custom.

The more fundamental causes of destoolment have been indicated in this and previous chapters: the rivalry among royals; the confused state of custom in a society in transition from a subsistence to an exchange economy; lack of definiteness about the chief's functions; his loss of economic resources; the emergence of the educated commoner or the successful cocoa-farmer; the presence of a superior authority. These and the other changes discussed have destroyed the old correlation between the chief's political power, religious authority, economic privilege, and military strength, with the consequent decline in his prestige and authority.

[1] See examples given in Chap. I, pp. 21-2.   [2] See Chap. VI.

The chiefs have tried to stop the frequent destoolments. In 1938 the Confederacy Council adopted the following rules:

1. Any member of a stool family who attempts to undermine his chief or offers or accepts a bribe for the purpose of inciting the destoolment of a chief shall be guilty of an offence and shall on summary conviction thereof be struck off the roll of the royal family, and shall forfeit all his rights of succession in the family.

2. Any subject of a stool who conspires with any member of a stool family, or offers or receives a bribe, or undermines or maliciously prosecutes a chief or sub-chief for the purpose of destooling such chief or sub-chief shall be guilty of an offence and shall on summary conviction thereof be liable to imprisonment for a term not exceeding six months with hard labour.

3. Any elder, sub-chief, or chief who conspires with any subject or royal of a stool, or receives or offers a bribe, or undermines or maliciously prosecutes a chief or sub-chief for the purpose of destooling such chief or sub-chief shall be guilty of an offence and shall on summary conviction thereof be destooled.

The Confederacy Council has tried to enforce these rules, and has dealt severely with those who have attempted to destool their chiefs. For example, in two instances in 1942, when the council acquitted the chiefs of Wenchi and Nkoranza against whom charges had been brought, some of those who had preferred the charges ('malcontents') were imprisoned, and the ringleaders were banished from their respective Divisions.

But the severe measures have not checked the deposition of chiefs. Formerly there were two ways in which a commoner could express criticism or dissatisfaction with the Government. One way was for him as an individual to lay his complaint before the elder, his lineage head, who represented him on the central authority. This channel was used for the expression of individual grievances. Secondly, the commoners could, as a body, express criticism of the chief and his council through their Nkwankwaa-hene, the commoners' leader.[1] This position has been abolished by the Confederacy Council, and there is no established organ for the commoners to express jointly any criticism or dissatisfaction with the Government. They may as individuals complain to their respective elders; but the elders are themselves members of the central authority and they are unable to represent the views of

[1] See Chap. I, p. 10.

the youngmen without incurring the chief's suspicion. They share a joint responsibility with him in the conduct of the affairs of the Division. The commoners now jointly express their dissatisfaction in attempts to destool the chief.

The frequency of destoolments may be seen from the following table. Vacancies caused by deaths are excluded, and account is taken only of destoolments or abdications among the twenty-one chiefs who are presidents of the twenty-one Native Authorities in the Ashanti Confederacy:

Name of chief	Native Authority	Year of destoolment or abdication
Akuamoa Boaten	Juaben	1942
Kwadwo Apawu	Agona	1942
Kwabena Kunadu	Suma	1943
Kwabena Kakari	Essumenja	1943
Kwaku Jarko II	Techiman	1944
Kwame Affram	Kumawu	1944
Kwaku Nkansa	Adansi	1944
Yaw Gyamfi	Bekwai	1945
Osei Akoto	Kuntanasi	1945
Asum Gyima III	Ejisu	1945
Yaw Boakye III	Bekwai	1946
Amoako Agyeman	Adansi	1946
Kwabena Wiafe II	Offinsu	1946
Kwabena Asubonteng	Dormaa	1946

Twelve Native Authorities out of twenty-one have changed their chiefs at least once during the five years, and two of them, Bekwai and Adansi, have had two changes within that time. On an average three out of the twenty-one chiefs have been destooled every year. Although there are some chiefs who have held their position for many years, it is evident from the above analysis that a chief's tenure of office is very insecure. It is an index of the disequilibrium of the Ashanti political structure to-day.

Yet as an institution chiefship is honoured and respected, and, judging from the keen competition for stools and the amounts candidates are willing to pay for them, the office is very much sought after. The people still look to the chief as their ruler and guide, the symbol, too, of their unity, traditions, and values. It is about his position and functions in the changed situation, what he should be and should do, that there is conflict.

The community attempts to resolve the conflict by now and again deposing one chief in order to try another; but, alas, though there are faults in every man, the greater faults are with the times[1] and the system. With the times it is fruitless to quarrel; with the faults in the system we may hopefully grapple. That requires the head, heart, and hand of all concerned.

Our analysis has shown that there have been two major changes in the political structure of Ashanti during the period of British rule, both the results of government policy.

The first is the trend towards centralization of administration on a territorial basis. This, as we have shown, has become necessary owing to new social factors such as improvement in communications, the presence in tribal areas of permanent settlers who are not members of the tribe of their place of residence, and, above all, because of the new functions expected of a Native Authority.

This centralization on a territorial basis we have seen to be at variance with the decentralization which characterized the kinship political institutions of Ashanti:—the small, more or less autonomous units of lineage, village, sub-division, or Division.

In the second place, as we have emphasized throughout, Ashanti chiefship is sacral. An important political development during the period of British rule has been the progressive secularization of the chief's office. Government has increased his administrative functions. The conflict between chief and people has centred round this development. The insecurity of the chief is a consequence of the secularization of his office.

These two processes in association with the other social changes to which we have referred in the preceding pages have caused the disequilibrium of the political structure.

In concluding this contribution towards the task of grappling with the political system of Ashanti as it is to-day, the author is reminded of an Ashanti proverb:

'Ɔman te sɛ adesoa, wonhu mu dakoro' 'The nation is like a load (with many things tied up)—one cannot perceive everything in it in a day.'

What he has perceived and attempted to describe and interpret is but a small portion of the load.

[1] See Chap. VI.

THE PRINCIPAL STOOLS OF ASHANTI ARRANGED UNDER THEIR RESPECTIVE CLANS

(Smaller stools omitted)

Name of clan	Head of clan	Member stools of the clan
1. Oyoko ne Dako	Asantehene	Asantehene, Juaben, Bekwai, Kokofu, Nsuta, Oyokohene Kumasi, Juaso.
2. Bretuo ne Agona		
(a) Bretuo	Mamponghene	Mampong, Effiduase, Jamasi,
(b) Agona		Apaa, Tafo, Nkawie.
3. Asona	Offinsuhene	Offinsu, Ejisu, Ejura, Akwamu Kumasi, Mansu-Nkwanta.
4. Asenie	Adontenhene Kumasi	Adonten, Amakom, Agona, Nkoranza, Wenchi.
5. Aduana	Essumejahene	Essumeja, Kumawu, Dormaa, Techiman, Agogo, Suma, Nsoatre.
6. Ekuona ne Asokore	Adansihene	Adansi, Asokore, Berekum, Manwerehene Kumasi.
7. Asachiri	Akrokerihene	Akrokeri, Asachiri, Abofuo.

ABUSUA GROUPS OF THE KUMASI CLAN CHIEFS

Kumasi clan	Groups within clan	Abusua group of clans
Adonten	Adontenhene	Asenie
	Amakomhene	,,
	Antoahene	,,
	Kwarmuhene	,,
	Akyiawkromhene	,,
Ankobea	Ankobeahene	
	Atipinhene	
Asafu	Akwamuhene	Asona
	Adumhene	Oyoko

Benkum	Tafohene	Agona
	Hyemanhene	Ekuona
	Tikromhene	Aduana
	Apiaduhene	Asachiri
	Apromasehene	Aduana
	Kwasohene	,,
	Boamanhene	,,
	Fomesuahene	Agona
	Assieninponhene	,,
Gyase	Sarmanhene (Gyasehene)	Oyoko
	Anantahene	,,
	Dadeasuabahene or Fantehene	Aduana
	Gyasewahene	
	Kronkohene	Asona
Kontire	Kontihene	Ekuona
	Nkawiehene	Bretuo (Agona)
	Toasehene	Asona
	Tredehene	Agona
	Apinanimhene	Asona
	Barmuhene	Ekuona
	Afarihene	,,
Kyidɔm	Akyɛmpemhene	,,
	Asemhene	
	Domakwaehene	Bretuo
	Sarwuahene	Oyoko
	Dominasehene	Bretuo
	Akroponhene	
	Hiahene	
Manwere	Manwerehene	Ekuona
	Asranponhene	Aduana
	Asebihene	,,
	Akomfurihene	Asona
	Nkabomhene	Ekuona
	Omantirehene	Agona
Oyoko	Oyokohene	Oyoko
	Etutuohene	,,
	Bremanhene	,,
	Denyasehene	,,
	Mampontenhene	,,
	Ahinkrohene	,,
	Awiomhene	,,
	Pampasehene	

APPENDIX III

MEMORANDUM on the relation between Christians and the State presented to Nana Sir Osei Agyeman Prempeh II, Asantehene, by representatives of the Christian Churches in Ashanti on 16 October 1942.

1. In the first place we wish to take this opportunity of placing on record our regret that so often in the past there has been a cleavage between Christians and non-Christians in this country, and our resolve to do all in our power to bring these two sections within the community together.

2. We must, however, state our conviction that in so far as some elements of the cleavage are due to difference of belief, the purpose of reconciliation cannot be furthered by any discussion which unduly minimizes these differences. We are forced to recognize that in some of its aspects Ancient Ashanti Religion asks an allegiance to certain spiritual powers which the worshippers of the God and Father of our Lord Jesus Christ cannot give.

3. Even so, we recognize that in the past there has been unnecessary cleavage, and we cannot hold individual Christians blameless for this. They have not always been ready to distinguish between those claims of Native Customary Law which had for them 'fetish' association and those which had not. They have therefore at times broken unnecessarily with Native Customary Laws and have not fulfilled their rightful allegiance to their chiefs.

4. On the other hand, we feel that Native Customary Law has not been widened to acknowledge the religious freedom which is implicit in British Law. In consequence there has been no general recognition of any procedure alternative to that laid down by Native Customary Law as possible for Christians in those matters which they regard as vital to conscience. These two together, misunderstanding on the part of certain Christians on the one hand, and, on the other, failure to make adequate recognition of good conscience in matters touching on belief, have led chiefs not unnaturally to question the loyalty of the Christian Community.

5. In order that this sense of division may be broken down we on our part pledge ourselves to impress ever more fully on the members of our Churches their duty to the State.

6. On the part of the chiefs we would ask that they accept as a fact the existence of Christians as members of their State and lay down ways by which they can show their allegiance to their chiefs without at the same time offending their Christian conscience (e.g. if a chief orders community work, say on roads, to take place on a Sunday as being the day most suitable to the majority of his subjects, he might at

the same time state that Christians may do their share of the work on the preceding Saturday. This taking of the initiative by the chief in remembering those of his subjects who are Christians would, we believe, go a long way towards relieving the strained feeling at present existing in such matters).

7. We believe that the Christian Community is large enough for the State to be the loser if Christians are cut off from a share in the country's political life. If no recognized place exists in Native Customary Law for those who do not believe in 'fetish', has not the time come in view of many changing circumstances for the adaptation of Native Customary Law in order that it may include in its provisions all loyal citizens? (e.g. if a new way of renewing allegiance to a chief is being considered on hygienic grounds, is it not more vital to the well-being of the State that new ways be considered which will not do violence to the conscience of many subjects?)

8. We therefore take this opportunity of suggesting to the Confederacy Council through the Asantehene that consultation may take place before any future codification of what has been up to the present Customary Law. Such codification seems to us to be foreshadowed in the discussion by the Confederacy Council of a document like that of the late Captain Warrington. By such consultation procedure in those points in which the Christian has difficulty, e.g. oaths, may be settled before codification rather than by appeal afterwards. Every such appeal puts the Christian and non-Christian on the defensive and increases the feeling of separation between them.

9. Against this background we look at the position of Christians in relation to the observance of Thursday. We recognize that this is an observance closely linked with ancient beliefs of the Ashanti people; beliefs which, however, are not to our mind wholly compatible with the Christian belief in God. Our members, if they observe the day, cannot do so for the ancient Ashanti reason. The question arises should they be asked to observe the day out of respect for the beliefs of others in the community. We feel that we cannot ask this of our members, in that to refrain from work on Thursday would be to them a confession of faith in Asase Yaa and her relation to harvest and famine and therefore a denial of the Fatherhood and providential care of God. A like difficulty of conscience holds in relation to other special days and observances which have a similar significance to Asase Yaa. If, however, the chief reason behind this observance is not so much the association with Asase Yaa as a desire for some communal act to express the unity of the nation, we would ask whether there is not some other act of allegiance in which the Christians could take part; an act which would not place the working life of farmers under the disadvantage of refraining from work on two days in the week.

We believe that a sympathetic understanding of the Christian position with regard to this day resulting in a dispensation from the present law would be the first step towards the new co-operation between Christians and the State which we earnestly desire to see. If at the same time some definite communal undertaking were suggested to the Christians by which they could show in concrete form their sense of unity with the whole nation, we believe that the chiefs would be re-assured of the loyalty of Christians to themselves and the State.

With the best interests of the Ashanti Nation in mind we submit this statement of our position for the consideration of the Otumfuo and the Confederacy Council.

O. M. RENNER (English Church Mission)
F. E. EKUBAN (Methodist Church)
T. A. BEETHAM (Methodist Church)
H. HENKING (Presbyterian Church)
E. M. ASIEDU (Presbyterian Church)
E. PAULISSEN (Roman Catholic Mission)
J. CORBETT (Salvation Army)
ISAAC SACKEY (A.M.E. Zion Mission)

APPENDIX IV

ASHANTI CONFEDERACY COUNCIL

Orders by Governor

1. THIS Order may be cited as 'The Ashanti Confederacy Council Order.'

2. There shall be a Native Authority to be called the 'Ashanti Confederacy Council' for the area specified in the First Schedule, and the said Council is hereby appointed to be the Native Authority for the said area.

3. The Ashanti Confederacy Council shall consist of the Asantehene and of the Head Chiefs of the Divisions specified in the first Schedule and the Chief of each of the seven Kumasi Clans specified in the Second Schedule, and the Tafohene of the Benkum Clan (Order 78/38).

4. The Asantehene when present shall preside at the meetings of the said Council, and when he is from any cause whatsoever unable to attend a Head Chief or Chief nominated by the Asantehene, or in default of such nomination the next senior Chief present, shall preside.

5. The said Council shall be deemed to be properly constituted for the transaction of any business, if in the opinion of the Asantehene or

of the person presiding in his absence the attendance of members is sufficient for the business to be transacted : Provided that in exercising his discretion the Asantehene or person presiding in his absence shall so far as practicable be guided by Native Customary Law.

6. It is hereby directed that the Ashanti Confederacy Council shall exercise only the powers conferred upon Native Authorities by sections 6, 7, 8, 15 and 16 of the Native Authority Ordinance. (Amended by 2 of 1936.)

First Schedule

The Divisions of Kumasi, Mampong, Juaben, Bekwai, Essumeja, Kokofu, Nsuta, Adansi, Kumawu, Offinsu, Ejisu, Agona, Banda, Wenchi, Mo, Abeasi, Nkoranza, Jaman, Berekum, Techiman, and Dormaa (Wam Pamu). (Amended by 17 of 1935, 34 of 1936, and 78 of 1938.)

Second Schedule

The Seven Kumasi Clans :

Adɔnten, Akwamu, Ankɔbea, Gyase, Korenti, Kyidɔm and Oyoko.

APPENDIX V

POWERS OF ASHANTI CONFEDERACY COUNCIL AND OF NATIVE AUTHORITIES

SECTIONS 6, 7, 8, 15, and 16 of the Native Authority (Ashanti Ordinance).

6. (1) It shall be the duty of a Native Authority to interpose for the purpose of preventing, and to the best of its ability to prevent, the commission of any offence within the area of its authority by any native subject to its jurisdiction.

(2) A Native Authority knowing of a design to commit an offence within the area of its authority by any native subject to its jurisdiction may arrest or direct the arrest of such native, if it appears to such Authority that the commission of the offence cannot be otherwise prevented. Any native so arrested shall, unless he be released within twenty-four hours of his arrest, be taken forthwith before a Magistrate's Court or a Native Court having jurisdiction over him.

(3) Every Native Authority receiving information that any native subject to its jurisdiction who has committed an offence for which he may be arrested without a warrant, or for whose arrest a warrant has been issued, is within the area of its authority, shall cause such native to be arrested and taken forthwith before a Magistrate's Court or a Native Court having jurisdiction over him.

(4) Every Native Authority receiving information that property of any description which has been stolen, whether within or without the area of its authority, is within such area, shall cause such property to be seized and detained pending the order of a Magistrate's Court or a Native Court having jurisdiction in the matter and shall forthwith report such seizure and detention to such Court. (Amended by 39 of 1935, s. 3.)

7. (1) It shall be the duty of every native subject to its jurisdiction, when so directed by a Native Authority, to attend before such Native Authority or before the Chief Commissioner or an administrative officer of a Native Court having jurisdiction over such native.

(2) Any such native who when so directed to attend before any such Authority, officer, or Court, shall without reasonable excuse, neglect or refuse to attend as and when directed, may be arrested in accordance with a warrant obtained under section 20 and taken before such Authority, officer, or Court.

8. Subject to the provisions of any ordinance or other law for the time being in force, a Native Authority may, subject to the general or specific directions of the Native Authority, if any, to which it is subordinate, issue orders, to be obeyed by such natives within its area as may be subject to its jurisdiction, for all or any of the following purposes:

(*a*) Prohibiting, restricting, or regulating the manufacture, distillation, sale, transport, distribution, supply, possession, and consumption of intoxicating liquors.

(*b*) Prohibiting, restricting, or regulating gambling.

(*c*) Prohibiting, restricting, or regulating the carrying and possession of weapons.

(*d*) Prohibiting, restricting, or regulating hunting and fishing.

(*e*) Prohibiting any act or conduct which in the opinion of the Native Authority might cause a riot or a disturbance or a breach of the peace.

(*f*) Preventing the pollution of the water in any stream, watercourse, or water-hole, and preventing the obstruction of any stream or water-course.

(*g*) Prohibiting, restricting, or regulating the cutting or destruction of trees.

(*h*) Requiring natives to report cases of infectious or contagious disease, whether of human beings or animals, and generally for the prevention of such disease and for the care of the sick.

(*i*) Requiring such natives to report the presence within the area of its authority of any native who has committed an offence for which he may be arrested without a warrant or for whose arrest a warrant has been issued, or of any property stolen or believed to have been stolen whether within or without such area.

(*j*) Requiring the birth, death, marriage, or divorce of any native subject to its jurisdiction to be reported to it or to such person as it may direct.

(*k*) Prohibiting, restricting, or regulating the movement in or through the area of its authority of livestock of any description.

(*l*) Prohibiting, restricting, or regulating the burning of grass or bush, and the use of fire or lights in any manner likely to ignite any grass or bush in contravention of any law or regulation.

(*m*) For the purpose of exterminating or preventing the spread of tsetse fly and locusts.

(*n*) Prohibiting, restricting, regulating, or requiring to be done any matter or thing which the Native Authority, by virtue of any native law or custom for the time being in force and not repugnant to morality or justice, has power to prohibit, restrict, regulate, or require to be done.

(*o*) Prohibiting, restricting, or regulating the construction of buildings.

(*p*) Requiring the removal of dangerous or ruinous buildings and of buildings constructed in contravention of any order issued under this Ordinance.

(*q*) Generally for the improvement of sanitation and for the better preservation of health within the area of its authority.

(*r*) For any other purpose, whether similar to those hereinbefore enumerated or not, which may, by notice published in the *Gazette*, be sanctioned by the Governor, either generally or for any particular area.

15. (1) Subject to the provisions of any ordinance or other law for the time being in force, a Native Authority, with the concurrence of the Native Authority, if any, to which it is subordinate, and subject to the approval of the Governor, may make rules providing for the peace, good order, and welfare of natives within the area of its authority, and imposing as penalties for the breach of any rule a fine of fifty pounds or imprisonment with or without hard labour for two years, or both such fine and imprisonment.

(2) Every rule made under subsection (1) shall be made known by publication in the *Gazette* and also in such manner as is customary in the area of the Native Authority by whom it is made, and thereupon, subject to any directions given by the Governor under subsection (5) of section 3, shall be binding on all natives residing or being within the jurisdiction of the Native Authority making the rules, and without prejudice to any other mode of proof, a certificate purporting

Q

to be signed by the Chief Commissioner or an administrative officer shall be sufficient evidence of the terms of any such rule, that the concurrence of a superior Native Authority, if any, has been obtained, that the approval of the Governor has been given, and that the rule has been made known as required by this subsection.

(3) The Governor may at any time revoke any rule made by a Native Authority under this section, and such revocation shall be made known in the manner herein prescribed for the promulgation of such rule and shall thereupon have effect.

(4) A native subject to the jurisdiction of a Native Authority who may be accused of an offence against rules made under this section may be arrested in accordance with a warrant obtained under section 20 and may be tried before a Magistrate's Court or a Native Court within the area of whose jurisdiction the offence was committed: Provided always that no court shall be authorized by this section to impose heavier penalties than such court is authorized to impose in the exercise of its ordinary criminal jurisdiction. (Amended by 39 of 1935, s. 3.)

16. (1) A Native Authority may, with the approval of the Governor, and shall, if so required by the Governor, establish a native treasury in the area under the control of such Native Authority. All moneys received by a Native Authority by way of dues, rates, fines, fees, grants, rents, or royalties shall be paid into such treasury.

(2) Where a Chief or a Chief with a native council has been appointed a Native Authority under this Ordinance for an area in which a native treasury has been established, such part of the revenues derived from properties of the Stool occupied by such Chief as the Governor may determine shall be paid into such native treasury and form part of the revenue of such Native Authority.

(3) The Governor may from time to time make rules for the general management, supervision, and control of such treasuries.

APPENDIX VI

A NATIVE LAW AND CUSTOM (ASHANTI CONFEDERACY COUNCIL) ORDINANCE, 1940

An Ordinance to provide for the recording and declaration of Native Law and Custom within the Ashanti Confederacy and for the modification of the same.

(30 March 1940)

1. This Ordinance may be cited as the Native Law and Custom (Ashanti Confederacy Council) Ordinance, 1940.

2. Interpretation:

'Confederacy' means the group of divisions under the supervision of the Asantehene.

'Confederacy Council' means the Ashanti Confederacy Council constituted under the Ashanti Confederacy Order as from time to time amended.

'Court' includes a Native Court.

'Division' means a territorial area within the Confederacy in respect of which a person is elected and installed as Headchief in accordance with native law and custom.

3. (1) The Confederacy Council may at any time record in writing a declaration of what in its opinion is the native law and custom within the Confederacy relating to any subject, and submit such declaration to the Chief Commissioner for the consideration of the Governor in Council.

(2) If the Governor in Council is satisfied that a declaration made under the provisions of subsection (1) truly and accurately records such native law and custom as aforesaid within the Confederacy, and that such native law and custom is not repugnant to justice, equity, or good conscience, or incompatible either in terms or by necessary implication with any Ordinance, he may upon the recommendation of the Confederacy Council by Order direct that such declaration shall be in force in any division specified in the Order.

(3) Upon such Order being made and published in the *Gazette*, the native law and custom set forth in the said declaration shall be deemed by every court to be a true and accurate statement of the native law and custom with respect to the subject to which such declaration relates within the divisions specified in the Order.

4. (1) The Confederacy Council may submit to the Chief Commissioner for the consideration of the Governor in Council any recommendation for the modification of native law and custom which it may consider expedient for the good government and welfare of the Confederacy.

(2) If the Governor in Council is of opinion that such modification of native law and custom is not repugnant to justice, equity, or good conscience, or incompatible either in terms or by necessary implication with any Ordinance, he may upon the recommendation of the Confederacy Council by Order direct that such modification shall be in force in any division specified in the Order, and such modification shall take effect in such division upon the Order being published in the *Gazette*.

APPENDIX VII

BIBLIOGRAPHY

I. *Books and publications quoted or referred to in the text*

RATTRAY, *Ashanti.*
—— *Ashanti Law and Constitution.*
—— *Religion and Art in Ashanti.*
CHRISTALLER, *Asante–Fante Dictionary.*
CLARIDGE, *A History of the Gold Coast and Ashanti*, vols. i and ii.
WARD, *A Short History of the Gold Coast.*
BOWDICH, *Mission to Ashantee.*
E. E. EVANS-PRITCHARD, *The Nuer.*
MAX GLUCKMAN, *Lozi Land and Royal Property.*
CASELY HAYFORD, *Gold Coast Native Institutions.*
STUBBS, *Constitutional History of England*, vol. i.
JOLIFFE, *The Constitutional History of Medieval England.*
POLLOCK and MAITLAND, *History of English Law.*
M. FORTES and E. E. EVANS-PRITCHARD, *African Political Systems.*
HAILEY, *African Survey.*
LUCY MAIR, *Native Policies in Africa.*
COLONIAL REPORTS: ASHANTI, 1905–26.
GOLD COAST LEGISLATIVE COUNCIL DEBATES, 1942–6.
SHEPHARD, *The Economics of Peasant Agriculture in the Gold Coast.*
RADCLIFFE-BROWN, *The Sociological Theory of Totemism.*
GODFREY and MONICA WILSON, *The Analysis of Social Change.*
Ed. RITA HINDEN, *Fabian Colonial Essays.*
R. FIRTH, *Human Types.*
MALINOWSKI, *The Dynamics of Culture Change.*
NATIVE AUTHORITY (ASHANTI) ORDINANCE (Cap. 79 of the Laws of
    the Gold Coast.)
NATIVE COURTS (ASHANTI) ORDINANCE (Cap. 80 of the Laws of the
    Gold Coast.)
HAVERS, *Report of Commission of Enquiry into expenses incurred by litigants
    of the Gold Coast and indebtedness incurred thereby.*
NATIVE AUTHORITY (COLONY) ORDINANCE, 1944.
KUMASI TOWN COUNCIL ORDINANCE, 1943.
NADEL, *A Black Byzantium.*
RAMSEYER and KÜHNE, *Four Years in Ashantee.*
FULLER, *A Vanished Dynasty—Ashanti.*

II. *Books and publications on Ashanti consulted but not mentioned in the text*

R. Austin Freeman, *Travels and Life in Ashanti and Jaman.*
Lady Hodgson, *The Siege of Kumasi.*
E. Smith, *The Golden Stool.*
Ellis, *A History of the Gold Coast of West Africa.*
Balmer, *History of the Akan People.*
Cruickshank, *Eighteen Years on the Gold Coast of Africa.*
Sir John Dalrymple Hay, *Ashanti and the Gold Coast.*
A. W. Cardinall, *Ashanti and Beyond.*
Reindorf, *History of the Gold Coast and Ashanti.*
Brackenbury and Huyshe, *Fanti and Ashanti.*
A. C. Beaton, *The Ashantees.*
Ramseyer and Steiner, *Dark and Stormy Days at Kumasi.*
J. B. Danquah, *Akan Laws and Customs.*
—— *Cases in Akan Law.*
T. B. Freeman, *Journal of Visits to Ashanti, &c.*
Baden-Powell, *The Downfall of Prempeh.*
Armitage and Montanaro, *The Ashanti Campaign of 1900.*
Bliss, *The Relief of Kumasi.*
Dooner, *To Kumasi and Back.*
W. M. Hall, *The Great Drama of Kumasi.*
Boyle, *Through Fanteeland to Coomassie.*
Henty, *The March to Coomassie.*
Stanley, *Coomassie and Magdala.*
Rogers, *Ashantee Invasion.*
Ricketts, *Ashantee War.*
'Daily News' Special Correspondent, *The Ashantee War.*
Winchwood Reade, *The Story of the Ashanti Campaign.*
Brackenbury, *Narrative of the Ashanti War* (2 vols.).
Dupuis, *Journal of a Residence in Ashanti.*

INDEX

oath fees, 108.
Odekuro, 5, 6, 13, 63.
Offences, 21-2, 55, 65 ff., 149-50, 152, 174, 177, 204, 223.
private and public, 67 ff.
sexual, 65-6, 70, 71, 72-3, 150, 154.
Ɔkyeame, 8, 11, 12, 13, 14, 15, 18, 19, 28, 31, 33, 35, 71, 81, 151, 152.
Osei Tutu, 4, 52, 76, 91, 92, 96.
Oyoko clan, the, 85, 86, 93, 97.

Patrilinearity, 38.
Penalties, 55, 66, 143, 144-5, 168, 170, 183.
Political system, viii, 85, 128 ff., 197-9, 217.
centralization, 198, 217.
decentralization, 22.
Population, 123, 147-8.
Prempeh, Chief, 29, 98-9, 101.
Procreation, two principles of, 1.
Property and succession to, 2, 43, 47, 125, 127.

Queen-mother, the, 9, 11, 13, 18, 19-21, 76, 97.

Rattray, R. S., viii, ix, 3, 6 n. 1, 8, 10, 12 n. 1, 13 n. 1, 18, 19, 21, 22, 23, 27, 28, 29, 39, 40, 41, 45-6, 48 n. 1, 49 n. 1, 53-4, 57, 60, 65, 71 and n. 1, 75, 76, 83-4, 151 n. 2.
Religion, 23 ff., 96, 220-2; *see also* Ceremonies; Missions.
Rites: *see* Ceremonies; Religion.
Roads, 74, 118-19.
Rubber, 120, 122, 174, 205.

Sacrifices, 13, 14, 15, 23, 26, 27, 29, 31, 34, 35, 36, 41, 42, 46, 49, 56, 63, 196, 197.
sheep and, 13, 19, 31-2, 71, 72, 73, 97, 149, 151, 204.
Sanctions, 11, 25, 55, 57, 60, 63, 91, 171, 186.
Settlements, early, 45-7.
Shrines, *see also* Stools.
Siblings, 127.
Social change and culture contact, vii-viii, 104, 124, 138, 177, 198-9, 216-17.
Songs and singing, 31.
Spirits, 23, 24, 26; *see also* Ancestors.

Stealing, 66, 67, 70, 74, 154.
Stools, 7-8, 12, 13, 19, 20, 26, 27, 28, 31-2, 33-4, 36-7, 44, 49, 95, 178.
ceremony of enstoolment, 12-13, 26.
chief Ashanti, 218.
debts, 49, 146, 172, 178, 182, 201, 205-9, 210.
funds, 214.
Golden, 17, 55, 57, 74 n. 1, 87, 91, 97 ff., 105, 113 ff., 172, 185, 192, 195; desecration of, 113 ff.
Ɔkyeame's, 18.
property, 49, 51, 73,
Silver, 87.
See also Chiefs: destoolment.
Strangers (settlers), 128-9, 130, 154-5, 157-8.
Suicide, 65, 66, 70, 71.

Taboos, 21, 26-27, 37, 55, 65-6, 69, 70, 71, 72, 74, 75, 76, 161.
Thursday, 40, 135, 136, 137, 174, 176, 178, 221-2.
oath, 8, 12, 75, 76.
Trade and commerce, 79 ff., 120 ff.
Treason, 66, 70, 73.
Treasure-trove, 45, 49, 57.
Treasury, the, and finance, 78 ff., 141, 156-7, 159-60, 161, 162-3, 226.

Villages, 4 ff., 7, 10, 16, 45, 46, 63-4, 78, 88-9, 94, 95, 148.
Odekuro and, 5, 6.

Ward, *A Short History of the Gold Coast*, ix, 4, 54 n. 5.
Warrington, Captain, *Notes on Ashanti Custom*, 174, 175, 178, 179.
Wenchi, 3 ff., 49, 76, 104, 147 ff., *et passim*.
Wenchihene, 5-6, 9, 16-18, 148.
oath of, 76.
Witchcraft, 70, 74.
Wives, 25.
Women, 20, 124.
menstruation and, 72.
Odwera ceremony and, 32.

Yaw Sapon, 53, 106.
Yefrefo, 3-4, 9.

For Product Safety Concerns and Information please contact our EU
representative GPSR@taylorandfrancis.com
Taylor & Francis Verlag GmbH, Kaufingerstraße 24, 80331 München, Germany

9 781138 492271